GW01044114

Cedar World

By
Barbara Bridgford

Dedication.

With special thanks to my
wonderful spirit friends and guides.

Introduction

Cedar across the world is about our full circle of life. We can try to imagine what we have been told from beings that exist in the higher realms of understanding, but this is not always easy. Nevertheless, they know more than we poor souls on this earth plane who are trying to feel our way in the darkness. Where better to obtain knowledge about life after death than directly from those who are already there.

I do hope that I will be able to bring a little comfort to those of you who have reached, or, who are reaching their mature years and are wondering what lays ahead beyond this existence. And to those who have lost someone, perhaps it will bring reassurance and peace of mind.

We have only our religious teachings to look to, and can only guess at the truth from a book written many years ago by elders and prophets of that time. As you know, we human beings are inclined to add our little 'bit' along the way especially over a long period of time!

There have been many communications over the years from spirit individuals, proving that life does indeed continue after the death process. It is when we reach old age and, or, have lost a loved one that we wonder and worry if they are happy, and about what lies ahead for us in the unknown. If I can give you food for thought then it may bring new concepts to your views of death and take away some of your fears.

We Say, such and such a person has died or we say they have passed on. I can tell you neither are true but what is true, is that a person has gone home; we all go home eventually, it's inevitable. What we need to do is to rejoice in the knowledge that they no longer have any pain or disabilities, no old frail bodies; they have been left behind. They have now received their well-earned rest, their promotion in the beautiful world where there is no cold, hunger, wars or suffering of any kind.

If you believe we have a soul, we are spirit beings and that we are here to learn, then it makes sense for us to leave this world when our schooling on this plane of existence is over. And if we are spirit, why shouldn't we communicate with our own kind either directly to our loved ones our family, or through the mediumistic faculties of a spiritualist medium?

We have long moved away from the dark ages when poor unenlightened souls would say that mediums were working with the devil and that they were witches, this certainly is not true. Mediums do not have a special gift; the ability to communicate with those who are living in the spirit world is natural. Think about it, how can it be otherwise?

The only difference with those who already communicate with the next world is that they have developed their sixth sense and are able to penetrate through their material bodies, letting their true selves, their spirit selves, see, hear and feel another vibration, the spiritual vibration. Everyone can train to become mediums and healers that is what spiritual development is all about and I have taught many people over the years. Naturally as with all things, some individuals are quicker than others to learn and develop, that is only because with some their spiritual ability is nearer the surface than with others. There is nothing magical or strange about this, it is our right, and it is the norm.

What a wonderful world it would be, if everyone could communicate with his or her loved ones and what a joy it would be to know your husband, sister, mother and father are well and happy, guiding and helping you. It is very simple, just a matter of heightening your vibrations so that the spirit world can reach you.

We are able to communicate with others too, such as, Doctors, Specialists, Teachers and those people who are wise in spirit knowledge. They are always there to help and guide you, because they love you.

I do not lose people in death, because they are with me all the time. I do not fear death because the spirit world is more beautiful than this world in all respects, and to become free of this material dense body and fly away must be a wonderful freedom.

12

My religion is, loving my neighbours and helping those in need.

We are now in the twenty first century, and there are more complementary therapists than there has ever been and many more people sensitive to spiritual truths.

As a child, I saw spirit people and thought this was normal. As I got older and started to develop as a medium and healer I found there were many questions that I needed answered.

It has been a difficult journey finding the truth, as each person I approached over the years seeking enlightenment could not satisfy my hunger for spiritual knowledge and truth. I soon realised it was down to me to find the answers and I spent the next thirty five years searching and I still am. I read as many books as I could get my hands on and eventually learnt a great deal from books and wise spirit teachers.

Dear 'Reader' this is a story of a journey of life, not only on the earthly plane of existence, but we need to go full circle and include the spiritual realms too.

The information given to me from spirit teachers along the way is factual, but it is down to you to try as far as you can to understand it or reject it, however, it make sense to put it to one side until later when I know you will be able to accept it as reasonable to your intelligence.

Understanding Universal Laws.

The Universal laws exist whether you know about them or not, whether you believe in them or not, they are in operation. When you are working in harmony with the Universal Laws your life will flow much easier.

The law of One or Oneness. Everything is connected, we are all one.

The Law of Vibration. Everything in the universe vibrates.

The Law of Attraction. You attract into your life what you send out in your vibrations, this is what you are offering, which comes back to you.

The Law of Allowing. The state of allowing is the purest state of manifesting. Allowing things to move without resistance and to evolve and grow naturally.

The Law of Resistance. Anything offering resistance will manifest itself into energy blockages or stuck energy.

The Law of Detachment. This is the law of releasing or letting go from your desire.

The Law of Abundance. There is more than

enough in the Universe for all, nothing is limited.

The Law of Intention. Directing energy as intentions is the first step of creation and desire, which then results in manifestations.

The Law of Action. Action must be taken in order to bring about a result in manifestation.

The Law of Cause and Effect. Every action has a reaction or a consequence.

The Law of Pure Potential. Everything and everyone is one of infinite possibilities.

The Law of Rhythm or Ebb and Flow. All things have a rhythm, a cycle, or an ebb and flow.

The Law of Polarity. Everything has an opposite to it, complementary opposites as part of a greater whole.

The Law of Relativity. Everything has challenges or tests that they will face allowing them to find strength within.

The Law of Dharma or Purpose. Everything was created with a purpose.

The Law of Giving and gratitude. The Universe

dictates that you must give in order to receive.

The Law of Correspondence. The Universe, or reality, cannot contradict itself.

The Law of Love. Love is Universal energy in its purest most powerful state.

Part one earth life.
Chapter One.

How it all began.

I have been a medium and healer for many years and linking with spirit people is a privilege on a daily basis. I have found a great deal of comfort in my work and during these years, the spiritual knowledge I received gave me the strength to cope with my hard and difficult personal life.

Previously, in the early days the only way I could have a conversation in trance with spirit guides was through automatic writing, and I must say that was after I had a couple of alcoholic drinks to make me very relaxed, therefore it was a bit up and down. I very rarely drink now so it was more difficult even though I did try. I never had any problems 'tuning in' for private readings and public demonstrations, therefore I continued with my mediumship and healing and gave up the automatic writing.

Since my conversation with Daniel I find I can now link with him very easily. As soon as I am on my computer and think of him we are able to converse. I have to type our conversation very quickly so that I have a record to refer to when I write this book. I then have to try to make what he has said easier to read because the aim is to reach out to everyone, even those who have had little or no education. By doing this I don't think

I have lost anything so far of what Daniel is trying to teach us.

I have learnt a great deal over the fifty years I have been an instrument for spirit, nevertheless I have asked Daniel questions even though I may know the answer so that those who read the book do not miss out. Some questions have been asked by circle members and, or, friends. I do hope you will enjoy the information given and will find it helpful.

Everything we do and think is subject to the law of cause and effect. Punishment is the result of wrongdoing and the sequence of sowing and reaping. Karma is one of many of Gods Laws, which my spirit guide will explain as we move along on the journey to discover our true purpose in life.

I decided to meditate to relax and to bring myself back to a positive way of thinking. As usual I made sure the telephone was unplugged and the doors locked and I changed the C D to a more suitable one. Making myself comfortable in the armchair, hands laying gently in my lap with palms facing upwards, I began to prepare myself for meditation. Taking several deep breaths, I started to unwind and link with my higher self.

I visualised my usual journey beginning with a shaft of white light in the centre of the room, seeing my body floating upwards absorbing the beautiful white light. After a while I arrived at my usual place that I had created for myself many years earlier; a starting place for meditations.

My back was resting against an old oak tree; the foliage spread above me like a beautiful canopy, the sun was shining with only a few puffs of white clouds here and there. I was very comfortable and warm and I could feel the cool thick green lush grass underneath my bare feet, my toes were deep into the green soft carpet.

The meadow sloped downwards, to a small stream that was spanned by a rather beautiful, but tiny bridge. On the other, side of the stream the meadow sloped upwards and at the top another lone old oak tree spreading out its branches. I took a deep breath and enjoyed the beautiful relaxing scene in front of me. I sauntered down towards the little stream picking up a few wild flowers on the way; I had not felt this good in a long time.

The stream was about six feet wide and very shallow, as I gazed down towards the bottom of the stream I found to my delight beautiful pebbles, they were all the colours of the spectrum. I placed my hand into the warm clear water retrieving one blue pebble. It was such a perfect oval shape, lovely and smooth to the touch, which made me want to stroke and fondle the stone as I sat on the bank with my feet dangling in the shallow water watching the ripples flow over my toes.

It's strange because each time I visited this place and sat by the bridge, I thought it was out of place, more ornamental than practical and it made me think that it must be symbolic, perhaps the intention of 'crossing over' to the 'other side'.

The only sound that broke the silence was the beautiful birds singing happily next to me, I could have stayed there forever. The birds flew down from the small flowering shrubs next to me unafraid and rested on my shoulders, hands and knees. I will never forget such a marvellous and overwhelming experience.

Gazing up towards the oak tree, I saw the figure of a person, who seemed to be enveloped in a bright radiant light. He was watching me as I enjoyed the lovely birds. Inside my mind, I heard the words 'please come and join me'. I Blinked and screwed up my eyes trying to see a little clearer as I proceeded to walk up the grassy incline towards the mysterious figure.

Once more I mentally heard "Sit down by my side child." This unknown person spoke in a gentle caring way. Excited and a little stunned, I obeyed, placing my back against the strong tree trunk, noticing the old oak tree opposite where I had started my meditation. Relaxing I said, "Who are you?"

"I am your friend and guide. Recently when you felt lost and touched the lowest possible depth and it seemed there was nobody and nothing in

the material world to help you, I came to your
side to give you the strength that you needed."

"Thank you!" As I responded, an indescribable,
incredible, loving tingling sensation flowed
through my entire body.

"Your soul has been very tired for some time my
dear. This is understandable living in your
heavy world of matter. It's not easy for those on
earth to face each problem with a smile, all you
can do is your best, then you must let it go."

"I have tried to be strong repeatedly. I have been
so disheartened struggling with all my problems
and I must say I have reached the very bottom of
despair. I thank God my faith is strong and it has
always kept me going but I must admit I was
down on my knees this time with sadness."

"Yes I am aware of your fears, it is not good for
you, it consumes you and it blackens you with
gloom. It makes it hard for us in our world to get
through the darkness to be close to you. If you
have fears, you cannot be at peace; this
negativity brings darkness around you, which of
course is the absence of light. You must raise
your vibrations and your thoughts and face your
trials, for they are opportunities for you to grow.
When you are in a state of calmness and peace
you are strong and then you are able to deal with

your problems and take responsibility for your life. You must learn to love yourself, by doing so you achieve peace and harmony. In order for you to grow spiritually you must change the way you think. Set your targets and keep your mind focused on your goals."

"That's not so easy and I do know it's all to do with my spiritual growth, which does keep me going."

"Life on earth is not easy, I'm afraid it is not meant to be, this is because you need to grow and develop strength and wisdom. However your spiritual growth means raising your vibration to a higher level bringing more light into your being and driving away those dark shadows because every thought, word, emotion and action is a vibration, this shows in your aura. Growth means purifying your thoughts and your emotions, choosing love actions in your everyday life, until you radiate at that higher level."

"Yes, it depends on the way I think and act, whether I will be able to raise my vibrations or not. Again I say it is not easy when you are down and depressed, but I do try."

"You have nothing to worry about; life has much to offer you even in your world. You have a long way to go on your journey; you have your own gifts to fulfil, to accomplish and books to write. The Great Spirits love will guide, sustain and cherish you."

Shocked at what he said I responded saying. "What do you mean, write books?"

"Ah! Yes, now is the time for you to pass on to others all that we have taught you and will teach you. I will explain how this will be accomplished later. You have learnt so much over the years being an instrument for spirit, and by doing so; it has strengthened the link that binds you to God. Your earthly life has not been easy, but there are natural laws which take care of these matters, those who serve will never want; that is to say, your essential needs are always supplied."

"That sounds absolutely absurd because I am not a writer, never have been. I hate writing letters never mind a book. I hardly ever attended English lessons at school I disliked it so much, the thought is very daunting."

"Yes I understand how you feel, you won't be alone I will be here to help you to write. My task is to teach you all aspects of spiritual life from the beginning, the full circle of life; this will include God's Laws. It is not going to be easy for we have a long way to go. Don't worry about it, all will be well. I will leave you now you have much to contemplate, we will speak again soon."

"But, but I still have one or two more questions to ask," I said looking into the white light, trying hard to see his face, an expression or image, something I could take away with me. Straining my eyes, I could just see the whiteness of his being blending into the brilliant light enveloping him. I said, "Thank you, I have a lot to think about. I don't know what else to say, I am speechless." Then suddenly he had gone.

I was feeling exhausted trying to take on board all that this wonderful person had said and I didn't want the meeting to end. Deep in thought, I walked back to my old oak tree and across the stream. I felt fantastic, my mind was all over the place and I realized I hadn't asked his name. I sat down at the oak tree and closed my eyes and in the blink of an eye, I was back in my armchair.

The following morning I sat with pen and paper trying to remember all that this wonderful spirit guide and teacher had said. And, I thought, if I am supposed to write a book I will need to record everything. Not an easy task although I told myself spirit would write the book, not me.

Loud banging on the outside door jolted me back to reality. I opened the door to find two

Jehovah Witnesses standing in front of me. Sighing I thought, that's all I need. They kept me at the door for quite some time even though I did say I wasn't interested; I tried to listen to what they had to say but I it isn't for me so I said impatiently. "I'm a spiritualist, I'm not interested. Goodbye." Not waiting for a response I closed the door. It wasn't very spiritual of me, but they intruded in my special thoughts. I felt ashamed at my impatience and thinking my spirit teacher would not approve, I also believe that religion should not be forced on anyone; it should come from the heart, mind you that is no reason to be rude.

It was around the time for dinner and I was feeling very hungry, I went into the kitchen and opened the fridge door to see what I could find. 'Ah! Gammon with eggs and chips, washed down with a glass of red wine that would be rather nice.

After dinner, I began to feel rather tired and I curled up in the armchair feeling very satisfied and comfortable. I was surprised to find within minutes my mind started to run riot again. I couldn't settle down at all, all I could think about was the conversation I had with spirit the day before. I tried to relax in my armchair taking slow deep breaths. It seemed to take forever for me to relax and then I felt myself drifting off.

"Hello, hello!"

Startled at hearing a voice, I turned to my right and saw my spirit friend standing next to me. "Oh! Hello how lovely to see you. Where am I?"

"You are in meditation."

"But I don't remember sitting for meditation. Am I dreaming?"

"Because you were thinking of me it made it much easier to unite the two worlds, and no you are not dreaming you just slipped into this state quite naturally; I helped of course."

"I am very pleased to see you, I was thinking about you."

"Yes I know every thought is registered in the spirit world."

"Oh dear, before I forget can you please tell me your name; I forgot to ask you yesterday."

"My name is Daniel, although names are unimportant."

"Thank you Daniel, I haven't been able to stop thinking about what you said. What happens next? What do we do? What am I supposed to do?"

"My dear child so many questions, you must not worry; I will direct you and explain everything to you as simply as I can. Relax and enjoy your journey. I will begin today explaining the time immediately before a spirit is united with a human baby and before the union of body and soul is complete. I will explain the whole circle of life from the physical birth and the reason you are on the earth plane, death of the body, spirit life and back again once more to the beginning; reincarnation."

"Wow! Wonderful! That sounds even more daunting but I can't wait to start."

"Good, I am pleased about that."

We talked for a while about my personal life and then he said good bye. I didn't tell anyone about my meeting with Daniel but it was killing me to keep such a secret. I knew eventually I would tell my development circle because I thought it would be nice for them and of course I wanted them to ask him questions for the book.

Our Creation.

Eventually after many casual meetings with Daniel, I told the members of my spiritual development circle. They were very excited and asked if they could meet him. When next we met

I introduced everyone to Daniel and started the questions with. "Daniel, can you explain to us, how we were created? I'm presuming you know."

"Good evening to you all I am very pleased to meet you. My dears, there is in existence an infinite sensitive, perceptive energy or presence which is all powerful, all-knowing, possesses limitless creative power and is present everywhere. This energy, this presence we call God, The Great Spirit or Mohammed and so on, decided to improve, to enrich its knowledge and desired to gather information and all the possible experiences it could ever imagine to enable the Great Spirit to understand more fully the magnificence of its own perfection. Because of the Great Spirits creativity, it developed a way to experience that which was not perfection. Therefore, it created the earth, a world that exists with both positive and negative energies, everything always having opposites present. In other words the earth allows human beings to be able to evaluate every human soul's experiences whilst in a physical body on earth.

The energy or presence of the Great Spirit has no form, no body that you can observe but is a loving energy that bathes and saturates everything with energy of pure unconditional love."

"Thank you for that. I am not sure of all the details but I have been told we were all created from the one energy, one spirit, and we all know deep inside that we are all part of the same spirit."

"Yes my dears. That is true. We are all energy; we are all part of the larger source of energy of our God the Creator. Even so, you are all unique special beings, distinctive from each other with your own special qualities; not one of you was created exactly the same. You have your own exceptional abilities, talents and gifts which help to express your individuality. You are all given the same spiritual opportunities including your free will, the ability to make choices; it is up to each individual how they choose to live their lives. In addition, you have been given the skill, the power and knowledge to flourish, to blossom, to grow within your own physical and spiritual existence. Therefore it is important that you take care and maintain a balance between the physical body and your spirit body."

I said cheekily. "One could say Daniel, that the Great Spirit is using us to gain knowledge."

"Yes, but I must emphasize we are one. The Great Spirit created us from itself and we were called souls. Every soul has a duty to incarnate and enter the experiences the lessons and trials placed before them. And as each soul resides upon the many planets and learns their lessons, both our souls and the Great Spirit would then possess a greater knowledge, greater wisdom of the less-than-perfect, therefore, we would have a better understanding and appreciation of that which is perfection. All energy in the spirit realms has the nature of perfect unconditional love. Do you understand? "

"Yes, thank you Daniel. We have a lot to learn."

"Yes my dear child, there is much for you all to learn and to understand but I am here to help you. Let me explain further, when you arrive in the physical world you are given all that you need to live in your new environment, you are given all the skills to achieve everything of which you are capable; you do not come into your new life without any knowledge, it is in your sub-consciousness, with experience you can 'tap into' through meditation.

Your lessons on earth are not easy, as I said earlier, they are not meant to be. Some souls attain what they came to earth to do; unfortunately, there are others, who do not. Progression, or, lack of it, is measured by the way each soul has lived their life, how they dealt with their challenges and all their trials placed before them. This is their spiritual growth.

When they have finished with their lessons

their soul leaves the physical world and returns home to the spirit realms. However, there are those who are taken early, who die through the acts of violence or, those who suffer bodily disorders. Spirit beings generally incarnate into a healthy, physically complete harmonious body unless they have a contract to the contrary. We will talk about pre-birth agreements at a later time.

What a shame that so many souls are ignorant to the things of spirit. Nevertheless, all of you will slowly make progress.

Before you were born onto the earth the physical world, you were as spirit beings, aware of the laws of the Great Spirit but this depends on the degree of development of the spirit individual. Although the laws still are imprinted in the spirits conscience however, those who are the lower instincts of man can often cause forgetfulness.

All the laws of nature are divine laws, because the Great Spirit created them, they are unchangeable. The Great Spirit cannot make mistakes; the laws of God are perfect.

I think before we move on any further you should also know the law of being. Like all laws, the Law of Being is a spiritual law; it is the Great Spirits Law. You are a spiritual being and as such you are not subject to the laws of the human being. Of course, you must obey the laws of the earth, but the spiritual being is governed by

spiritual laws. These laws are?
1. The 'word' of you is law.
2. The 'word' of you creates.
3. The 'word' of you moulds the physical body into either health or dis-ease.
4. As a man thinks in his heart, so is he.
5. You live in your consciousness; there is nowhere else you can live.
6. You make your heaven, or hell. Your thinking makes it so.

As a pure being a pure spirit you are the perfect image of the Great Spirit. Where your attention goes, your energy flows, all thoughts create energy therefore you shall build, you create that which you imagine. This is the law of being. Think on this and you will understand how this law works.

I will continue on a similar note with the law of evolution. Like the cocoon that evolves into a beautiful butterfly, so does the soul of human beings forever evolve by degrees to perfection of the Creator; the aim of a spirit is perfection. This is law, you cannot stop it and it is the fulfilling of God's law.

There is a way for you to quicken the process, since you all have been given the power of thought and since thought creates, you can become whatever you want. Suppose you would be an illuminated body of light, very well, this very desire is the fulfilment. If your heart longs for illumination, you should work for it, believe it and you shall fulfil the laws that bring illumination. These are the laws?

1. You must know that all Light of Being is within you.
2. As you dwell on the Light IT must express itself in the physical body.
3. As a Light Being then you would live with Lightness and you would drive back all thoughts that are of a negative nature. This is the cleansing which is necessary. Cleansing means cleansing of your consciousness or ridding of the negative ideas that are in the subconscious mind.
4. All race thoughts must be uprooted. How? By looking at them, by analysing them. Ask yourself; is this thing of the Great Spirit? Is it real? No. Then it is no part of me for I am a spiritual being. I accept only that which is pure, truth, good and constructive. All else is not a part of my consciousness therefore, I release it into the nothingness from which it came.

It would not be long by such a thought effort to clear the subconscious mind of all negation. Then shall the Light of Understanding shine through. That is illumination. Complete understanding of all that was, is and is to be."

"Thank you Daniel, it's good to know you are there to help us, and feel it's going to be hard to remember what you have just said, but I am sure we will all try hard." Emma said.

Problems with some babies.

"I know someone who has lost her child, so I was wondering if you could explain to us please about miscarriages, stillborn, physically and mentally disabled babies? I feel it would help mothers who have experienced anything like that to understand why it happened. Also can you tell us what happens if the spirit decides to leave the body, if it changes its mind, would another spirit take over?" Jean asked.

"You have asked me four questions, I will answer them all. It is always sad for the parents when they have lost a child, but there is always a reason for a baby not to be born. It is dreadful for a parent to lose a child at any age, it is excruciatingly painful for them, when parents have not even had a chance to cradle the infant in their arms and they feel an intense sadness.

Grieving parents often blame the Great Spirit first and then each other for their unborn child that has been taken from them. They ask themselves what they could have done to prevent it, were they to blame. The truth is no one is to blame it is predestined.

Premature deaths are the cause of imperfections of the body and in such cases the deaths are often intended mainly as a trial for the parents, lessons they agreed before coming to earth. If the body of the child dies through miscarriage before the spirit has the chance to complete the incarnation, the spirit will choose another body. If a spirit fails to incarnate, unless another immediate existence has been arranged beforehand, then it would have to wait and make a new choice. Is that clear to you?"

"Thank you. I'm not sure if it's clear but we will give it a lot of thought and if we have questions we will come back to you if you don't mind? What can you tell us about stillborn babies?"

"As I have just said, both miscarriages and still born babies are usually trials for the parents."

Carol spoke and asked Daniel. "I was wondering if there could be another reason for both these deaths of a child, such as the foetus never having a spirit allotted to it."

"No, no that could never happen because every child to be born is predestined to have a soul, otherwise it would be pointless. Nothing is created without design."

Carol went on to ask. "I understand from

Barbara that when we are in the spirit world we choose our body and our family. Is that correct? Oh! I am not questioning what Barbara has told us, it's just better coming from you. And is it possible that some spirits may regret their choice of body because of all the trials that lay before them, and if so what happens?"

"Yes you are correct in your thinking. However, once a spirit has completed its incarnation it has no memory, therefore it cannot regret a choice that it is not conscious of having made in the spirit world. Although, at first the links between spirit and body are weak therefore in very few instances before the memory has been erased the soul assigned to the foetus may decide that it is not ready to come to earth and at that time breaks connection with the foetus, causing it to cease functioning.

Often souls who are not happy with their incarnation and remain on the earth plane could later on in life find the burden too heavy, beyond its strength, and may eventually resort to suicide."

"How awful!" Emma exclaimed. "Although I can understand why some souls have had enough and want to die. It's a hard life sometimes here on earth."

"It is not meant to be easy my dear. Earth is a

heavy difficult planet, with hard and difficult lessons, that is why you are here."

Brain damage and disabilities.

Elsie spoke this time. "Thank you Daniel. We haven't discussed a child that is born with extensive brain damage, and, or drastic physical disabilities. What would be the purpose of such a life when it is too damaged to make the right decisions?"

"I continue to repeat myself; it is because such births are permitted as a trial, either for the parents or for the incarnated spirit. As I said these deaths are often intended mainly as a trial for the parents. This seems so cruel, but it is what they chose for themselves, all of them. Whatever the cause, when a spirit has failed to accomplish a planned incarnation, another existence will be provided, in most cases immediately. However, some spirit beings need time to make a new choice, if an immediate reincarnation had been previously decided upon that is what will happen.

Usually, the spirit knows beforehand that the body that was chosen, for whatever reason has no chance of living long. If they chose it for those reasons it is because they are afraid of the trials they have foreseen and they will have to pay a price. Once they are absolutely united to an infant's body, it is too late for them to refuse this union."

Abortion.

Elsie thanked Daniel and went on to ask. "Could you please tell us what are the penalties of abortion for a baby and would this be karma?"

"Yes it is karma, and I am sure you will see things much clearer when we speak later and discuss this subject.

This topic is a very emotional issue for many human beings. I must point out that the soul never dies. A miscarriage or an abortion is not the death of a foetal soul; it is the termination of human cells the physical.

Miscarriage is usually the result of a contract made by the mother and father of the unborn child to deal with all of the emotional results of losing a baby at an early stage of development or even right up to birth, which is a stillborn baby. In addition the act of having an abortion is a lesson that some souls wish to experience. All the emotions of selfishness, guilt, regret and much more, come flooding in from within and from their family members.

The consequence of a spirit due to abortion is that the life on earth has been ended. The answer is that it must be commenced all over again, because the chosen spirit has been prevented from undergoing the trials it set out to do. On the other hand, when during the pre-birth plan discussed with the Elders an abortion is arranged as a life event, a soul may not even have been selected to that foetus.

If no contract or a pre-birth plan has been agreed and arranged, the mother, or any other person who takes a life of an unborn child, has committed a crime. Abortion is the wrongdoing of the law of our Creator, therefore a crime. Every violation of the law of the Great Spirit is a crime.

We will discuss Gods Laws later so that you will be able to understand fully what I am teaching you."

"Thank you, we will look forward to that. What if by having the baby, the life of the mother is at risk?" Elsie continued.

"If the life of the mother is at risk by the birth of the child, it is better to sacrifice the one whose existence is not yet complete rather than the one whose existence is complete. Does that make sense to you?"

"Yes it does, thank you very much. I am finding all this absolutely wonderful; I think we are very lucky to be included in these teachings. I am sure we would never have thought about all these things if we hadn't had you and were left to get on with our lives."

Children born in poverty.

The circle members talked amongst themselves and then I spoke. "Thank you Daniel we understand now. What about all those poor babies born in poverty and slums? Surely no one would want to choose a life of such hardship.

Some poor children are born to parents who drink or have mental or moral problems. They have to live in filth and are faced with a hard life, while others grow up surrounded by beautiful things and have a wonderful life. This seems very unfair."

"I'm afraid life does at times seem unfair, nevertheless, every soul has its own spiritual growth, its own evolution. You are thinking and judging with material earthly standards and not by what is best for the soul, the soul has to express itself in its own way. All souls whether born into luxury or poverty have opportunities for their soul to discover itself and to express its own divinity.

That is the only standard of judgement; true compensation is the reward of the soul, which learns to express its self through all difficulties. I must stress again, most spirits choose their challenges and trials before they arrive on earth so that they can grow spiritually, without these lessons on earth the spirit would be stagnant. "

"Thank you Daniel, I thought as much, but we needed confirmation from you. I suppose we have all had good and bad times. Thank you Daniel for your time and patience with us, it is all very interesting but it is getting very late and we have to close the circle. Reluctantly we must say goodnight and look forward to our next session with you."

"It is my pleasure. Good night."

Everyone was very excited and overwhelmed at what they had witnessed. Jean said she wouldn't be able to sleep because she was too excited; the rest of the circle agreed. They all wanted to sit and talk but it was very late, and their partners would be worried. We said good night and arranged to meet again the following evening to discuss all that Daniel had told us.

As soon as they left I went to bed. I was so tired I thought I could sleep for a week but that wasn't to be. I had a long restless night, my mind was all over the place wondering how on earth I could write a book and then my mind would jump back to what Daniel had said. I saw every hour until about four in the morning when I finally dropped off to sleep. In my dream state I was with some very wise spirit people, I remember them talking to me about all sorts of wondrous things, so much information.

When I woke up I felt exhausted as if I had been working all night. An overload of information I couldn't remember, and then I remembered the scene and talking to those people but it was very vague. I tried hard to remember what was said; I knew it was important but I couldn't bring it forward in my mind. I felt as if I had let spirit and myself down and wondered if I could ever write this book. It was beginning to be a nightmare and I hadn't even started yet.

After I showered and got dressed I made breakfast, just some toast and coffee, I felt down in the dumps and decided to meditate after breakfast and see if I could recall what was said to me during the night. I thought whilst I was relaxed I might remember or even see those spirit people again.

I made myself comfortable in the arm chair and prepared myself by breathing very deeply and slowly imagining the shaft of white light coming into my crown chakra. I sat for over an hour trying to meditate but my mind wouldn't stop racing. I eventually gave up.

All day I couldn't get the events out of my mind, although it's not every day one has a conversation with spirit teachers. I had in the past experienced automatic writing, but never asked questions before. I must say I always found it impossible to relax enough to talk to them through automatic writing, for this type of phenomena one has to be totally and utterly relaxed, which was near impossible for me. However I found when I had had a few alcoholic drinks I was able to link with them and do automatic writing. It was great, but I couldn't keep on drinking for that purpose. Therefore when Daniel spoke to me so easily during my meditation I was 'gob smacked'. And now communicating with me directly through my mind or typing on the computer.

Years ago I had a circle for physical phenomena and during the 6 years we sat together we experienced transfigurations. This is when spirit people replaced their facial features on my face and showed their characteristics and mannerisms through gestures and sometimes speaking directly to the relative.

During those years and with the correct sitters we received some wonderful proof of survival. My guides also spoke through me, although with difficulty, but it was wonderful. The circle eventually broke up because I moved away; the members of the circle were upset but understood my situation. I have never had such a good harmonious and balanced circle since.

It was time for the circle members to arrive and I had been looking forward to the gathering all day. They arrived on time at 7 pm full of excitement, I made tea for us all and then we settled down to an evening of discussions. I began by telling them what happened whilst I was asleep the night before.

"Come on then, tell us all about what spirit said and don't keep us in suspense any longer." Emma said all excited.

I responded with, "Sorry ladies there isn't much to tell, I can't remember anything that was said." I went on to explain what had happened and could feel the disappointment in the room. "I'm sorry. I feel just as disappointed as you."

"Never mind Barbara better luck next time. Let's talk about what Daniel said, I think it's absolutely wonderful and I feel very privileged to learn from the spirit world direct. And I must say I am pleased to be part of this circle and I am looking forward to hear more." Emma said.

Jane chipped in saying. "Yes I feel the same but can we start now because I can't stay very long this evening."

"Yes OK." I said. "What shall we start with? Daniel said such a lot? Is there anything Daniel said that any of you cannot accept? I think that is the place to start."

"No I don't think so it all makes sense to me,

although I don't know how I would take the information about being responsible for having a stillborn or miscarriage if I had experienced it. I think you may get some backlash from readers if you write about that, don't you think?" Jane said.

"You could well be right." I said. "However I will write everything Daniel says he knows best. And I must say truth is most important and I am sure after some thought others who read the book will accept it. We must remember Daniel did say he would explain everything to us from birth to physical death, the spirit world and back again to reincarnation. I feel it is important for those who read the book to read all of it and not pick things out, this will enable them to get a fuller picture and a better idea of the truth of why we are here, why we exist."

Elsie spoke up. "I agree with you Barbara, but I also think you could get some flack which will not be very nice for you."

"I think I will have to get a thick skin, having said that I trust my spirit guides implicitly and I am sure they would help if that happened. And of course it is my duty and yours to pass on knowledge to those less fortunate than ourselves. Don't you agree?"

"Yes." They all said at once.

We talked for a couple of hours discussing everything that was said and made notes of questions we need to ask. I also asked Elsie to record everything of our meetings with those in spirit. She agreed, and she would re-type it out for me; what a relief!

We all had a good chat about everything and there was much laughter and the atmosphere changed; they said they felt uplifted.

Our circle sat every Wednesday evening at 7.30pm.

The next meeting with Daniel started during my meditation when I asked "Are you there Daniel."

He responded with. "Yes my dear."

Adoption.

"Daniel we have discussed everything you said to us and we were wondering when you said there is a pre-birth plan of our next life, do we choose our parents and do they choose us, if that is the case why would anyone want to plan to be adopted and why would parents choose to adopt rather than have their own children?"

"I am pleased you talked amongst yourselves. I

do not want you to accept anything that is contrary to your intelligence, if so, you must put it to one side for a later time when you will be able to accept it.

Now I must answer your question. There are numerous reasons why people in your world have their children adopted and on a soul level there are also various reasons why the incarnating spirit requests not to have their own children.

Before incarnation, spirits discus their next life with their guides and those who are trained to assist spirit in their pre-birth planning. They discuss which path is best for them to take that will give them the opportunities, challenges and experiences necessary to heal their past karma.

Regarding adoption, there is more than one soul to be considered here. The soul who has chosen to be adopted, and the mother who has chosen to have her child taken for adoption, there are also those close family members who are affected by this action.

For example, a soul may have had a bad experience, felt unwanted with biological parents in a previous life, therefore chose this time to be adopted. On the other hand, in a previous life the parent who gave their child up for adoption may wish to experience the feeling of rejection that the child perhaps felt when given away. Alternatively, a spirit who wishes to adopt children in their next life may have chosen to return to earth in service; this will often happen when spirit beings wish to help other souls to heal their energy brought from a previous life, either the mother of the child, or the child itself.

All spirit people have their own experiences in previous lives that determine the reasons for wanting particular challenges; they make their own choices, therefore, there can never be any victims. Do you understand; all experiences on earth are planned before re-birth?"

"Thank you, yes I think that answers my question. It is quite complicated isn't it? I said."

"When you think about your life experiences and how it affected you and others then you will see that what I have said is not complicated at all. It's very simple, what you sow, you reap."

Adult soul in a baby's body.

"I have often wondered, and it is puzzling me if we have lived many times before, we must be an adult spirit who animates the body of a child, and if that is so, why doesn't the child behave as an adult? I have spent quite some time since we last spoke thinking about this, and it doesn't make any sense to me." Jean said.

"My dear I am pleased I give you food for

thought and it is a very good question. However, not all souls are mature, there are new spirits born into your world all the time. Nevertheless, it is the imperfections of the human bodily organs that prevent the soul from revealing its true self as it would like. Do you understand the spirit can only act according to the state of the body, the instrument it is using? Therefore, because it is a baby it can only think as a child with that small organ of thought. Does that make sense to you?"

"Yes I think so; you have a wonderful way of explaining everything to us, thank you so much."

Daniel continued. "I am very pleased you understand what I am saying otherwise it would be pointless.

Later as the child reaches its teen years and the organ of thought has grown the soul is more able to show its true character and individuality. There is something else to take into consideration, often the spirit of a child born to the planet earth could be from a world that is different from yours."

"Wow, another world, another planet?"

"Yes that is correct, but I will talk about that on another occasion." Do you have any further questions?"

"Not at the moment. I'm sure we are all eager to hear more about other planets."

"I will speak to you later regarding other worlds in the galaxy. If you have no questions at this time I will say good night and bless you."

"Thank you and goodnight Daniel."

The circle members were over the moon and yearned for more, including myself. We talked for a little while and then they left.

I was pleased and less worried about writing the book; everything seemed to fall into place with Elsie transcribing all the text written on my computer. I did simplify most of what Daniel said because it took a lot of absorbing, too wonderfully 'spiritual', but difficult to read for a beginner; I was told by Daniel at the beginning to make everything readable for those who have had very little or no schooling, therefore reaching out to everyone who seeks to know about spiritual and earth life.

During the rest of the week some of the girls in turn rang me and asked questions; needing clarification on certain points about what was said at the last meeting with Daniel. I am pleased I was able to answer in a positive way. What seemed simple and natural to me, was difficult for the circle to understand. I am afraid I cannot remember how it was for me in the early days of development.

I had a hectic week including the weekend seeing those who needed healing and those who wanted proof of survival. I was feeling a little tired when circle night came around. Having said that I do get a great deal of upliftment talking with Daniel.

Chapter Two.

Abuse and Cruelty.

The girls arrived as usual on time with their big beaming smiles; it's wonderful to see them and know how much they appreciate Daniels efforts. We meditated for a little while to relax and 'tune' into spirit. I then went and sat down at my computer and asked. "Daniel are you there?"

"Hello, hello. I am here waiting for you all." He said.

A circle member asked Daniel. "It is wonderful to be able to talk with you, I feel very privileged. If I may tell you a story about my childhood and perhaps you can give me some advice about karma? "

"Yes please do, I am here to help you all."

"Thank you. Most of my childhood was spent being afraid of my father; he shouted and lashed out at my mother. He worked away a great deal of the time coming home at weekends until his job changed then he could be home during the week too. When I came home from school and saw his car parked outside of the house, the fear inside me made me want to run away; I sort of withdrew inside myself.

The shouting between them especially when I was in bed petrified me because he had hit mum several times before and she had to be taken to hospital with deep cuts and bruises. It was horrendous for a small child to cope with, and I feared he would eventually kill her. The police were always being called out due to the physical abuse, but they seemed to be on my dads' side, sat down drinking tea and laughing. I remember thinking how awful they all were.

On one occasion mum fought back, I remember she stuck the poker into his knee before he had chance to thump her. I must say it was really hell to witness all of that.

Mum told him to leave on several times, which was a waste of time because she kept on taking him back over and over again, despite all the pain she had gone through. She divorced and married him twice; she never showed interest in other men. I find it hard to understand why she continually put up with his brutish behaviour. What are your views Daniel?"

"My dear child, you cannot be at peace if you give another the power to hurt or anger you, to frustrate you. If you blame anyone for what their actions have done to your lives or for how you feel, you are victims.

My dear in truth, there is physical abuse and verbal abuse because words and thoughts are energy and the energy of abusive words penetrates the victim's chakras, their energy centres, thumping and pounding the body as if being physically thrashed. There can be no verbal abuse without physical abuse.

Difficulties and obstacles including abuse are one of many trials of the soul; usually it is karma, which is as you know payback time. What you have told me sounds as though your mother felt she had not learnt her lessons, therefore continuing to suffer until such time she felt the lesson or debt had been fulfilled.

Because of the amnesia of past lives the soul is unable to understand what is happening. As each of the contracts and lessons are completed the soul will take away the blinds from their eyes to reveal the hidden lessons. The soul may understand why something has occurred and choose not to repeat it.

On the other hand spirit return in a particular gender to see what it is like, to see how the spirit would cope, perhaps to experience the feelings of being abused, bringing inner strength, self-worth and so on. Or the soul may complete a lesson, such as being abused by their partner, and learn to get out of the situation, but still fail to learn why it happened and therefore get into another domestic abuse situation.

This can repeat as many times as necessary until the lesson is completely understood. Lessons may be even carried over into a subsequent lifetime if the lesson never gets understood. Lack of memory will keep it hidden until understanding is complete.

With a lesson such as domestic abuse, when the partner appreciates that he or she does not deserve to be a punch bag any longer, and understands the lessons that he or she is equal to their partner, they can walk away and will never have to look back. Any further similar issues of lack of self-worth will start to clear so that they may see the whole picture around those issues. I am not saying this was your mothers' situation but I feel you need to know why sometimes this happens.

Eventually when a soul masters all their lessons or debts, they become stronger, more purified, and more highly evolved. The events in their lives, sometimes of hostility, of despair, of pain and misery, all play their part in preparing the soul gradually for the path that it has to tread.

However hard it was, and is for you, you need to accept that all your experiences and your mothers are part of the soul's evolution and spiritual growth.

One day when you leave your body and return home to the spirit world freed from the restrictions of the heavy physical body, you will look back and evaluate the life you have lived on earth. You will be able to see how everything fits together just like a jigsaw puzzle and how every experience, every trial was a lesson for the soul, bringing greater knowledge and understanding.

My dears, you must understand there are always opposites as I have explained to you. Do you see you can only enjoy happiness when you have experienced the very depths of despair for as low as you can fall in life, so you are can rise above into the sunshine. Do you understand?"

"Thank you for that, yes I can understand now. I have looked back in my life many times when I made silly mistakes and had to suffer the consequences, so I do have some idea of what you are saying. However, words do not take away the pain of my childhood."

"You must let yourself think of spiritual things, rather than be like some who live at a purely physical level of understanding. They believe only what they can see, hear and feel, plodding through life living by human laws, cursing and blaming others afraid of change and the consequences.

Can't you see how lucky you are to have the knowledge of spiritual things, there are so many souls walking the earth in darkness not knowing life does indeed continue after the death of the physical body. Eventually they will come to understand how wonderful life can be. This is why you should spread your knowledge to those less fortunate than yourselves.

As you become more open and aware of spiritual matters you begin to live your life in a relaxed and trusting way following your intuitions, working on a higher vibration.

When you realise and accept that you are spirit first and are part of the Great Spirit, you can take control over your destiny and your existence. Your spirit, your soul will shine and radiate outwards in all direction with love. You will feel much lighter, your entire heavy load has been left behind and each step you take will be much easier as you journey onward through life helping others.

Surely understanding karma must help you all, you are able to overcome anything and face up to it. If there were no difficulties, no trials, no troubles, no pain, no suffering there would be no evolution, no progression, no spiritual growth only stagnation. Do you see how it all works for the benefit of every soul wherever they are?"

"To be without all the problems sounds wonderful but surely sometime in the distant future the earth would be a much better place when more experienced souls are able to live without suffering?"

"Possibly in time, Although, as you know there are some spirits who are already on earth who see opportunities to serve and plan their life challenges to be of service to others."

"If we were shown clearly the full picture of our existence and the reason why we are here, we would then have something to look forward to and something to aim for."

"All will be clear when you have completed your incarnations to gain knowledge, until then your missions will not be revealed to you."

Beth, a member of the circle said. "So you are saying that we only find out when our karma is completed and only then we will have our answers. I'm afraid that doesn't give me any encouragement, in fact the thought of having to come back over and over again not knowing how many more lives I may have to endure depresses me terribly."

"My dear children you will understand soon, the key lies within you all, then you will be able to unlock the doors and set yourself free. You must free yourselves from mental and emotional striving this will cause you to be chained to negative unproductive thoughts.

When you are free you will then be able to spread your wings and move forward and upwards. And the more aware you become the freer you are and the higher you can rise and greater the understanding you will have earned. Being here today, listening to me shows that you are on the correct path, wanting to learn, having a thirst for knowledge.

The responsibility for creating your reality, your thoughts, words, emotions and your actions in life are directly down to you, when you accept this, your life will change totally and you will begin to understand your mission. Do you see how easy it can be?"

"Thank you, it sounds easy but in reality it is difficult for us poor souls on earth."

"My dear, I do understand what you all have to endure, however every single moment of life offers an opportunity for spiritual growth that is why you need to observe and master your thoughts. That's not too difficult, is it?"

"When you put it like that, probably not."

"You see my dears, all you have to do is control your thoughts because every thought, is constantly raising or lowing your vibrations. That is why you should start your day and make it a habit of thinking calm and positive thoughts. No matter how difficult your problems are, try and imagine a positive outcome. Your mind does not know it is imagination, therefore, it believes all is well with you and relaxes your body. You know how this works in meditation, as you think, you create pictures.

I know life is hard at times but you can make it

better if you can try to understand. Every word creates a symbol and each word you utter has a shape, therefore, stop and think, only send out nice thoughts, do not hurt or be harsh with words, instead make sure they strengthen, heal and comfort. Take care what you say, think and do, because it will stay in your aura, where it will attract more of the same, good or bad. You have heard the expression, 'actions speak louder than words, or thoughts', this is the truth; they do.

You asked for help, now you need to develop caring, kindness, generosity, acceptance, courage and good positive actions, these are things you should do naturally. I know it is not easy when someone hurts you but try and bless them, remember you have all done bad things during your many lifetimes and it could be payback time. We are all part of the Great Spirit our Creator so stop blaming others when things go wrong. That's what you can do; it's not very hard is it?"

"You make everything sound so easy and it is not. Not for us poor souls living here on earth but I will try to do better. Can you tell me, do we all have the same lessons and trials to overcome?"

"We all started on the bottom rung of the ladder, it is up to you how fast you climb to the top. Everyone is different in their level of spiritual growth and understanding; therefore lessons must differ from one soul to another. One person may need to learn how to love and accept a person or a situation. Another may need a challenge or even to face rape, cruelty, abuse or even murder.

Human beings must look at their lives, go within to understand the tests they already have experienced and handle new challenges appropriately as they arrive. It is OK to mourn, grieve, or rejoice you are human and human beings have emotions.

Whatever you sow, that's what you shall reap, without exceptions. I am trying to teach you this, helping you now to understand what we give from the heart is always returned to us tenfold and in many different ways.

You may give a meal and receive a book from someone else. You may give money to one person and receive a holiday from another. Having said that, you must never expect something back from the person you give to, because it negates the Law of Abundance! Moreover, receive everything that comes your way openly with a sense of deserving and gratitude.

If you give something away thinking, 'I'm always bailing him out', or 'I always pay', you are withholding. Generosity is a quality, and that means giving away freely and from your heart. This ensures more will flow in."

Sighing Beth said. "Thank you Daniel. I wonder, will we, can we ever master all these things."

"But of course you will in time. All you have to do is your best to live in abundance, which means flowing with love, happiness, prosperity and success, when you have all this you will have wonderful health, ill health comes with negativity and bad thoughts.

The Great Spirit made you all the same, and within your being you have the ability to make your life on earth a happy place of beauty. You all belong to the one spirit the Great Spirit; therefore you have all that the Great Spirit has. It is up to you, you have free will.

Whatever you see around you, you express in your life whether it is poverty, illness, beauty this is what you hold in your consciousness. In other words, what you think or do is what you are. It is up to you how you live your life how you think, positive or negative thoughts because what you visualise, you create therefore it must come into being. As you think in your heart, so it is. This is the law of abundance.

To master prosperity is to believe that there will always be plenty and thinking positive, talking and acting in that way knowing more will flow in. Do you see?

Abundance dwells within each individual. Everyone has within themselves all the things that will make their life on earth a heavenly place of joy and of beauty. The Great Spirit does indeed want all that is good for you, for everyone. If you as a child of God and are heir to all that the father has, and if you are the beneficiary, then how or why should you lack anything for which you have need?

Human beings live in their consciousness, it is only in your consciousness where you can lack any thing, if this is true, and then what are you conscious of? Have a good look around you, in your surroundings, what do you see? Do you see poverty, illness, and disharmony?

Whatever you hold in your consciousness must express in your life. In other words, what you think becomes reality because thought creates. Therefore, abundance can only flow with the right positive thoughts, words, emotions and deeds. It is also receiving with the right thought, words, emotions and deeds. Because of the Law of Flow, you cannot do one without the other or you block the river of abundance.

Are you beginning to understand the law of abundance does indeed supply every possible need? Look around you my dears, see the abundance of nature, and accept it. The earth does indeed give forth of her abundance. You must accept the abundance.

'As within, so without' means what you think or visualise must come into appearance. This is the law: As a man thinketh in his heart, so is he.

My dear you have to believe, to be positive in what you desire, if you do not believe then whatever it is it will not flow to you.

You must love yourself to live the law of abundance and give to yourselves, and feel comfortable in your own company.

If you do not and cannot love yourself, then how can you love others, your fellow human beings? And if you give to everyone except yourself, it is time to question your motive for giving.

I'm afraid, and it is quite common in your world that some people over-compensate by giving more because they are unable to love, you must not do this for your lack of love and self-worth; this will block the law from operating.

How many times have you heard someone say 'my mother or father didn't have time for me when I was a child, instead they gave me plenty of money to spend to do what I wanted, but I would rather have had more of their time.' Therefore, do not over give to others; keep a balance in giving and receiving.

When you are a success you have a feeling of fulfilment and self-worth, of peace and joy within.

God's Law of Abundance does indeed supply every possible need. All you need do is look around you and see the wonders of nature. The earth brings forth her abundance."

"So, what we think manifests." Jane said.

"Yes that is what I said. If you find yourself in a difficult situation, a serious problem, you should pray. Pray for the qualities you need and for a positive outcome. Once you have faced the problem, learnt from it and what it has to offer you automatically raises your vibration, therefore, you will never have to face that lower-vibration challenge again. It is so very simple my dears."

"In other words we must stay positive at all times even when we are facing the depths of despair?"

"Yes you must. When you begin to feel yourself slipping into a negative way of thinking, start correcting your thoughts and take deep breaths, deep, slow breaths help you to reconnect, apart from the oxygen you breathe you breathe in Paraná, this is the universal life force. I am sure you will have heard of Paraná before.

The Universal Life Force (Paraná) works on the physical body and your astral and mental levels, this is the first two of seven layers of your spirit body (we will talk of this later). Its manifestation on the human body depends on the sunlight, because Paraná radiates/emanates from the sun; most people feel better when the sun shines, it is like a tonic to human beings.

On a sunny day Paraná is abundant, on a cloudy day it is greatly reduced. At night your body uses the Paraná which has been manufactured the previous day; liken it to a storage heater. When you sleep your nerves and muscles relax, and the absorption of Paraná can take place. This is why sleep, even a short nap, is so recuperative, 'people say 'they are going to have a power nap' because they absorb the vitality from the atmosphere.

My dear you did this when you were bringing up your children and it worked, didn't it? Now you know Paraná was at work."

Daniel was talking to me about my younger days with a growing family. I must say my ten minute naps did work. I felt so much better I just took it for granted.

"The universe is a vast energy system of different vibrations just like the different frequencies of a radio, for example when you tune a radio to one station you will hear music, when tuned to another the news, yet another will give you the shipping forecast! All are radio frequencies and have different characteristics, energy has different vibrations too.

This is also how mediumship works; the mediums change their vibrations to 'tune in' to the spirit world that vibrates faster than the human body. However, you choose to perceive energy it is ever present and all-powerful. All emotions vibrate at different levels; love is the strongest energy vibration than any other. The spirit world, your home is of unconditional love.

The non-physical energy known as Paraná animates and flows through all living things, and is the life force, without it everything would wither and die. All healers use this energy helping the sick. In other words, you are breathing the Breath of God."

Interrupting, Beth said. "Thank you for that, I will try and remember to take deep breaths."

"If you feel dispirited, take yourself off to a place of beauty with clean, fresh air. Then you can breathe in the energies of the Great Spirit."

Jean said. "I must admit, when I meditate on a place of beauty, without actually going outside, I always feel much better afterwards. Thank you for everything; you explain things so simply, even I can understand."

Another member of my development circle asked. "You mentioned the law of karma, the law of abundance. Are there any other laws and who made them?"

"Our Creator made the laws. The laws are many and as I continue to teach you I will explain these laws when it is necessary to do so."

It was very late so we said good night and thanked Daniel for his help.

Drugs. Addiction.

During the following week I saw a young women for a reading and healing, she told me how worried she was about her son who was on drugs; she asked me if I could help in any way. I told her I would ask spirit if they could help and I would let her know.

The following meeting with Daniel came very quickly. All my circle members arrived on time very excited wondering what spirit had in store for them from the beyond. Most of the questions they wanted to ask were to do with their own and family experiences.

When I was tuned into Daniel I asked the question. "If a person was addicted to drugs, alcohol, or cigarettes whilst on earth would they still need them when they are in a spirit body?"

"My dear you do not change when you leave the earth life; you take all of your characteristics, your mannerisms including good and bad habits with you back to the spirit realms. However, if you want to smoke, drink or use any other addictive substances you may do so, but the satisfaction does not last, it is not meant to, but you can have it as long as you require it."

Jokingly Jane said. "Oh! Great I stopped smoking because of my health, so I will be able to smoke again without having to fear of getting cancer."
I'm not sure what Daniel thought to that outburst, he didn't make any direct remarks to Jane.

"Addictive drugs have a ruthless, harsh grip on those poor souls who are the victims of a serious drug habit. The desire for drugs has become deep rooted in the soul itself, and the agony of spirits is heart breaking to see. Some of these poor souls are then earthbound because they need to satisfy their cravings.
They frequently obtain some satisfaction from being close or even controlling human beings on earth who have similar addictions, similar vibrations. They can force them to become addicts to various drugs. Earth bound means those who do not want to leave the earth vibration, therefore living in the lower astral level, which is closer to earth.
It takes time but eventually those poor souls will find their way out of their hell, the hell they have made for themselves."

"Oh dear, I feel so sorry for them, I thought their habits would disappear or become easier to get rid of once they were in the spirit realms." Jane said sheepishly.

"No, I am afraid not. However, hopefully some good will have come out of this experience, perhaps a karmic debt or lesson for the parents. You must decide what you tell the questioner."

"Thank you for that." Jane said

"It is always a pleasure."

Suicide.

"I suppose there are a number of addicts who take their lives in desperation. What would happen if someone took their own life because of drugs or, in the hope of arriving sooner at a happier existence? Those who believe in life after the death, are told, that the spirit world is a place of beauty and of love, therefore I can understand why a person could well be tempted to do this." I said.

"My dear, suicide is a life-lesson that may be chosen by the soul, when contracts have been made between souls to experience the heartache, trauma and emotional upset of a swift, unexpected ending of a life, suicide is generally the way they choose.

Remember all souls have freedom of choice, if they decide on suicide for an early return home because they are overwhelmed with their human existence; it is the choice of the soul.

The soul may think it can stop its continued frustrations by leaving the existing physical life by killing the body in some way. Sadly, that is not so for those spirits will eventually see the error of their ways and soon request a return to the earth plane. If they are allowed, it is in order to complete the life that they cut short in pursuit of a mistaken idea.

Suicide is not the ultimate sin as some humans belief systems teach. Once the soul leaves the body it returns to a world of unconditional love to evaluate what went wrong and how to experience the desired lessons in a new way; it will eventually come back to fulfil the lessons.

The beautiful realms of those who have lived a good life cannot be opened by cheating, no matter what may have been the motive; suicide will delay the entrance into a better world.

Those of you who care for their fellow man and do good helping those less fortunate than yourselves will be much surer of reaching a higher and more radiant realm."

Emma put the question. "Some people have taken their lives due to terrible grief they have suffered after losing a loved one, expecting to re-join them in heaven. What would happen to those poor souls?"

"Oh! My dear what a pity, there is no excuse for suicide, because this is an act of cowardice and they will have to pay for their stupidity. I am sad to say, in such cases the result of their suicide will not be what they expected, they will not be reunited to their loved ones, and they will find themselves separated from them."

"How dreadful, it's so unfair. So what you're saying is that we do not have the right to end our life, for any reason?" Emma said sadly.

"That is exactly what I am saying, no one has the right to take their life, or any other person's life, that right belongs to the Great Spirit alone. Those who voluntarily commit suicide violate Gods laws. Nevertheless, most spirits when they arrive here immediately regret taking their lives especially those who were physically healthy."

Emma jumped in quickly and said. "You said voluntary? Isn't suicide always voluntary?"

"Human beings who are mentally ill and kill themselves do not know what they are doing. Is that voluntary suicide?"

"I don't know, perhaps not." Emma said. "What are your thoughts of those who commit suicide because they are fed up, sick of life?"

"It is extremely foolish, why didn't they get involved in some useful work? Hobbies, charitable work for example. If they had done so, life would not have been as tiresome for them, but could have been very rewarding."

Emma continued. "Yes I can see that, can you tell us what happens to those who resort to suicide in order to escape from the troubles and disappointments of this world; is that the same as my last question?"

"I do not wish to give the impression that I lack understanding, for that is not true. But in my opinion they are weaklings and cowards who lack courage of their existence. You have heard the saying 'God helps those who help themselves,' this is very true. The Great Spirit does indeed help those who suffer bravely, but not those who have neither strength nor courage.

One of the reasons why we must pass on knowledge to the unenlightened is to help them understand that their troubles, their problems of life are trials or lessons that they chose to help themselves either to learn or pay back a debt. My dear if they were to endure their troubles without complaint great will be their reward.

The more knowledge that is received will help

those who are in turmoil. All it needs then is to think about what they intend to do."

"Yes I see. I understand what you are saying, but what about those poor souls who die out of despair, would that be suicide?" Emma asked rather hesitantly.

"But of course it is, can you not see self-abandonment, wallowing in self-pity is suicide? The souls have been lacking in courage, grit, purpose and commitment, or had failed to make the best of their intelligence to help themselves out of their difficulties.

I am sure you are aware that there are souls who would rather die of hunger than earn their living by manual labour because it is beneath them. I have heard human beings say 'you won't get me doing that job, it's for stupid people.' It would go still harder with them if they had been one of those who were too proud. However, those who caused the person to commit suicide, or those who might have prevented it, would be more to blame for the act than the poor soul who took his life, who would therefore be judged leniently; they would not."

"I feel we need to talk over all reasons of suicide with you so that we might help all those who read this book. Therefore, can you tell us please, what is the cause of weariness of this life that causes suicide?"

"Yes we must do that. In most cases weariness is idleness, overindulgence, lack of confidence, sitting around doing nothing. Those who seek employment and use their natural talents in the search of some useful work in a pleasing occupation will find their time passes quickly. Therefore, they are more capable of tolerating unexpected changes of life, with patience and resignation. "

"Thank you. Can you tell us if there are any other reasons why people commit suicide?"

"Yes, I am sorry to say, there are a great number of suicides due to the obsessing or possessing influence of earthbound spirits. I talked earlier about drug addicts making the life of those on earth a nightmare. Some of these spirits are driven by a desire to torment their victims on earth until they have had enough of the hell and take their lives.

There are others, who have committed suicide and find when they reach the spirit world they are not dead and believe themselves to be still alive. Because they have no knowledge of a spirit world they believe that their suicide attempts have failed and continue trying to find ways of ending their lives again through an earthly human being.

When these poor confused souls come in contact with human beings whose natures are sensitive and sympathetic they cling to that physical body and impress on the minds of that person, depressive, dark and morbid thoughts, to instigate them to take their own lives."

"Thank you Daniel but that sounds horrific." Jane said.

Homosexuality and Heterosexuality.

"If we have time I would like to tell you a about a young man I knew years ago if that is OK?"

"But of course my dear." Daniel replied with his wonderful gentle voice.

"Years ago I owned a health hotel, apart from hotel guests, we had clients who came for a day of beauty, the gym and or for specific treatments. During that time, we had a rather nice man who came regularly for treatments on a Sunday after he had his two boys staying with him for the weekend. He must have felt the need for relaxation following a hectic time with the children.
After many weekends the beauty therapists and I got to know him pretty well, or so we thought. I don't know how the conversation turned to homosexuality, but he began to tell us

that he was gay. We were dumb struck, he had two boys, and therefore how could he be gay? One of the therapists blurted out. "How can you be gay, you are married and have two children?' Before he had chance to answer the first question she went on to ask, 'Does your wife know you are gay?' I thought this very rude of her and give her a telling off when he had gone.

One day when I was alone with him, I don't know why, he told me the story of his married life. He said, 'I always looked at men but it never dawned on me that I was gay, perhaps I closed my mind to it; I think I must have. I loved my wife very much, and still do, therefore it wasn't a problem making love to her, and because of that I didn't believe I was homosexual.

It was not long after my second son was born that I started to feel sexual thoughts towards other men. I must say it was a bit of a shock to me. However, after a great deal of thought and analysing my behaviour as a heterosexual, I began to realise that I was living a lie.

To cut a long story short, I told my wife, in the gentlest way I could, that I was gay. She could not believe it, but when she knew I was serious; she said nothing but sat and wept. We eventually agreed to split up, it was very hard for us both because we still loved each other, but it would have been impossible to live together under those circumstances.

We are still friends and I have the children

every weekend.'

I felt so sorry for them both, and often think of them and their lives. Can you tell me if there is a karmic or other reason for this to happen?"

"There could be many reasons why a soul chooses to incarnate as a gay or lesbian person, knowing fair well that their life would bring them mental and physical abuse from those who do not know any better. The soul could be paying back karmic debts, perhaps lack of understanding for homosexuals or bullying a gay or lesbian in a previous life, or simply wanting the experience and knowledge of same sex relationships and all the problems that goes with it.

As I have always said, you cannot understand a situation until you have experienced it. Generally, the main reason why spirits return to earth is to learn and to pay back karma debts, or finish something left undone.

It is possible the spirit had a traumatic experience in a previous life whilst in the body of a woman, such as rape, physical abuse from a husband or other male persons. Therefore, before incarnation to earth again, the spirit may have decided to take the sensitivity and gentleness of a female human being and be protected from all the things that happened in a previous life.

I do not know, whatever the reason, there is no

escaping, what you sow you will most definitely reap. This is cause and effect.

Spirit is both male and female; however, a spirit usually will be inclined towards one sex rather than both; the person mentioned above, most likely preferred the female gender."

Incest.

"Thank you. That sounds easy to take in.

My friend told me, when she was a child her father sexually abused her. This dreadful nightmare has left her with terrible emotional scars. At the moment on the television we are hearing about so many men committing child sexual abuse. I find it hard to understand why anyone could do such a thing, and some to their own children. Can you tell us why incest is allowed to take place?"

"Yes, it is dreadful and I will try and explain this to you. However, I must say again, all incarnations good or bad are chosen by the spirit in a pre-birth plan, and agreed upon by all those taking part in that life situation, prior to their incarnation to earth.

I cannot know everyone's life challenges, and or, trials; therefore, I cannot say exactly why your friend experienced this traumatic time in her life. Obviously, the 'energy' of incest has been carried into this new life to be healed.

Your friend could well have been the perpetrator of sexual abuse in a previous life, and he or she decided when in the spirit world this would be the way to heal the problem; it was their choice. Karmic debts will hold you back from moving forward; therefore healing that situation is necessary to enable a soul to progress.

Never judge another human being, we have all be there and done terrible things in our many lives. This is why it should be easy to forgive a person no matter what they have done. It could have been you in a previous life. Try and look beyond the physical body and see the poor soul who doesn't know any better."

Jane said rather shocked. "Wow! I didn't expect to hear that. The information has given me an awful lot to contemplate. We human beings don't think like that and I am pleased you told us."

"I am also very pleased to hear that, I want to make you think and understand what life is all about." Daniel replied.

Feeling tired I said to Daniel "I would like that very much but I do feel a little tired now. There is so much to take in to understand and we like time to have a cuppa and discuss what you have taught us before they have to go home. So we must say goodnight."

"As you wish, you must rest. Good bye."

Everything Daniel said tonight was very deep and in some ways quite hard to digest, that is why we had to talk whilst it was fresh in our minds. Thank goodness all that is said at these meetings is typed on the computer and recorded as I repeat the words Daniel speaks to me so nothing is lost. There might be a few misspelt words and no grammar but on the whole it is OK.

The circle members stayed much later than usual dissecting all that Daniel had said. I must say some of us were getting a little heated at times.

Elsie said. "Daniel makes everything sound so easy, perhaps it is, but knowing and doing are two different things! I wish all the talk of positivity, the way in which we think and so on was as easy for us."

Carol responded. "When we talk to Daniel I for one thinks I will practice what he is saying in my everyday life. But it's not long before I'm back on my physical earthly way of living shouting at the kids, moaning and groaning at life. Maybe I have a long way to go before I can truly practice a spiritual life, a true spiritual life like Daniels. And what if we have to incarnate thousand more times to get there? Oh my! I feel beaten before I start."

Smiling I said. "That's a defeatist attitude, think positive girls. I bet Daniel is listening to us and shaking his head. I bet he despairs of us, especially me; he's been with me for many lifetimes. Oh dear! I must try harder."

"Well at least you have been working for spirit a very long time, healing, your mediumship work and teaching, so you must have some brownie points."

Laughing I said. "I don't think it works like that. Remember what Daniel said about having lots of knowledge but may not have other good characteristics, such as morals. There will be things I need to learn otherwise I wouldn't be here."

"Yes but you probably won't have as many incarnations to suffer." Elsie said.

"None of us could possibly know what is in store for us. You must not think like that, if you do you will not sleep tonight. And we have a lot of work to do developing our spiritual gifts perhaps that is where we should concentrate our energies for now?" I replied with confidence.

I had to call time because I was very tired and I think they would have continued with their friendly banter until morning.

When they had gone I got ready for bed and sat in my dressing gown for quite some time. My mind was now active and running riot again so I decided to try and meditate for a little while hoping to receive a little inspiration.

I curled up on the sofa and closed my eyes, which really is the wrong thing to do for meditation but I was tired. Within seconds, I had fallen asleep.

I dreamt that I was sitting on a bench in a beautiful garden full of fragrant flowers; it was peaceful except for the singing of the birds that settled around me. The perfume from the flowers made me feel quite intoxicated, suddenly I noticed a visitor sitting next to me, when I turned to look to see whom it was the image faded.

"Hello. Who's there? Is it you Daniel?" I enquired in my dream.

"Yes my dear child. When you wake, meditate and listen, it is here that you will find your true self. Meditation allows you to free yourself, to open the door for the divine energy to flow and as you raise your vibrations, you will attract help that is more spiritual. You must remember also, the power of prayer."

"I responded to the invisible presence. Yes I know how powerful prayer is. My prayers have been answered many times."

"Yes that is good. Prayer is communicating with the Great Spirit and is like a telephone line. Every word and thought you send along is a prayer. Continue with your book and do not worry. Telling God how impossible it is, is being negative you must direct your thoughts in a positive way."

"I will try." I said sighing.

"Have faith dear child. Faith is an active ingredient in bringing your prayers about. God the Great Spirit always answers those who pray from the heart. Sometimes God answers your prayers in a practical way rather than with miracles."

"But I do have faith; the human side of me keeps letting me down. I get very tired and find it hard to pray at times."

"Many people pray without really expecting the prayer to be granted, so they take no action."

"Yes, I know because I feel like that at times."

"The Law of Prayer is to ask and then believe it

will be granted. Always thank the Great Spirit and prepare to receive what you have asked for."

"Yes I will. Thank you. Does it help if there are a few people gathered together in prayer asking for the same thing?"

"Yes it does. If more than one person joins in with your prayers it strengthens the power of the prayer. When you offer a prayer, try to keep holding the vision of perfection, meditate and listen."

"Thank you very much. I feel better already."

"Bless you. There are many natural Laws and this is the Law of Prayers. Good bye."

"What are the other Laws?" There was no answer. "Hello." I said again but he had gone.

I remembered all that Daniel said to me when I woke up in the morning. Although it took quite some time for me to get my bearings, and then I started to remember it all. Fantastic I wondered if this would happen every time I went to sleep and decided to do what Daniel said, although I thought I was already doing that.

Chapter Three.

Forgetfulness of the past.

The following week we meditated as usual and when I felt ready we all greeted Daniel and talked about everyday things with him and some asked about personal problems.

"Oh I have just remembered a question." I said quickly before Daniel had time to talk. "I understand there is a loss of memory with incarnated spirits. Can you tell me please why we lose the memory of our past and how we can be responsible for our actions and atone for faults, of which we have no memory? Surely it would make our life here much easier if we knew what mistakes we had made in a previous life."

"Let me explain my dear, as the incarnating spirit comes close to the unborn child, memories slowly fade in the confusion as the union takes place when the spirit attaches itself to the unborn child. Once the chosen spirit has completed the union with the unborn child all ideas and remembrance of the past has gone.

This is very important, because of this the soul is more fully itself with each new life; therefore, a soul is better able to distinguish between right and wrong, good and evil. If the soul remembered its past it would not have the freedom to choose and would not be true in its actions and there would be no spiritual growth to take place. However, there are times when a soul does recall events from the past, but it takes many life times of learning and sensitivity to recall this information; it has to be earned. Do you understand?"

"Yes, I think so. We would pretend to care and do the right thing even if we would rather do the opposite. So it wouldn't come from the heart." I said.

"Exactly, that is correct. You live your lives on earth and when you return to the spirit world, all your actions are shown to you, you are able to see your faults, and where you went wrong and how you could have prevented them.

When it is time for you to incarnate again, you are able with help, to choose your next body and the lessons needed to make you more equipped to repair and heal the mistakes you have made in previous lives and at the same time improve your spiritual growth.

You are never alone, superior spirit beings help you in your new tasks and guide you on your new road."

The circle chatted amongst themselves for a

minute or two about amnesia in the new life.

"Would you like to ask me anything or shall I continue?"

I answered. "We were just saying we understand and appreciate the way you explain things to us in such a simple manner. Thank you and please continue."

Free Will.

"I will speak to you about free will now. A spirit individual may have lived a long time, many incarnations without having improved morally and yet advanced in intelligence.

You must experience all things for you to understand life, to strive for perfection. Knowledge is good but not without acquiring good moral standards."

Again Elsie interrupted Daniel. "I never really thought about spirit morals being separate to intelligence, I suppose I thought if you were intelligent spiritually then you would automatically be an honest, honourable person. That has given me food for thought. Thank you. Oh! I'm sorry again."

"I am pleased about that, all knowledge should make you think and to help you make the right decisions in life.

As you know, you are all given free will, but remember to use it wisely and trust in the universal energy to guide you on and through your difficult path ahead. It is a wonderful gift; however make sure you travel on the correct path and not in the negative direction. It is very important that you use your free will for the good this is all part of your evolvement and of your learning process.

You must try to create balance and harmony between the mind spirit and body, because any negativity is always a destructive energy, which can make you become ill and depression could take hold, which could take a long time to shake off.

You know yourself my dear, when a patient comes to you for help you are able to see the imbalance within their chakras and their auric field, hence their illness. Just by living in a heavy physical world can cause you to be unbalanced, or not to be in harmony with your spirit, mind and body.

You must try to think positive to maintain your natural strong connection with your spirit self. Always create pictures of good outcomes in your life in the physical world to achieve the very best mental, emotional and spiritual health.

I feel that you should know how to protect yourselves therefore I will explain the law of fortification.

Fortify yourself with the All-Mighty Power available to you. Consciously surround yourself with this universal energy. See it swirl clockwise and counter clockwise, a force so powerful that nothing can penetrate it. Protect yourself morning noon and night. Use this consciously. You must be aware and believe of this protection before it can become real to you. Only as you ask can you receive. It is the law.

Apply the Universal Life Force to protect you against all negative energies, all disease, and all things that are not for your highest good. This is your heritage, your gift of God the Great Spirit. Before you were sent to earth, the Great Spirit knew the problems you would have to face and gave you this protection.

My dears this has always been yours to use but you have not remembered. Now the curtain is being slowly drawn aside, and many things are being brought for you to remember. This mighty protection is yours to use, but, of course you have free will to use or reject it. This is the law of fortification.

And now my dear children good night and bless you."

I met Daniel on my own a couple of days later at 7pm. I started to meditate at my computer with Daniel in mind. It wasn't long before I felt him over shadow me. (Come into my space, my auric field.) "Hello Daniel." I said.

"Good evening my dear. I understand your circle members were not happy when we last met. Do not worry, they will think about what was said and feel differently by the time we meet again. It takes time for people to understand the workings of spirit and of course we must remember they have not had your experience, they are new to spiritual teachings."

"Yes you are right Daniel. What is easy for me could be very difficult for them to understand at the moment. I find it difficult to remember how I felt in the beginning of my development; it is over fifty years ago."

"Yes it is a while in earthly time, and my dear you have come a long way. So today you will learn and pass on what I say to all those who are less fortunate than yourself. One of your roles in this life is to teach. Therefore I will talk to you this evening about the law of action.

Many human beings spend time praying and sit daydreaming about things they would like to do. However, unless they put these things into action, their praying and daydreaming is of no use. Action is the only thing that accomplishes anything and without action, you have static or abortive ideas. Do you see, any idea you may get, unless it is acted upon, is a total waste of time and energy?

The Great Spirit does, indeed, answer your

prayers, you may not think so at times, but it is true. The Great Spirit and you are one and the Great Spirit guides you to 'do' that which our Creator directs, and so, that is working with God. 'All things are possible with God, the Great Spirit!' But what does it really mean?

Everyone knows that the Great Spirit can do all things, therefore you also can do all things and you are the only one who must do it. Then, and only then are you working with God, and all things are then possible to you. You will not be the one doing it, it will be the Great Spirit within who 'doeth the works.' Know this: Nothing is accomplished without action. This is the law of action. Do you understand my dear?"

"Yes I do, thank you. When I was a young girl my mum and I would 'pipe dream' about what we would do if we won the football pools. Looking back it was rather silly, however because we were so poor it gave us innocent pleasure. We would talk for hours dreaming of nice things that we didn't have. I know it's not really what you are talking about, it just brought back memories, and the point I am making is that in those days most people would 'pipe dream' of better things in life. And most people wouldn't do anything to improve themselves or act upon it."

"Yes I remember when you did this. I will now

talk about the law of Compensation. Every act of goodness has its compensation. Since human beings are a law unto themselves, you are the giver and the receiver. You give of all that you have; and all comes back to you. You give love, compassion, money or yourself, your time, energy, wisdom, joy and laughter.

Do you understand you indeed have all things within you? Human beings need never beg the Creator for any good thing, for all that the Great Spirit has, is yours. The Great Spirit is Love; you are love also. The Great Spirit is substance; there is only one substance, from which all things are made. If there is only one substance, how can you differ in any way from God the Great Spirit? God is pure Spirit. You are also a spiritual being. Do you believe it? Can you accept it? You are a divine being made in the image and perfection. Think on this perfection that you are, and as you keep this picture before you, you will be that I AM THAT I AM. This is the law of Compensation.

Take your time and digest what I teach you, it will them become easier in your everyday life."

I repeated what Daniel said, I suppose to help it to sink in. "Are you saying what you give out you will receive? We are part of the Great Spirit, therefore whatever God has we also have. We, the human race and God are one; therefore we can use the power within us."

"Yes. But think on it a while. We will move on and talk of karma, which is generally what life on earth is all about. Are you writing this down?"

Karma.

"Yes thank you, if I may say something first? I understand our lives are all to do with karma. I have read many books on the subject each author with differing opinions. I would like to understand exactly how it works, in your words please. I believe it is about things we have done that have affected others, good or bad in our past lives, debts we have to pay back. I hope I am right because this makes sense to me."

"Yes you are correct. I will explain so that everyone will be able to understand the workings of karma. Karma is the natural justice of the universe that controls the actions of all living beings. The operation of natural law cannot be cancelled or changed under any circumstances; it is the law of cause and effect.

Since all of us have been give free will, it is always our choice, or will to choose the way we shall live good or bad. Therefore what you do, how you live will affect the Natural Law.

The simple way to explain this to you is that spirit beings incarnate over and over again because they do not have the wisdom of the experience unless they have performed, lived through, or been a part of the experience itself.

For example all souls have knowledge of wars, cruelty, floods, famine and so on throughout your world, but only those souls who took part in one way or another have complete knowledge and wisdom of the physical, mental, and emotional traumas of the events caused to the human and spirit body.

Human beings often say to someone who is going through a traumatic emotional problem or illness, 'I understand how you feel'. That cannot be true unless that person has experienced that particular situation. In other words, living through an experience is the only way possible to gather wisdom from that experience. Can you see how it works?"

"Yes thank you. Please continue."

"Furthermore, to truly have the full wisdom of a situation the soul must understand why each person behaved as they did. This can only be done when the soul feels deep inside it and evaluates the experience.

Natural law is both impersonal and impartial; it is sometimes understood as a karmic debt. The natural law ensures that everyone receives spiritually exactly what they are entitled, what they have earned in that lifetime.

This law applies not only to individuals but to all nations, all countries, everyone on the planet. Therefore, karma maintains balance through the laws of cause and effect, which ultimately means that if you are good and kind to your fellow human beings and other living things you will be rewarded, but if you behave badly then no bad or evil act goes unpunished, whether in this life or the next.

Do you see it is through karma that each soul works out its own salvation, by its actions? No one else can do it for you; it is the part of your lives to put straight unfinished business from the past; these conditions influence all that you do.

Most spirit beings incarnate because they want to balance their past-life energies just as they had planned before they came to earth, but sometimes it doesn't always work out.

There are souls who are not ready to learn and refuse to accept the opportunities their new earth family offer them for their spiritual growth and the changes in their karma. Therefore, they will continue to carry on the old ways, the disputes, wars, addiction, cruelty or feelings towards others.

They allow their lower natures to dominate their higher instincts, and then they must pay the price, just as every goodness and kindness automatically means they are better as a result.

Things that are worth doing cannot be easy, if they were, then they would not be worth having.

Does this make sense to you thus far?"

"Yes it does. We always discus what you have said, which always makes things a little clearer. If we have any questions we will ask, thank you."

"Yes you must understand what I teach, otherwise it is pointless. I will continue.

You may have karmic debts with members of your soul group, these souls are at the same spiritual development, the same evolutionary stage as you and with whom you have shared many lifetimes. Because you have lived many times, you have been playing the roles of husband, wife, daughter, son, brother, sister, mother, father, friend, and enemy to the same spirits. I will explain all about group souls at a later time.

My dear as an individual soul and for your personal evolution there will be particular lessons you need to learn for your growth so that you can move forward.

All your thoughts, actions and your intentions including everything you say, every word is recorded; this is what creates your karma. You make choices with everything you feel, say, or do, and these choices you make will produce a current of energy, a ripple effect that will travel throughout the whole of the universe and through time. This again is your karma, good or bad if not in this lifetime, future lives. Therefore, can you understand, it makes sense that what you did in your lives is carried forward to your present life, which determines the events you are experiencing now. You have no one else to blame for your karmic trials but yourself.

You can see how your life on earth is very much like a play on a stage and how you act out your part, your role in your present life determines the way in which you progress. You are all responsible for your actions, there are no excuses, and no one is exempt.

Human beings can only do what they believe is right and good. As long as they believe in their own heart they are doing right, it is, indeed, right. However, if you behave in a bad way you shall receive bad results. If you are good, then good will always follow you. This is the Karmic Law.

Remember, if you give out love you will get love in return, if you show compassion you will receive compassion. You always get what you send out."

"Thank you very much for that. I will explain to the circle all that you have said this evening. And of course it is all transcribed so they will be able to see it word for word themselves. It will help them to understand why they have to experience certain things in this life; I feel sure this will help them, and to all those who read your words.

I am feeling tired again, can we please close our meeting now."

"But of course, rest my dear and we will speak again soon. Good night dear child. Bless you."

There is so much Daniel teaches us and in a very simple way. Nevertheless we have to digest it so that it all becomes a natural way of living. However we must not have our heads in the clouds we still have to live on earth, this heavy world where cruelty and bad things continue.

I met with circle members again to discuss what Daniel had told me. Time moves very quickly these days, it must be getting old that makes it seem so. The girls arrived on time again all excited. After they settled down we talked for quite a while and then Jean said. "It would be much better if we knew what was in store for us, don't you think Barbara?"

"Well it would, but what Daniel said makes sense, if we knew why we were here then I am sure we would behave to our detriment. Nothing at all would come from our hearts we would just play along to get extra marks, so to speak. Then of course we would have to come back time and time again; it would be much harder for us."

"I suppose you are right Barbara. It's such a toil

learning these lessons and working through traumas, hardships, trials and so on. I have had a rotten life nothing has ever been easy for me." Jean said miserably."

I said. "I think we should print out copies of the pages of what Daniel has told us then we could all have a copy and read it every time we feel down. I know we shouldn't feel like this but we are only human. Daniel would say 'if you try hard and you fail to do what you started, it doesn't matter pick yourself up and start again.' The Great Spirit just wants us to try, to do our best that is all we can do.

I do feel in time when we know more about spiritual things we will do better with our lives. Don't you agree?" They all agreed with me and I continued. "I don't want any of you to go home defeated before you start, you must think of the wonderful outcome, your rewards in the spirit world from your efforts."

"Your right again Barbara, we are thinking in a very negative way we must stop and be grateful for what we are receiving from the realms of spirit, we are so fortunate to learn all that Daniel is teaching us. He would be very disappointed listening to us. Although he did say that anything we are not happy with we should put it to one side until we can understand." Beth said.

We talked generally and they went home late once again. It wasn't long after they left I went to bed and thought about all that Daniel had said. I always found it difficult to sleep after a meeting with Daniel, too much information to digest.

Not sleeping made me think about a few months earlier when I couldn't have a development circle at home because I didn't get much peace and quiet in my life, mostly during the spring and summer months because of where I lived.

The street comprised of old stone back-to-back terrace houses with a new complex of town houses and two story flats at the top. At first sight, it didn't look too bad having its own car park, courtyard and gardens that were serviced; it had to be a bonus.

I moved in to be near my mum who was suffering with senility and she was unable to walk or do anything for herself. She had some help from social services but not nearly enough. It wasn't long before I found my new home and lifestyle had become a nightmare.

The neighbours were from hell. Loud music bellowed out at night, shouting and carrying on in the streets was a daily occurrence. To make things worse most of the neighbourhood children used the courtyard as a playground. I had to tolerate twenty to thirty children playing football, skating, cricket and other childlike games after school, weekends and school holidays, with toddlers playing the remainder of the time.

I hardly ever had any respite from the noise. Listening to the radio or watching television was near impossible, no amount of complaining helped at all, in fact, it made things worse with nasty obscene letters posted through my letterbox.

Parents didn't care; in fact some parents brought their children by car and dropped them off to play with the children already living on the street, only too glad to get rid of them for an afternoon. I might just as well have placed my lounge suite and bed in the middle of a public playground. It wasn't that I disliked children, I adored them, but this situation was unacceptable.

Perhaps looking back I needed to learn tolerance.

It was winter time, so I started to have some peace and quiet and moved the circle from mums to my place as the children were at home indoors. I had started to catch up with my sleep, however now for wonderful reasons I couldn't sleep. I'm not complaining really but I will have to find a way of stopping my mind jumping from one subject to another, never still. On these nights meditation didn't work either.

Wednesday soon came around and I was feeling

a little more rested. The girls arrived on time as usual, smiling from ear to ear.

I said. "What are you all smiling at? You all look like the cat that got the cream."

"Where just excited Barbara and can't wait to talk with Daniel." Jane said grinning.

Her smile and laughter was always so infectious and once we started laughing we couldn't stop. And this time was no exception for some unknown reason we found ourselves in hysterics. Could it have been spirit presence and upliftment, I don't know?

Elsie had typed and printed copies of what Daniel had taught us and handed them out to all of us. I had to tell them quickly to concentrate on this evening and leave the papers until later and read them at home.

We settled down and as usual when everyone was comfortable I sat down at the computer and said "Hello Daniel are you waiting for us?"

"Yes good evening to you all, you sound very happy."

"Yes I suppose we are." I said still wanting to laugh.

"That is good; laughter is good for the soul. Do you have any questions for me before I start?"

"No thank you Daniel, we are eager to hear what you have to say this evening." Beth replied.

"Very well I will talk this evening about giving thanks. My dears we should all give thanks, let each day of your life be a day of thanksgiving. Give thanks for all things, all things great and small, good or bad because as you know all things are for a purpose. If you are faced with a problem give thanks, I know it is not easy but give thanks anyway because there are no problems there is always an answer.

If you meditate on the problem you will receive the answer in your gut. Always go with your gut feelings usually they are correct. If some disaster comes upon you, give thanks because when it is has gone you will be stronger, well equipped to help another through a similar experience.

Know this my dears, no one comes to earth alone; you have your guardian angel by your side, always; remember this. Never rush headlong into a situation that is not good for you, calmly reason it out and then go ahead if it seems right for you. This does not mean it shall always be right, but if you take a wrong turn, it doesn't matter, start again.

You have so much to learn through experience. If you do not experience the 'thing', you cannot truly know it. The greatest of all teachers is the one who has experienced the thing he speaks of, for he speaks from the heart. Therefore, give thanks for all that was, is, and shall ever be.

Do you understand, when I have said 'you need to experience a lesson to understand it?' Give thanks for your difficulties for you are learning that is why you incarnate so many times on earth. This is the Law of Thanksgiving"

Light Workers.

Usually we discuss what we are going to ask Daniel at our weekly meetings but on this occasion Emma asked out of the blue. "I was on the internet and came across some talk on light workers. Can you please explain what light workers are?"

"Light workers my dears are wonderful devoted spirit people who volunteer, before their incarnation, to help and to heal the planet and all those who live there.

Each light worker is dedicated to serving others; however, life on earth causes a form of amnesia in light workers, similar to everyone else born on earth. Therefore they forget their true spiritual status, their identities and plans, and their abilities to assist the earth and all living creatures.

They are very enlightened souls and have within themselves the ability to attain spiritual awaken faster than most other souls on earth because they are older souls with more experience.

Most light workers discover naturally their inborn spiritual gifts, spiritual communication skills such as clairvoyance, mediumship and spiritual healing abilities. These are the gifts that they volunteered to use, to heal the earth and the population.

These brave souls have a deeply strong inner desire to spread goodness, light, love, healing and knowledge on your planet earth; this is their plan, this is their mission. They chose to do this by the means of writing, teaching, counselling, healing and talking about their spiritual experiences, they want to help the world's problems; social and environmental. They do this through their spiritual belief systems and usually work as healers in some way.

They consciously choose to become well-versed in the understanding of the law of karma, which is the mechanism, the workings of all life: There are many of Gods Laws to become familiar with and to live by.

I must say that light workers are not all the same, there are various levels of spiritual enlightenment and expertise. However, they are all wonderful souls who have a deeply strong inner desire to spread goodness, light, love and knowledge on your planet earth; this is their plan, their mission.

Most light workers do not have an easy life

with many obstacles and challenges to overcome for the benefit of humanity as a whole. For example, a soul may plan, for instance, to be ill most of their life on earth or have a number of various problems so that others close to them who lack compassion are given the opportunity to learn and express themselves fully in a more compassionate way.

They do this to understand fully the trials of earth, which enables them to fulfil their mission. Can you see yourself in this situation?"

"No not yet but I think Barbara is a light worker."

I chipped in saying "Yes. I have always had an inner feeling of being a light worker and you have definitely described my life."

"It takes courage and strength my dear for a soul to make their way through the karmic burden, and at times you have questioned all the trauma you have had to endure; now you know and others will realize eventually that they are essentially beings of light.

They have to go through the hard trials themselves so that they will be able to help others in finding their own true selves. This generally requires great determination and perseverance within, on an inner level, when many light workers have become depressed and in a state of self-doubt, self-denial and even hopelessness. Only by going through all stages of earths, challenges and trials are they themselves able to eventually understand how to help others achieve a state of true happiness and enlightenment.

With their controlled intention and thought vibrations, they can heal anything; mind over matter. There are no limits, except those they place upon their healing abilities. They are already aware of the power of their thoughts and they are continuing to learn that their thoughts are even more powerful than they suspected! Remember this when you are healing, you can do this work."

I said. "Thank you for that. Every word you have said applies to me, I have gone through so much hardship and traumas in this life, it has sometimes been beyond my strength and ability, but somehow I got through it all. You have confirmed what I felt, which makes me feel a great deal better."

"I wonder why souls would wish to come back to earth to suffer all over again. I don't think I would." Carol said.

"I have already said these spirit beings have a desire to help mankind and want to pursue this amazing, loving mission, knowing they will have to endure the heaviness and confusion of earthly life. They feel drawn, like a magnet, to help people; they are kind-hearted, sensitive and empathic and as I have already stated are likely to be healers, teachers and in a caring profession."

Beth spoke. "That is very interesting thank you for that. Can you tell me if light workers are very religious souls?"

"Their religion is spiritual, living Gods Laws to the best of their ability. However, they can make mistakes out of temporary states of ignorance and confusion as anyone else.

As you know we have all lived many times and light workers were deeply involved with spirituality, and, or religions in the past, some light workers were witches, shamans, priests, priestesses, monks, nuns, mediums and so on.

They built bridges between the two worlds, your world and the spirit world; as you do now, which of course in those days were a mystery, they were rejected and persecuted and many of them were sentenced to burn at the stake for the gifts they possessed."

Laughing I said. "Thank you Daniel, that makes me smile because I am always joking about being burned at the stake."

Beth went on to ask. "I also saw on the internet something about our vibrations. I didn't understand so could you please explain to us what it is?"

Your energetic vibrations/karma.

"Yes my dear. All things vibrate at various rates of vibration. If you find oneness or joy with another body or person it means you vibrate to their thought vibration and there is a bond established or a like thinking which makes for harmony. All things gravitate to a like vibration. That is what is meant when our Lord spoke of 'many mansions.'

When you are on the earth plane, you function on a certain vibration. When you pass from, or out of this vibration, you naturally by the very law of gravitation, gravitate to your own rate of vibration.

Each one is forever exactly, where they belong. They could not function anywhere else in their present state of consciousness, or vibration.

As you rise in your consciousness, you raise your rate of vibration; it fluctuates as you think. That is why you are up in the clouds one minute or in a high state of vibration or you may be at the depths of despair in another moment. You may choose this day in which state of vibration you wish to function. This is the law of vibration Your soul vibrates at many different levels, and many different things can affect your vibrations.

For example, when you feel good and are in harmony with your whole self your spirit, mind and body you vibrate at a perfect level and as your moods change so does your vibrations either lower when you are negative and higher when you are positive. When your soul vibrates, an energy pattern is sent out by you to the Universe for all to see.

Not only your soul vibrates, animals, trees, every living thing vibrates, they all move and vibrate at the rate that is correct for them. The city vibrates differently to the quiet peaceful countryside. You may not notice but the earth also constantly vibrates although on a different level, in fact everything in the Universe vibrates at their particular level.

You must have noticed that some areas, some places you feel better than at others, this is because the vibration of that particular place is more harmonious to you than when in other places.

Can you see how simple it is? Think and behave in a positive manner and all will be well, you will be happy and healthy. I know it is not easy for you but it is very important for you to understand and for you to be aware of your own vibrations when you are not in harmony with your soul. You will need then to put it right by altering the way you think and behave, sending out positive energy rather than negative and try to live within the laws of the Great Spirit. Have I made it clear for you?"

"Yes I do understand, but it is not an easy task to continually be aware of your vibrations and living as you say within Gods Laws. Surely if we did then we wouldn't need to be here, would we?"

"You are correct, if you live a perfect life you will not create any karma or debts to pay, or put right. Although prior to that you have to experience situations, trials, trauma and when you have done all of this, learnt all those lessons you came to earth to do, perhaps then you will not break any of Gods Laws and will no longer have to incarnate unless of course you wish to assist someone in need. Therefore, you are here because you still need to learn, you have not evolved enough to remain in the spirit world, unless as I said you are here as an act of charity.

'Whatsoever a man soweth, that shall he also reap'. 'Do unto others, as you would have others do unto you'.

What you give from the heart is returned to you tenfold, not necessarily the same way; you may give someone a meal and receive flowers from someone else. You may give money to one person and receive a day out from another. You may give someone a helping hand and get tender loving care from someone else.

That doesn't sound too difficult does it? You must try to live by the Laws of God, as I said earlier there are many, do not worry I will explain them to you.

To live the Law of Tenfold Return you must of course love yourselves and give to yourselves. If you give to everyone except yourselves, it is time to question your motive for giving. You are most likely to over-compensating for your lack of love and self-worth and naturally, this blocks the law from operating.

If you give something away while thinking, 'I'm always paying, I'm always bailing him out', you are withholding. Generosity is a wonderful quality and means giving away freely from your heart. If you do this, it will ensure more will come back to you. Would you give more to others if you trusted more would flow back to you? Then give from the heart and it will. You must never expect anything back from the person you give to; it negates the Law of Abundance! Moreover, receive everything that comes your way openly with a sense of deserving and gratitude. You then have the key to greater 'wealth' than you can imagine.

Do not hoard money for fear it will be taken away, or that there will not be enough to go around; this is not affluence, it is being ruled by money. On the other hand, prosperity is having plenty, knowing more will come and believing that there will always be plenty: Then you master money.

Success is not striving for material things or outside recognition; it is a feeling of fulfilment and self-worth, happiness, peace, harmony and joy within.

Unconsciously, without thinking you may 'remember' that you have made a past-life agreement to help someone at some point in their life. If you do not keep your promise, contracts and commitments made in this life, a past life, or even between your Higher Selves, you will attract frustration, disappointment and loss into your life. When you honour these promises, you are rewarded tenfold.

Remember to watch for the manifestation of the Law of Abundance in your life for it is a key to spiritual development.

This is the Law of Tenfold Return and the Law of Flow; you will notice the majority of Gods Laws complement one another; These Laws, like all other Spiritual Laws, are exact."

"Thank you Daniel."

"Before I leave you I must say there is a purpose for all things, all things that make up the body of human beings.

Let me give you an example of why you have fingers and toes; your fingers are magnetized it is through them that you draw the Universal Life Force. When you stretch forth your hands

114

horizontally, left palm up to receive, right palm down to give, the life force flows through the left palm through the entire body and out of the right palm carrying with it all things not to your highest good. Now, of course, you must know this, for nothing can hinder this flow except your doubt. You must believe or it will not work, this is practiced in many forms of healing, such as to empower the Reiki practitioner.

Now the toes: Ten toes to keep you well grounded, connected with the earth. Your feet are more than just something to stand on; they are your understanding also. You 'pick up' through the soles of your feet, earth vibrations; your oneness with earth. You are an earthly being from the waist down; a spiritual being from the waist up. The spiritual part of you reaches upwards, always. However, you cannot live in the clouds, and so your feet shall always keep you well-grounded when you understand their purpose. Therefore, take good care of your feet, for while your fingers reach upward, your feet shall keep you grounded and in balance, for all things work together for the good of man. This is the law of the physical.

My dear children I will leave you now to consider what we have spoken about this evening. Good night."

"Good night Daniel. You always give us much to consider. Thank you."

"Good night dear children. Bless you all."

We talked for quite a while and Jean said. "It would be much better if we knew what was in store for us, don't you think Barbara?"

"Well it would, but what Daniel said makes sense, if we knew why we were here then I am sure we would behave to our detriment. Nothing at all would come from our hearts we would just play along to get extra marks, so to speak. Then of course we would have to come back time and time again; it would be much harder for us."

"I suppose you are right Barbara, well yes you are right. It's such a toil learning these lessons and working through traumas, hardships, trials and so on. I have had a rotten life nothing has ever been easy for me." Jean said miserably."

I said. "I think we should now go over what Daniel has said. We found having copies of our lessons with Daniel worked a treat and we could read it every time we felt down. I know we shouldn't feel like that but we are only human. Daniel would say 'if you try hard and you fail to do what you started, it doesn't matter pick yourself up and start again.' The Great Spirit just wants us to try, to do our best that is all we can do.

I do feel in time when we know more about spiritual things we will do better with our lives. Don't you agree?" They all agreed with me

I continued. "I don't want any of you to go home defeated before you start, you must think of the wonderful outcome, your rewards in the spirit world from your efforts."

"Your right again Barbara, we are thinking in a very negative way we must stop and be grateful for what we are receiving from the realms of spirit, we are so fortunate to learn all that Daniel is telling us. He would be very disappointed listening to us. Although he did say that anything we are not happy with we should put it to one side until we can understand." Beth said.

We had another cuppa and they all left. They left me feeling a little down due to their attitude. I think it's because all the wonderful information has been too much for them to take on board. When all said and done, it has taken me about fifty years to learn quite a lot of this information. I pulled myself together and started to sing, it has always been a good way of making me feel better.

It came to mind that the circle hasn't sat for development since we started speaking with Daniel. I am sure they will be missing their 'connection', with their spirit guides. I decided

to talk with them after our next meeting and sort
something out.

Chapter Four.

Accident and Disease and 'The Law of Communion'.

"Good evening my dears, I hope you have had a relaxing time thinking on what I said last time we met.

I heard you talking about an accident earlier. I must tell you truly, there is no such thing as an accident because any such event is what the soul chooses to learn about itself and its lessons.

You see dear children, accidents and disease are all ways for souls to learn their lessons. Disease is best called 'dis-ease' because the body is out of balance with itself. It is the effect of the choices the soul has made. The physical body is composed of a life-force of energy, which is the soul and is covered by flesh and bones, which I prefer to call your school uniform.

Everything that human beings do affects the flow of energy, around and through their being. When people become anxious, the bodily system fails to work efficiently and it creates extra-acidic conditions, thereby creating stomach problems such as ulcers. And when a soul becomes depressed it creates blocks within the body, preventing the life force to flow through the chakras, therefore the person becomes ill and dis-eased. I am explaining to you what you already know, because when you are healing you are able to feel the flow of energy going into the chakras of your patients and this tells you where their sickness is.

As you know my dear holding back on emotions or thinking only negative thoughts will also shut down the flow of energy. This prevents areas of the body from getting the natural nutrients it needs to survive. A correct way of thinking will help the flow to resume."

"Thank you Daniel. Yes I can feel the universal life force flowing into the chakras when I am healing; it has always been an accurate way of finding out where the problem is. For those who do not know, it is a lot for them to absorb."

"Let me now talk to you about the law of communion. My dears you did indeed come from heaven, only to learn your many lessons through experience, then slowly work your way back to your God self.

When you came to earth you were, and at no time separated from your God. Your silver cord is the connecting rod, or string that makes you one with God. This being so, then the cosmic string, or cord, is your communicating link with your God. You cannot ever be separated. This, then is your first and greatest awakening, First the realisation that you are one with your God, and second, to establish this oneness through communication.

How to do this: Sit quietly, feet touching the floor, hands loosely on knees. Now see, or imagine your-self sitting in a great golden sea of light. Visualise this cosmic cord, or string rising from the top of your head, up, up, into all Light. There in the stillness your God will speak to you. This is the Law of Communion."

"Thank you for that."

Akashic records.

"There is a lot of spiritual knowledge to learn. You will see eventually that it is really quite simple. Let me explain, everyone has a balance sheet, which is a record of your karma known as your Akashic record.

All of you have a knowledgeable spirit being that looks after you this wonderful being, which you call a Guardian Angel looks after your personal record and is with you throughout all your many lives. It may be easier for you to visualise your Akashic record as a computer disc, which is held in the Universal Computer.

These beings are incredibly evolved spirits that look after all Akashic records, they and other wise elders help your spirit to make important decisions in your next life, including your choice of parents and all that you need to learn and accomplish in your new existence on earth. This is because your karma good and bad is carried forward from lifetime to lifetime.

In order for you to evolve, to grow and to climb the spiritual ladder you will need to balance your record sheet, this is your karma of past lives. As you know, karma is a balance of good and bad thoughts including all your actions in previous incarnations. Watch for events that continually repeat, this will suggest it is karma. Therefore, it is important that you should try and learn from them.

I must explain that at no time during the life of a physical body is the soul one hundred percent encased, captured or imprisoned in the physical human body, a portion of the spirits energy always remains behind in the spirit realms and also forms what humans call the unconscious mind, what we call the higher self. Do you understand thus far?"

"It's a bit hard going." Jane said.

"I will try to make it simple for you. The higher self, the unconscious mind has access to the wisdom that the spirit has gained in prior lives from the Akashic records. When a soul has completed the lessons it has learned on earth and in the spirit realms, it finds it can bring to the fore wisdom from its higher self to help teach other souls how to experience life. At the same time they can be more in touch with their own higher selves."

Daniel talked a little slower and emphasized some words, which made it easier for my circle members to grasp.

"Once you understand the karmic patterns of your earth life you can start to work with them instead of against them. I must emphasise, nothing, in your life happens by chance, even the most horrendous acts are all part of the scheme in life."

Emma asks. "It doesn't seem fair, some people look to have a great life, nothing seems to go wrong for them, plenty of money, no worries. When there are others who have a life of continuous suffering one way or another. Why is that?"

"Some people do seem to have all the luck and attract good things, those who have all the money, happy marriage, good jobs, and lovely homes. Whereas there are others who struggle continually throughout their lives, some live in poverty trying hard to earn enough to feed themselves and their family, to keep a roof over their heads.
Human beings tends to notice others good fortune and their own bad luck, thinking that the

other man's grass is greener. This is not good, you must focus upon your own life your own pathway, never mind what others are doing. When you understand what I am teaching you, you will see how it all works.

Karma is about experience, not about punishment. The idea that you are punished for your sins is wrong, you choose; with the help of highly advanced souls, how you will best learn the lessons to balance your karmic debts. You choose whether a crippled body, blindness, poverty etc., would be beneficial to your progress.

When you come to a time in your life, when you do not know which way to turn, take time to sit quiet and pray, or meditate and you will receive subconsciously the help you need to move forward. When you are feeling negative and life is not treating you very well you are unable to think clearly, therefore you should take time to count your blessings; you will find they are many. If you did this each morning before anything else you will find your day full of positive thoughts and actions.

My dears, the Great Spirit created the universe; the earth plane for you, which is your class- room. I continue to say that you are here to learn and the training is often harsh, however, as long as you are good spiritual beings do all the right things and live within Gods laws then you will have harmony and peace. However, if you live contrary to the laws you will have to face that when you return home to the spirit world. It is better to do it now and save yourselves years of needless difficulties.

When a soul has to undergo the necessity for suffering and sorrow in their life, some like you, would misconstrue this as being hard, callous. It is not so, suffering automatically brings its own rewards because you are the beneficiary, it touches the soul."

Emma said. "I am trying to understand what you are saying but it is still hard to live here, even when we know it is beneficial to our spiritual growth. It is difficult to think positive at times. Some people's lives are unbearable full of pain and suffering, how can they be positive?"

"I have never said your life on earth would be an easy one. It is sad, your world does not understand the function of pain, the function of suffering, the difficulties and hardships, but all these play an important part in the evolution of the human spirit. You know yourself, when you look back at your life and see how often the greatest crises, the most difficult problems, the darkest hours, were the stepping-stones that led you to a greater understanding.

Do not think these are unfeeling words that I bring you. I am aware of your world and I do comprehend the sheer scale of the problems you have to endure, we have all been there, I have been there. It would be wonderful if you always felt the sunshine, and did not have a care, where all difficulties were automatically taken away. However, you would not evolve; it is in the facing of all your challenges, your trials and it is by rising above them that you all grow.

When you return to the world of spirit and see all the things you have done, all the karmic lessons and trials you have overcome, you will rejoice and you will thank the Great Spirit for the opportunities given to you for your spiritual growth. And I do know that you think this is impossible for you, but you do not realise how strong you are, how strong your spirit is in dealing with your lives."

Poverty, shanty towns.

"Thank you Daniel." I said. "Can you explain to us why anyone would choose to live in poverty and what would be the benefit of this choice?

I would like to tell you the story that made me want to ask you this question. I have always been drawn to South Africa, very much like a magnet, I have always had the feeling of wanting to go back home. (Perhaps this could be a previous life memory.)

I have been back to South Africa three times to live there but it never worked out for me. What always stands out in my mind when I think of being out there is the terrible situation of poverty. There are thousands and thousands of human beings living worse than animals in hovels; Shanty Towns. Their homes made of corrugated iron sheets and cardboard boxes.

When I drove past on a dark cold night the hovels in the township were lit up with candles, they had no electric lights or heating and only communal toilets and water facilities and when it rained their homes were flooded. I went home and cried for these poor souls.

On another occasion I was on the waterfront having a drink with friends and I saw a young girl about nine or ten wearing only a short sleeved cotton dress and bare feet begging in the cold night alone. I talked to her and asked where her parents were, she didn't answer. I gave her some money and told her to go home. I was afraid for her safety, a young vulnerable girl out on her own; it doesn't bear thinking what might have happened to her. There was a lot of begging on the streets but this was different, it was dangerous.

The fact I could do nothing about it haunts me even now years later. I am sure there must have been a lesson for me in that experience. What can you tell me about such a life?"

"It is always sad to see suffering and hardship, however it is what those souls chose for themselves before they incarnated to earth, and they needed to learn from their trials to enable them to grow spiritually.

One of the lessons would be hopelessness, and how they dealt with their lives in that situation. Perhaps she was one of the wealthy people in a previous life and needed to understand poverty. I do not know.

Some could give up, commit suicide and learn nothing from their trials, whilst others would look inside themselves and meditate on all the good things of life, such as love.

One of the lessons for you could be to experience helplessness along with the compassion you already have. There are many reasons that a soul chooses that life challenge. Do you understand?"

I went on to say. "Yes I do thank you for that. It helps to understand when you realize they had a good reason to be born in that horrible life situation. Whilst we are talking about poverty, there are homeless people who live on the street for no fault of their own and there are those who have lost their business and money and end up homeless. What have they to learn from this situation?"

"My dear there is always a good reason for all life situations. As you know, these souls chose this life to learn what they needed for their spiritual evolution. One example would be that the person who lost all their wealth probably needed to learn that money is not so important there are other things in life more important, such as spiritual growth. In both cases they could go on and help other poor souls who are homeless, they have first-hand knowledge and experience of the suffering and life on the streets.

Turning a negative situation into a positive outcome by helping others is truly a good way of moving further up the heavenly staircase.

As I said earlier, it is beneficial for you all to acknowledge karma and be aware of creating future karma with every thought and action; therefore, you should aim to always create good karma.

Good karma is always concerned with your spiritual progression and making your soul available to more advanced lessons, rather than continually making the awful lessons time and time again like some do. It is as simple as that.

Creating good karma works immediately by returning to you what you have given to others. If you love another, you will be loved in return. If you are friendly to others, you receive friendship. If you help and care for people, it will be returned to you when you need it.

Be positive as this creates good karma in your life, you are the only ones who can do this. You are not alone, everyone has their share of problems, burdens, challenges, you have blessings too, to lighten the load.

Remember, the higher your vibration the quicker karma comes to you. If you never get away with anything, you are subject to instant karma. Your soul is not allowing you to accumulate any more karmic debt. Whatever you give out comes back to you instantly; it is a sign that you are becoming more evolved. Your karmic records are kept up to date; it is as simple as that.

My dear children, it is easy for you to test this by looking back on your lives and you will see where there is instant karma, then you will know without doubt we in the spirit realms bring only truth.

What you need to do when there is a problem is to look at it, face it, meditate on the challenge and ask yourself what can I learn from this, why did I choose this trial; you will find an answer because you will remember what I have taught you."

Jean responded with. "Thank you I do believe the words of spirit teachers. You keep saying 'it's as simple as that' but you are not living here."

"But my dear, I have lived on the physical plane many, many, many times and I do understand your lives and situations."

Free will and animals.

I said to Daniel. " I was thinking last night in bed, if all spirit beings behave correctly as you said, can you tell me why some animals in this world are being born to be tortured, slaughtered and misused by human beings, they haven't done anything wrong?

I saw on television a teenage boy kicking a small puppy up and down just like a football, I wanted to cry and still do when I think about it. It makes me feel sick; surely, animal spirits have behaved correctly, so surely that must be a contradiction."

"It is always terrible to hear of such cruelty. However, animal spirits are not in the same category as a human spirit because human beings are given the responsibility of making right choices; that is your free will.

My dear child your physical world is full of abuse and cruelty to animals, it cannot be otherwise if human kind is to progress. If they were deprived of their free will, they would not have the chance to evolve their character, their individuality and progress. But remember what I have said, what you sow, you eventually reap, there is no escape and the teenager will have to pay for his act of cruelty."

I wasn't happy with the answer and said. "Sorry

Daniel, I cannot accept that. We are told the Great Spirit is all loving and just, therefore surely all life would be precious. I cannot accept your answer; I still think it is contradictory."

Animal cruelty.

"It is good that you challenge me and you don't accept everything you are told like a sponge. Anything that is not acceptable to your intelligence put to one side for a later time.

My dear, we in the spirit world are constantly striving to fight wars between the forces of good and evil, in your world there are those who are greedy and selfish and who are ignorant and there are those with knowledge.

There are many who do not realise the part animals play on earth, they have as much right to be on your planet as you human beings. We will continue to fight until the battle has been won. It is gradual but we will win in the end."

"I do not think that boy will ever stop being cruel to animals."

"You must not judge, remember we have all be there at one time or another. Negativity does not help, as I have just said there will be a gradual awareness of human beings responsibility to other forms of life. You are evolving and so is the planet. There will be many highs and lows and ups and downs, because the effects of evolution is twisting and turning. However, you are moving towards progression slowly, if not there would be no evolution.

The plan of life is created by the Great Spirit with infinite wisdom and love, therefore, provision has been made for everything and everybody.

It is up to human beings to take responsibility for their actions to ensure that all who share the earth with them are treated with kindness. Whatever happens there is always compensation as part of the natural law. You have the responsibility of ensuring that animals should progress and grow according to their path of evolution. If you give up, abandon your responsibilities then you must pay the price for it. Those who practice cruelty will have to pay by spiritual laws for everything they do."

"Thank you for that, although I will have to think hard and long about what you said. If an animal on earth develops human qualities, such as feelings and intelligence will it remain just an animal soul without any chance of further evolution, or could it possibly in time move into the human kingdom? I would hope so." I said.

"As you know, evolution is part of the natural law, Gods law. Your spirit and the animals is the same substance of the same Great Spirit. In essence there is no difference only in the degree. Being infinite, the spirit can achieve tremendous expression, which is latent in both man and animals, but spiritually it is all part of the same path."

I continued with this subject and asked. "Have human beings an unlimited right of destruction in regard to animals?"

"The right is limited to providing food and safety; no abuse can be a matter of right."

I wasn't satisfied with the answers and continued to question. "I don't think you have answered my questions, however what do you think of destruction that goes beyond the limits of providing food and safety; for instance, hunting, when it has no useful purpose and no other motive than the pleasure of killing?"

"All destruction that goes beyond the limits of your needs is a violation of the law of the Great Spirit. The animal kingdom behaves much better than the human race in that they only destroy according to their necessities; but man, who has free will, destroys unnecessarily. This is an act of bestiality and those who hurt and kill the animals of your planet purely for pleasure will be called to account for abusing the freedom given to them."

"I am sorry to say, progression at any cost I cannot accept and I find it is so difficult to understand how this is allowed to happen".

"If you disagree that is not a problem, as I said before, you must put it to one side until such a time as it is acceptable to your intelligence.

My dear would you rather humanity was robbed of its free will? If human beings are deprived of their free will they will cease to be anything but robots, machines and would be unable to unfold the spirituality within them.

I must remind you, that you are put on earth because life is your school, where you will learn, it is the training ground for the soul. You can only evolve when you experience trials and challenges and overcome them."

"There must be some other way rather than hurting our animal kingdom and still have free will. I am not sure that I would like to evolve at the cost of harming defenceless animals. It seems to me there is something amiss when we do the wrong things and the animals have to pay." I said disapprovingly.

Carol went on to ask Daniel. "Can you tell us anything else about animals in the spirit world and where they go?"

"All wild animals are grouped together for

example, whales, dolphins and seals are together cows, horses and zebras are together. Animals have their own way of bonding with their community."

Carol continued to question. "If that's the case I won't be able to have my animals with me, will I?"

"Those of you who love animals on earth believe you can communicate with your pets in small ways. When you return to the spirit world and see your pets again and when you build your home and garden in the spiritual sphere you may have your loving pets with you, because it is natural for them to be there. You and your pets have a bond, of mutual love and respect for each other. Therefore you will be able to renew your relationship."

"Oh thank you Daniel that makes me feel much better."

"Domesticated pets are able to extend love and affection to human beings, which of course you need, and I must say they are much less complicated than human souls, whereas the wild animal souls do not understand you very much at all.

All human and animal souls require freedom of expression. Therefore pets are more willing to give up some of their freedom to bond again with humans in exchange for love, protection and affection. Do you understand?"

"Yes thank you. Where do they go and does anyone look after them whilst we are on earth?" Carol continued."

"My dear, there is always some highly evolved spirit being to look after them, they are not alone. They are called Caretakers who are specialist spirits who love animals. You have no need to worry."

"I am so pleased to hear that, it broke my heart when I had to have my little dog put to sleep. Will I be punished for that?"

"No my dear, you put your pet to sleep out of love, the motive was good therefore no karmic debt was created."

"Thank you."

"There is no reason for you to thank me; it is always my pleasure to help those who seek knowledge."

"Reluctantly Daniel it is time for us to close once again. Thank you so much, we do appreciate what you say and look forward to the next time."

"It is always a pleasure. Good night, sleep well."

I don't know why but I started getting headaches after a meeting, I think it must be the psychic energy used and the concentration of trying to remain linked with Daniel; sometimes harder than others.

It was getting late and I knew everyone wanted to discuss what had been said before they left for home. We talked for a time and we all agreed to make the most of our sessions with Daniel and ask questions next time we meet that could help all those who read the book and were looking for guidance.

Reluctantly I explained to the circle that I needed to go to bed. They left feeling very disappointed; I did promise to see them during the following week.

My head was thumping and I felt a little sickly so I went straight to bed. I felt awful not doing my distant healing and praying but I felt too ill. I knew spirit doctors would continue to look after my patients. I slept sound and had a good night's sleep.

The next morning my headache and sickness had gone so I knew it wasn't a tummy bug, I thought it was as I said something to do with my psychic energy. I decided that I should spend less time linked to the spirit world in one session; perhaps I would meet with Daniel twice a week, once on my own earlier in the week, which I had done before. It was always a wonderful experience chatting to my spirit guide who gave us such a lot to think about.

It was a strange week and I thought I would 'test the water' so to speak. I found myself analysing everything that had happened in my life and finding possible answers to do with my karma. I tried to analyse people who came to see me for healing and readings and found it very interesting because I felt that what Daniel was teaching us would be very helpful to those who came to see me. I must say it gave me even more to think about. I suppose this is what Daniel wanted us all to do, to find comfort in knowing we chose all the trials that we have had to endure, and possibly much more to come.

I think it does help to know why some of us have a hard life and others don't. It also gives us a different way of looking at serious crimes such as murder.

I look forward to my future talks with Daniel and learning first hand from those who know and we can trust, what life truly is all about.

My intentions were to talk with Daniel on Friday but I couldn't because I felt unwell, so I meditated and apologised to him for my absence.

I rang all the circle members to arrange a meeting, some wanted Friday and others Monday so we had a vote and agreed Monday, two days before circle night. I decided to link with Daniel on the Sunday then we would be able to discuss both evenings.

Chapter Five.

Jesus.

At our next meeting and before we spoke to Daniel we talked for quite some time going over all that was said previously, and we tried to see things differently, as Daniel had told us.

It's strange to find that we are actually thinking before we speak. It can only be good to check ourselves against saying things that we do not mean, therefore not creating the negative thought being sent out into the universe.

Before I sat at my computer we all sat in a circle for meditation and Prayers, sending out love to all our spirit guides and helpers. After about thirty minutes and 'tuned in' to a higher vibration I asked for Daniel to make his presence clear to the circle. Within seconds I felt Daniel over shadow me, I was by then in a state of light trance. I asked Daniel. "Do you know what Jesus looks like?"

"Yes, I have seen the Lord Jesus in all his radiance. At Christmas time we, teachers, guides and other higher spirit beings retire to a place to be with Jesus. We discuss all that we have done, and how we could have done things differently to get better results. It is similar to when spirits go to visit the elders for guidance; we are counselled just as you are but with our Lord

Jesus.

Whatever picture you will have of Him in your mind that is how you will see him."

"I have been with Jesus, it was a wonderful experience. During meditation, we walked down an avenue of beautiful white flowers with a wonderful intoxicating perfume. On the opposite side were white doves they flew onto my hand and I could see their little hearts beating in their tiny chests. Jesus put his hand across my shoulders and the most powerful love energy filled me from top to toe; a truly magical moment for me and I will never forget it. I just had to tell you."

"That is wonderful for you, you were truly blessed. The energy from Him is beyond description there are no earthly words to explain this to you. But you already know don't you my dear?"

"I most certainly do."

Love story.

One of the circle members asked Daniel. "I wonder if I can explain something to you Daniel and if you would tell me what you think."

"Yes, I will do my best to help you."

"In my dream, which was Chinese orientated, I fell in love with a man who loved me very much. I had never felt so loved before it was wonderful. We were so much in love that eventually we were together despite the fact that he was married.

Somehow his wife disappeared and was no longer in the picture. I am not sure if he left his wife, or got rid of her in some way. I remember he was quite a powerful man.

This dream continued for several nights beginning where the story left off the night before.

When I woke up the following morning, I had a strong feeling I was living a memory of a previous life.

I have given this a great deal of thought and believe my life now is in some way paying me back for taking this man from his wife and breaking up their marriage. Maybe there could be other parts of that life of a similar nature, I don't know. The reason I believe this to be correct is that in my life now I have always been looking for love, even though my husbands, partners have said they loved me it has not been good enough, not what I 'know' it should be.

When I was a child, about 7 or 8 years old my grandmother said to me one day. I love your bother but your granddad loved you; he died when I was around three years old. I remember him vaguely, but what a cruel thing to say to a little girl. She hurt me so much I have not been able to forget what she said to me. No matter what I said or did for her, it was never good enough. I was not a bad child, I was good and thoughtful towards everyone, and therefore I could not understand why she treated me that way.

My mother behaved the same way towards me and treated me very badly. I had to do such a lot of chores for her I never stopped, it was as if having a wicked step mother just like the story 'Cinderella'; my brother could never do anything wrong in her eyes and got away with everything.

I am wondering if I have been paying back karma for taking another woman's husband. I would appreciate your views Daniel"

"My dear child, there could be many reasons for the lack of love in this life. However, I have said before, I am not in a position to know everything about everyone, but I do feel it is most likely lessons you have to learn to enable you to grow spiritual by paying back karma from a previous life.

It may not have anything to do with what you have just told me; it could be that you did not show love to anyone in a previous existence, as I said there could be many reasons for this. One thing is definite, there is no escape from wrong behaviour and it creates karma."

"Thank you so much Daniel for your help. I hope I have learnt the lessons and I have moved on spiritually."

"If you have learnt the lessons, then you have indeed started to shine a little more. Let me explain the power of love. The power of love never dies; it never dies because it is part of the Great Spirit. Divine love spreads across the whole of the universe and wherever love exists, it is the very heart of life and within each soul seeking expression."

"Can you please tell me more about love?"

"Yes, my dear. If you desire love, you must give out love. If you are in need of peace, be peaceful, if you require harmony, then you must live harmoniously. You attract, or draw to you only the qualities you possess, because like attracts like. Your energy is like a magnet force, therefore you draw to you what you desire, and you repel all other things. This is truth. Nothing will ever come to you unless you draw it to you because the same thing is within you, even if you do not know it."

"Goodness me, so what you are saying is that everything that has happened to me, I brought on myself by attracting it?" Beth said sounding puzzled.

"Yes, you have drawn towards you everything and everyone who was and who is still in your life. You are like a magnetic force, if you have magnets stuck all over you, you would expect things to stick to you, would you not?"

Replying Beth said. "Well yes I suppose so, but all the same I cannot imagine attracting some of the things that has happened to me."

"Some of your qualities are magnetic, and others repellent. Everyone unconsciously transmit their energy. You are a transmitter, you broadcast by sending out emotional energy, likes and dislikes and much more. You send out into the atmosphere your personal pictures. People who do not vibrate on your frequency simply are not attracted to you. They pass you by."

"What do you mean by frequency?" Beth continued.

"You vibrate and the vibration you emit is made up of your conscious and unconscious energy, some of which is repellent, some magnetic and some neutral. If you allow things to happen to you, which you don't like, then you must stop sending out thoughts that it is OK, therefore you are the only one to blame because you didn't object to this 'thing'.

Do you see some things may of course be a

return of karma, which is the inevitable balancing of right and wrong over many of your lifetimes? Therefore, my dear you must start drawing love to you. The laws of the Great Spirit are exact, they are unfailing laws.

Your lack of love is probably a karmic debt, because it does work in all things, for LAW IS! This is the Law of Attraction.

True love is unconditional wanting to care for your fellow human beings, love means accepting people exactly as they are, without judging them. It is always seeing the good in others, having compassion, understanding and empathy.

True, genuine love is like a magnet and has a strong pull, a quality that anyone radiating it draws people to them. When you are able to love unconditionally, you then have the greatest spiritual wealth and it is much more than you can ever imagine.

This is another of God's laws; it is the Law of Tenfold Return. This law, like all other spiritual laws, is exact."

Jean spoke up this time. "Thank you. Again you make it sound so easy, but loving unconditionally is very difficult, especially those who treat us badly. But I am sure we will all try."

"I am pleased to hear that my dear. The undeniable love between man and woman is the natural law of God; they are two people but one in harmony. You must have heard people say 'we are like two hearts that beat as one.' That is true, those who are united by the bonds of true love will find one another again no matter where and despite all the hurdles, the handicaps and obstacles that may be in the way.

Even in death true love cements two beings even when one is parted from the other. There is an attracting, magnetic pulsating power that pulls them together. It enables the one in the spirit world to manipulate the conditions the atmosphere around them so that they are able to draw near to the one on earth, crossing the bridge between the two worlds briefly. They want to help and assist spiritually whilst they are in the heavy world of matter.

There are different types of love that takes many forms and is one of the most misused words in your world. Some say 'give my love to so and so' when they are indifferent to that person. Others perhaps believe infatuation or physical passion is love.

There is the love of a mother, the maternal instincts, which are believed to be love, an expression of affection, devotion and the desire to provide for their children's needs.

The undeniable love, between man and a woman and there is the love of friendship, which is founded on mutual attraction and understanding."

"I'm not sure if I understand what you are saying. How do you know when it is real love between a man and a woman? People think they know but I don't think they do" Asked Carol.

"There is also the love of two souls from the same soul group and are incarnating at the same time on earth. There is complete harmony between them; they are parts of the whole. I will explain all about this later.

To answer your question, real love is so magnetic; it is so overwhelming in its attraction, that it must find itself. There is always an opposite; there is a negative to everything. For example, there is good and bad and there is light and darkness.

There are many human beings who manipulate friendships, or relationships. They blackmail them so that they will stay with them; that is not love. Love is not making people dependent so they will not leave you, or pleasing others so they will like you.
Do you understand?"

"Yes thank you. I hadn't really thought about how many ways a person could love."

"There is of course divine love. Where advanced spiritual beings return to your cold, grey, heavy unattractive world to help those who need it, they are driven by the divine love which envelops the whole universe.

You are not an evolved soul until you can say, and believe it, I repeat really believe 'I love all mankind'. There are many souls in your world who think what they have is love but that is not always the case. Every soul evolves continually but to those who love selflessly in its highest form embraces the whole of humanity. But sadly, my dear children, people of the earth are a long way from doing that."

I said to Daniel. "It is difficult for some in this world, it has taken me a long time but I now can love my neighbour. I look beyond the physical and imagine their spirit body, their soul unfolding and learning."

"That is good; all the Great Spirit asks is that you do your best. Love is not physical it is spiritual; love can never die because it is eternal and part of the Great Spirit our Creator.

The whole universe exists because of Gods laws, which are many. You cannot see the power, the energy of love, but love does exist. Love is the greatest power in the universe; it guides the destiny of every living creature and every life form. It is the very breath and essence of life, if there were no divine love, there would be no life in the universe. Real love is so magnetic, is so overwhelming in its attraction that it must find itself; the two halves must recognise one another.

This does not necessarily happen on your journey through earth's lessons because this is of the spirit and is often blind; however you must try and get rid of the imperfections of the physical, so that you can see the spiritual. Is that clear to you?"

What is Spirit and what is the purpose of the soul?

"Daniel I have not been well my energy level after speaking with you seems to drop, I feel exhausted."

"You are not as well as I would like nothing serious but run down, your healers will help you. I feel that we should meet twice a week, little and often would be better." He said.

"Yes I think you are right, we will do that. We must not waste valuable time so please would you tell us the purpose of the soul and why we are here?"

"You ask the purpose of the soul. The spirit world is the real world it is the eternal world surviving everything else. This is where we all came from and this place is where we will return on the death of the physical body.

Souls incarnate to earth because they have to experience duality that is opposites, positive and negative; earth is the only planet that offers this. You are all destined to attain perfection by learning and passing through different spheres and realms, to reach the level of degrees of the purest spirits.

Spirits enter the earth plane of existence with no memory of their personal past lives, their mission, or of their planet of duality.

All experiences are kept in the Akashic records which have recorded volumes of every spirit. Therefore, whenever a soul is back in the spirit world it has instant recall of all these entries. This does not apply to those in the lower realms.

Souls need opposites so that they can evaluate all their experiences, it is the only way they can measure and value their tests and trials, to know their worth. One has to experience all aspects of a situation and to dissect it until each action and each part is played to fully and completely understand it. By doing this, eventually spirit can reach perfection. The knowledge in the Akashic records has accumulated over many lifetimes in the physical world; the wisdom of them-selves and of the Great Spirit is then added together."

"Goodness me!" I said interrupting. "I would have thought every planet would have opposites, you say just the earth has negative and positive. Will you be explaining what they have on other planets to us?"

"If you remember my dear, I said I would discuss other planet with you all later."

"Sorry Daniel, I forgot."

"You must try and remember what I say so that you will be able to ask me questions later.

The earth plane is a heavy planet and the only one that has different species of earth life. However, the Great Spirit chose you human beings for the incarnation of spirits who are at a certain level of development.

Human beings are superior to all other species, morally and intelligently; this is produced only by reincarnation. How fast you grow depends on what you learn in your life on earth, your school.

You are all human beings with a brain, a mind and over the years and many lifetimes have created your own characteristic and habits. You all have your own tendencies, desires and ideas, these are so vital that they rule the way in which you think and behave.

Human beings comprise of three parts, a physical body, which is animated by a soul residing in a body, and there is the perispirit which is a link that joins and unites the soul with the body and is what you know as the silver cord.

Human beings have two natures. They have the instincts and base nature of animals and their soul contributes in the quality, the nature of spirits. The soul is an incarnated spirit that inhabits, dwells in a material body this being the clothing what I call the school uniform.

Your spirit body radiates out in all directions which is what is called your aura. My dear child this is the purpose of the soul, to grow and to learn. Does that answer your question thus far?"

"Yes I think so."

"Spirit people are beings that have incarnated many times into physical embryos on earth and other planets to learn lessons and by doing so gain wisdom and knowledge.

They belong to different classes residing in different spheres and are not equal to one another either in power, intelligence, knowledge or morality. This of course is down to their spiritual growth and how they have learned their lessons and dealt with their karma.

Spirit beings are everywhere, in space, around you, seeing you, mixing with you. An invisible world as tangible to them as your world is to you. They are attracted to you by their sympathy to your moral quality, in other words, they are attracted to your spiritual light, which is what you are.

There are other experienced spirit beings that come with love and a desire to help and improve you. Spirit beings of the highest order are more refined from those below them, by superior purity and knowledge; they are all pure angelic spirit beings. This is the aim of all spirit beings."

"I see, thank you for that Daniel, now we know."

"My dears you can be so much more, you are what you think and believe, not only in the realms of spirit, but wherever you are. All things are yours, your heritage; claim it. I say to you, you are a joint heir with Christ the Nazarene, you are all part of the Great Spirit therefore, claim your heritage and then it is forever yours.

There is a great law involved here because whatever you affirm for yourself IS the law of your being. You have heard the expression; 'You are law unto yourself' it is true. You build into your consciousness that which you believe of yourself, or affirms. Therefore, let the weak say they are strong; let the poor say they are rich.

If you say, 'I am strong,' you must carry it through, but if you act like a weakling, you are indeed weak because you must know you must believe that what you say is Truth, regardless of appearances. Stand firm in this even though you appear to be week, affirm your strength, because all power is within you to use, and command.

Say then, 'I am strong!' and know it. It shall always be done unto you, as you know it.

My dears do you understand, it is simple. Think about it. This is the Law of Affirmation."

"Thank you we will discuss everything when you have left us. I need to ask you questions even if I know the answers so that others get the benefit from what you have to say, is that acceptable to you? Having said that Daniel, you always add something extra that makes me think."

"Yes of course, that is the correct way to move forward in our discussions."

War, murder and accidental death.

"I have been reading a book about physical deaths. Can you explain if there are such things as accidental deaths? Such as people who die due to natural disasters such as a floods, earthquakes etc. Are these accidents or are they pre-birth plans?" Jane asked.

"You must always ask me if you have read or heard something that you are not totally happy with and I will try to answer your question.

The answer is no, there is no such thing as accidental because there is only cause and effect in operation. Whatever you regard as accidental can be due only to the operation of the law of cause and effect.

Let me say that most spirits, in the overwhelming majority of cases know when they should go back home, the period of their earthly life, it is discussed with council elders before their incarnation. However, because you all have free will, the individual soul may decide to exercise their free will and alter the time of the death of their physical body however I must say this action is in the minority. Every accident is the effect of a preceding cause; you cannot separate one from the other. Does that answer your question?"

"Yes it does thank you. I understand. It makes sense when you think of the workings of karma. It has to be worked within the natural law, Gods laws. In fact everything to do with life is also to do with karma. Is that correct?"

"Yes that is correct, except when a soul incarnates to assist another soul out of love and compassion. That is not due to karma."

"Yes of course, I had forgotten about that. May I tell you a story and perhaps you will explain this to us."

"Yes you may, that is why I am here."

Murder story of a Leeds United supporter.

"A young woman came to see me for a reading, her name was Sue; her friend had recommended me to her. She arrived looking rather depressed but yet hopeful, not knowing how the reading may go. I greeted her and asked her to sit down and relax. We talked generally for a while until I felt she was less tense and appeared to feel more at ease.

Reading 06-04-2000.

I started the reading by saying there is the presence of a young a man, in the spirit world, he gives the name of Kevin and he said he died suddenly in terrible circumstances and he had trouble breathing. He continued saying he didn't die straight away and his death was unexpected; he was very emotional.

I told her that I could see him a bit clearer now; he looks to be quite stocky in build. He is telling me his death is not over. I couldn't understand what that meant, but Sue nodded and seemed to understand. (After the reading Sue told me it was because the trial was still in progress.)

I said, he brings with him the feeling of a husbands love and he is sending a lot of love to you, George and Holly. He is telling me his death was linked to a football match overseas. I asked Sue if this man was her husband, she said yes.

Changing the subject he went on to say eighteen months to two years ago they started up a new life together which took a lot of financing; sadly it is now over. He went on to ask me to mention scooters, which I did. (Sue told me later he always had scooters rather than motor bikes).

He told me he is very close to her, and now he is showing me a picture of a Brown Horse, which he says she has links to, he also says he liked a drink or two. (The new life was buying a pub called 'The Bay Horse' and he did like to have a drink.).

Kevin is now talking about a birthday or a celebration; he is giving you a beautiful bouquet of red roses. (It was Sue's birthday on the day of the reading).

He went on to talk of his death; he says it was around 9 pm. when he was attacked. Sue didn't know what time he was attacked. (This was confirmed later when she checked it out with the other men who went on the football trip with him).

He also spoke of 'having three children. (Sue confirmed they had two living children George and Holly and one child in the spirit world due to a miscarriage). He was worried about Sue because she felt lost and empty, saying she must move on. He says 'he has met John who is linked to the Bay Horse pub. (Sue didn't know who this was).

I continued to explain to Sue there was another gentleman present in the spirit world; he looked to be aged 60-70years old, with white hair and who passed with a chest condition. (She told me this was her husband's father).

Kevin went on to show me mental pictures of a house; I described a through lounge without furniture and needing a lot of work. (Sue confirmed this was the house they bought before he died; they were in the middle of decorating the house. He then went on to describe a bedroom in another house. (This was his mother's bedroom) he said she must move on, she is holding a grudge that is eating away at her and it is making her ill. (All this was confirmed).

I continued to say there was another gentleman in spirit drawing close, wearing glasses, dark grey hair also around the age of 60-70. He says he is very close to you trying to give you strength to cope and gave the name of Jack. (This was Sue's dad).

Kevin talked about George his son, saying he was having trouble concentrating at school, but not to worry he will be OK. He can see Holly his daughter, with lots of tears, softly weeping. He says 'he is always around them and was at the caravan with them earlier in the year.

He is concerned about Sue's future and says he will talk again about this. He sees her playing with her rings on her finger when she thinks of him. He says she misses him at night. Kevin goes on to say how much he loves her. (Sue confirmed all this to be true). He is very upset about hurting her; he always loved you and always will. (He was referring to a bad patch they went through during the year of 1996.

He says he likes Holly's new hair style, and he shows me him giving her a silver key, placing it in her hand and closing her fingers around it. He sends love to his mum - he is alright, tell her to let the incident go.

He is concerned and sad that Sue is going through a bad time with so many problems, and says they have not ended yet. He says 'he has to go now, love to you and the kids, more love given with the bouquet of red roses for her birthday.

Other things mentioned:-The names of David twice, Spag, June, Carol, Hazel, Joe, a ticket, watch with a broken strap, Ireland and Florida.

Since then she has confirmed that David is the name of a cousin who died. Spag is Kevin, her husband's nick name. Sue went to Ireland for her 40th birthday. Other things not confirmed yet.

Reading June 2001.

I started the reading again with her husband showing me he is unable to breath, he talks of his life been taken suddenly and says he is still trying to get over it. I can see him clearer, average build, thick set, was murdered, stabbed. He is showing me Leeds United Football Club colours. He says there has been no conviction - it is not ended. He says he loves you.

He talks about a photo & plaque, he says he likes it. (A plaque in memory of him was placed at Leeds United, Elland Road, Football Ground on the 1st anniversary of his death.)

He changes the subject again saying he was with them all on holiday in France at Christmas time. And goes on to say she had her nails done on Friday - he was with her and watched. He is now wrapping his two children up in cotton wool and holding them close together.

I go on to tell Sue about a lady he is showing me with blond hair, he says it is his mother, he says she has settled down a bit, but she is still not happy and full of resentment. Tell mum, he says, she must put what happened to me out of her mind, because this brings a lot of darkness around her, which prevents me from drawing close to her. He can see she has fits of rage and I try to calm her down. Tell her I am in a lovely place and that I know about the dried flowers from my grave.

I also know Sue that you get up each day wishing it was over. Life is too short, you must start to live again soon the sun will shine on you again. Love to Holly and George, by the way, he says he likes Holly's new school.

Kevin now talks of 'being in the spirit world

with his dad who had a stomach problem.

He can see children gathering up newspapers, these will have something associated with his death.

He goes back to the problems in their relationship, Kevin again says he always loved you and regrets what happened it was a big mistake, and says Sue will not let it go.

He Talks again of Turkey walking down a street with two friends, one ran off, he is very upset about this. He says his transition is slow and he finds it hard moving away from the pull of the earth. (This could be caused with the way he died, and, or the long drawn out problems with the trial, also grieving relatives can pull him back to earth).

Sue asked if she should move house, Kevin replied saying not yet. Sue asked when and Kevin gave the number 10. (Sue has since moved house to number 46; she says 4 plus 6 equals 10.) I personally do not like to make things fit.

Kevin said Sue should move on, don't worry there is nothing wrong with her having a new relationship. He leaves her with much love to her the children and his mum.

Other things mentioned: - Name of Jim/James, November, Chrystal Decanter, Silk Flower and a White Rose. Confirmed later. Chrystal Decanter bought for Sue by the new owners of the Bay Horse. White Rose carved on the bottom of the grave stone and the dried flowers mentioned earlier from his funeral flowers.

Reading December 2001.

I started the reading by saying to Sue that she should try and feel Kevin, as he is very close to her and he is still learning to communicate. He says I have to mention your car tax and insurance try to get a better deal. (Sue did). He is happy that you are coping much better now; he says you are doing OK.

He now talks about Patience Strong who writes verses. (Sue had one or two given to her). He says in about two years Sue will have a new man in her life and will move house. Spoke of Sue having moved since he passed into the spirit world and having more space, but to watch what she does with her money and to keep her savings.

Kevin says he was with Sue on their wedding anniversary in October. He went on to say he was very pleased Sue had spoken to his mates to confirm the time of his attack in Turkey (as I stated in the previous reading was 9pm).

Sue's dad came through again talking this time about his finger to prove as always that I was speaking to him. (He chopped off his the end of his finger whilst working on his car.)

Kevin wants Sue to keep his Scooter. He is pleased she is at last starting to move on, but he is very upset that his mother is still grieving. He told Sue about George's school trip to Ingleton, went on to send is love to both his children.

He has looked back on his life and feels he could have helped Sue more and been more sensitive and caring towards her. He went on to mention that Sue had a boyfriend and that everyone needs to have someone. Everything will go well, and in two years she will have put everything behind her, she will meet someone else who will be better for her.

A brief visit from Jack, Sue's dad arrived with big hugs for her mum as she is a little depressed at the moment.

Kevin says he is OK now and settled down to spirit life, when he arrived in the beyond he was in a state of shock, but he has moved on himself now. He asked about the new boots Sue bought; make sure they are not too tight he says. (She had just bought a pair). He went on to talk about George's teeth not growing straight. (This is also correct).

Kevin said he wasn't worried about her any more she would be just fine. He left leaving his love with her. Sue's dad gave her a hug and left too.

Reading June 2010.

Kevin came through and I could see him playing with a bracelet, (one of Kevin's, Sue now wears). He was probably saying he knows she wears it.

He says he loves these reunions with her.

He said he forgives the Turkish men who killed him. (Sue says this would be out of character). However, this is what happens when we go to the next world we see things differently. (There is an explanation from my guide Daniel later.)

He changes the subject talking about Sue getting drunk when she went out with her friend Julie; he saw her dancing and falling over. He said increasing her hours at work suited her. (True) He spoke of the money, paid out to Sue earlier in the year and that she had put some to one side. He talked about her being alone, no longer in a relationship. He said next summer things would change drastically for her she would have someone and be much happier.

He went on to talk about York Minster. (She had booked a night out in York). Said he watched her change the furniture around in the lounge but wasn't sure about it. (This is true). He said there were still some things to do in the house. He said since she decorated the hall, the picture is no longer there. (Sue used to have their wedding photo on the wall). He knew she had the chance of a holiday later in the year. He said go for it. (True)

Kevin says George has 'shut down' feels put out. Perhaps if you get him a cat or a dog to dote on he would feel better. He also explained that their computer printer had broken down. (When

Sue got home a few days later, George had to get it fixed.) Says he is good at designing and it would be a good move if he went into some sort of creative work.

He talked about wallpaper been put on upside down. He also said he was pleased to let Barbara put this in her book. He gave his love and left.
Sue's dad came and gave his love. He has no worries about her mum she seems to be OK alone. He gave two names this time, Jack and John. (He was known by both names). He gave his love and left.

Other things mentioned: - Names Mike/ Michael, Aunty Ann says Hello. Windsor.
Sue went to Windsor for a long weekend.
Mike/Michael Cousin who died 3 years earlier.

These are some of the details I found out after the readings. Kevin Speight, aged 40 Born 1959 was murdered on Wednesday 06-04-2000, stabbed...died at approximately 9pm, on the operating table, Istanbul, Turkey; he never saw the match.

Leeds United Fan went to Istanbul, Turkey to watch the match on Thursday 07-04-2000 Leeds United versus Galatasaray. He has a wife Sue, children George and Holly and 1 child in spirit.

I am sorry it sounds a bit disjointed but I have told you as it was said to me. I hope you can understand it? I would appreciate an explanation as to what extent a human being is allowed to kill and what happens to the victim?"

Killing, murder.

"Thank you for the story. As I have said many times everyone is given free will, this does not mean this enables individuals to do everything they would like to do. The gift of free will is part of the Creators plan, the natural law, so that you all have the opportunity of living in harmony with everyone and everything, achieving all that is good.

Only on earth can you have an experience of negativity, negative emotions represent the most dramatic opposite of love that can exist. The more you evolve spiritually the more you realise that you must act in accordance with the knowledge of spiritual truths.

Killing or any negative behaviour, such as murder and hate, is breaking the laws of the Great Spirit; negative behaviour is unique to the earth plane of existence.

Most people feel compassion usually for the victim; however this can be very misleading. You see when someone is murdered; the assailant could well be the one better off. The person who committed the murder may have agreed to help the victim pay back karma, before they came back to earth, during a pre-birth plan. Therefore, by helping the victim, it could be seen as a charitable act out of love. I will explain more about pre-birth plans at a later time, when you will be able to understand how the natural law works."

"I wonder if Spag the young man I told you about who was murdered overseas at a football match had a contract with the killer in a pre-birth plan. It would make sense when Spag said to his wife that he forgave the man, which wasn't like him. Yes that would definitely make sense. I will wait to hear what you say later about pre-birth plans. Thank you."

"Yes that is a possibility. It gives me great pleasure to be able to pass on to you my knowledge. I feel that God's law of Sin and Justice is now appropriate for me to explain to you.

The sins of the spirit are many, such as anger, hatred, criticism, jealousy, and so on, when you believe and know you are part of the Great Spirit you will love all people, things, and conditions. You will not sin, because you will know all is of God and that all is good! This is the Law of Sin.

We all have been given free will, which is the greatest gift from our Creator. You all have this great power of choice to do what you will, good or bad. As you can see from what we have been discussing, there are those who do not always use their will for good, and therefore, the law of justice works.

The Great Spirit does not punish you; you punish yourselves. Since the law of justice is a 'just' law, this law for wrongdoing punishes you. Therefore you already know the outcome, for within everyone is your conscience, which tells you right from wrong.

If you work with your conscience, you will not be able to wrong anyone; because you know when you harm your fellowman you also harm yourself. Because as you sow, so shall you reap. This is the Law of Justice. My dear do you understand?"

Capital punishment and wars.

"Yes Daniel I do." I went on questioning about murder, and said. "Surely soldiers that take life in a war situation are committing murder? Would this act be karma or murder?"

"That is a very good question my dear. The natural law, Gods law, determines the period of the life of a soul on earth. However, it is possible, that free will and other factors may arise and can change the life span of that soul.

I will say again, and I will say it many times, human beings have free will, therefore wars are not predictable, your world must resolve for them what they must do. They cannot have all the benefits of free will without some of the disadvantages. If human beings choose to wage war on each other that is their responsibility. However, they will have to pay the price."

"Daniel, there seems to be fighting all over the earth and I feel it is getting worse. Terrorists are committing terrible acts of violence, some of which is against innocent people being killed or hurt in some way. Our country have sent in soldiers to try and bring these wars to an end but this doesn't seem to work, peace seems to be a long way off. What is your opinion of bringing capital punishment back to protect the innocent victims?"

"It is always wrong to take human life; therefore committing another murder does not help in any way the one who has been murdered. And I doubt very much that capital punishment would work".

"Wouldn't it help to save future innocent lives?"

"No my dear, life is sacred and spiritually there is compensation and retribution, and perfect justice will always be done. No one will get away with breaking any of the laws of the Great Spirit they will pay a price. Those who commit those acts will learn how foolish they are in so doing.

You must always practice those spiritual principles on which all life is based. No one can cheat the Great Spirit, or the laws devised by infinite intelligence of love and wisdom."

"I understand, thank you. Are you able to tell us, why we are experiencing so much terrible violence?"

"What can I say, my dear it is many things, dissatisfaction, it is greed, selfishness and hate, all these feeling are being expressed. It is human beings who are more interested in materialism rather than the finer things of spirit. As long as materialism rules your world, so automatically it brings the penalties that must accompany such acts."

"You are saying murder is a crime in the eyes of God no matter what the reason is?"

"God's Law of Destruction has been broken. Yes, murder is a terrible crime; for the person who takes the life of another human being, who cuts short a life of karmic balancing or preventing a soul that has a mission to complete."

"Are all murders equally wicked? If that's the case how can a man go to war and fight for his country when there is this law of destruction, or murder? And is a man answerable for the lives he takes whilst at war?"

"Killing another human being is a crime in the

sight of God. However, the Great Spirit is just and judges the intention rather than the deed. It all depends if the soldier is forced to fight or not; nevertheless, if he commits any cruel acts he would be answerable, however, he would be rewarded for his humanity."

"What if someone had to kill another in self-defence, would God excuse that murder?"

"Yes but let me say, only if it is in self-defence and the only way to preserve their life."

"What about all the soldiers who have killed many people during the onslaught of wars? I often wonder what it is that makes men fight."

"I have already answered the first part of your question. To answer the second part of your question, Human beings fight because they allow their animal nature to overrule their spiritual nature, and to satisfy their wild passions.

There are some who wage war because they want to be seen as the strongest; therefore, war starts between nations. As people of earth progress spiritually, war becomes less frequent, and when it becomes inevitable, they behave more humanely."

"Will wars ever cease on earth?"

"Yes; when human beings understand and practice Gods laws, only then will humans be at peace. Sadly it will take a long, long time."

"I find it hard to understand why God the Great Spirit allows wars and murder. Why has war been allowed?"

"The answer is freedom and progress."

"I don't understand Daniel; I think that is a poor answer. If war is destined to bring us freedom, how does it happen that the outcome is so often the opposite, suppression of the defeated?"

"It is permitted in order to tire those who have been overpowered, and to urge them forward more quickly."

"I'm not sure I understand that. What about the one who incites war for his own gain?"

"The human being who instigates a war is guilty, the aggressor will have to undergo many incarnations, many trials in order to compensate for all the murders caused by him, furthermore, he will have to answer for every man who has been killed to satisfy his own evil desires."

"Thank you Daniel there is a lot for us to think about and discus."

"Yes there is my dear. Now let me talk of destruction, which is another law of the Great Spirit. You see destruction brings re-birth; it is necessary that all things should be destroyed; all things must come to an end, that they may be regenerated, spiritual renewal, new life. What you call destruction is only transformation, the plan of which is to renew, improve and perfect human beings and all living beings.

For example, animals destroy each other for food; as a result maintaining a balance in reproduction. It is only the body that is ever destroyed, and this body is not the vital part it is the soul, which is indestructible."

"I don't wish to be difficult but if destruction is necessary for the regeneration of beings, why then does the Great Spirit provide us with the need for self-preservation? Why does nature provide this?"

"That is a good question. The answer is, in order that their destruction may not take place before the proper time. Have you forgotten they have lessons to learn? And their time on earth has been agreed. It is for this reason that God has given to each being the desire to live and to reproduce itself."

"It's so complicated. Since death is to lead us to a better life, and it delivers us from the evils of our earth existence, and is therefore to be rather desired than dreaded, why do we have the instinctive horror of death?"

"Most human beings have no knowledge of spiritual things, which is one of the reasons they are afraid, afraid of the unknown. We have said that human beings should seek to prolong their life in order to accomplish their lessons. Therefore, God has given them the instinct of self-preservation, and this instinct sustains them under all their trials.

During the earthly life of human beings they sadly measure everything by the standard of their physical life; but, after death, the soul understands and sees things differently, and feels that the life of the body is a very small matter.

The spirit world is the real world and you are the children of the Great Spirit your creator therefore, you survive everything. If you consider an earthly life as it is and how small a thing it is in comparison with the unending life of spirit you would see how un-important it is.

The victims of war will find in another existence compensation for their sufferings. This is the Law of Destruction. I hope that answers your questions?"

"Thank you Daniel yes, you have taught us so much. Reluctantly I have to end the meeting, I am feeling tired. I will talk to the circle members tomorrow when we can discuss all that you have said. They don't know we are having a meeting today so they will be very excited to learn what we have been talking about. Thank you again and I look forward to speaking to you again on Wednesday."

"There is no need to thank me, it is my pleasure."

We all said goodnight and then we made a cuppa and had the usual discussions until late.

After they had gone home I made myself another cup of tea and thought about my evening with Daniel.

I am so lucky to have the ability to link with those in the spirit world and I love my guides and helpers very much. They have used me as an instrument to heal the sick and to link with peoples loved ones and to prove life after death for about 40 years, so they are part of me now. I don't know what I would do without them.

I am always tired when I have spoken to Daniel, I must be doing something wrong. People say to me 'you shouldn't be poorly or suffer in any way, after all the work you do for the spirit world.' I tell them, 'I know why I am always in pain, I am not excused my earthly trials and lessons and I know it is my karma. I have said jokingly 'I must have been a bad one in a past life;' there is a lot of truth in that saying.

I do at times breathe in the universal life energy, to make me feel better but I am my worst enemy, there is always something else I have to do. I need to do what I tell others and find time!

I woke up the following morning feeling great. I had several people to see for healing and readings, finishing in good time to have a meal and to see the girls.

They arrived on the dot at 7.30pm very excited. They took off their coats and sat down in their usual places. It's very important to always sit in the same place and at the same time each week when you sit for development, as each sitter gives their energy to the circle and creates a good balance for spirit guides to work with. It takes time for the spirit world to make adjustments to get the correct vibration and balance in the room.

I made a cup of tea for us all and sat down for our relaxing discussions and update. The meeting was always typed so they could read for themselves what was said. Most of them felt a little cheated because I talked to Daniel without them; I explained about my tiredness and said we would be having less time but twice a week instead of once, I also said they would be welcome if they could find the time.

We talked for a very long time going over what had been said on both evenings. It's quite funny really to see grown up ladies looking agog just like young children listening to an adventure story. It reminded me of the times I spent as a child sat on the back steps of a neighbour's house telling ghost stories to a large audience of under ten years olds. They never wanted me to stop either.

Chapter Six.

Cruelty.

Wednesday came very quickly and again the girls were on time as usual. Daniel was waiting also. I said "thank you for coming Daniel. We always look forward to our time with you."

Jean said to Daniel. "Can you tell us please your feelings towards cruelty?"

Daniel replied. "Cruelty is abhorrent and always the result of an evil nature."

Jean went on with. "I was wondering if you could tell us, is cruelty the foremost part of the character of unenlightened human beings?"

"Among the unenlightened races, as you call them, are souls who do not know any better, their physical part rules over their spirit side? They care for nothing of life, they abandon themselves to the instincts of their brutal, animal nature as they think only of themselves and their own life, and this generally renders them cruel. Eventually advanced souls help them to move forward and upwards. You must remember we have all been in some form of un-development, we have had to grow and we continue to do so."

"Thank you I understand." Jean said. "Can you tell us if cruelty is the absence of morals?"

"The moral sense exists in all human beings but in some it is not developed, it takes some time for undeveloped souls to show kindness and humane traits. Human beings are progressing all the time, although some slower than others.

Those who have the instinct of evil are out of place among good people. Slowly their evil tendencies will disappear as they become more experience and get a clearer understanding of what is good and what is evil. It takes many, many lifetimes for the improvement to become complete.

Karma is not always something you have to pay back when you have done wrong, karma is also to learn and experience new feelings. For example, how can you be truly compassionate if you have never seen or felt compassion? How can you give love if you have never felt loved? How can you truly understand those who live in poverty if you have never experience it yourself? How can you truly feel for those who have been victims of cruelty when you have never experienced it?

There is always an opposite for every action and emotion. Think hard about situations around you, yourself, family and friends and you may find the reason for your karma and their life lesson within that family circle.

Especially if the same thing happens again and again, it is telling you that you need to learn from this to enable you to move forward."

"Thank you Daniel, the more you explain things to us the more we begin to see things much clearer. And I can now see and understand, cause and effect." Jean said.

All the ladies confirmed what Jean said.

Rape.

I asked. "Can you please explain to us what happens to the person who commits the act of rape? A long time ago a friend told me she had been raped and after all these years she still 'feels' the scars from this horrible act."

"Any act of violence is terrible and contravenes God's law. Sometimes however, rape victims know their attacker when they were in the spirit world and before incarnation. They may have agreed to the rape during a pre-birth plan and made a contract with the soul, who out of a charitable act agreed to be the rapist by sacrificing their time in the spirit world to go back to the heavy earth plane to help a spirit experience a very important trial in their earth life, perhaps to balance karma, perhaps she did something similar in a previous life; better to be raped by someone you know rather than a stranger, these are free will decisions by both parties. Not all rapes are planned.

Let me say here, all of us at some time have committed serious crimes such as rape, murder and such like, in our past lives and dealt with our karma, enabling us to grow. Without these trials how would we truly know what it is like to love if we haven't experience hate? How do we know what cruelty is in less we have experienced it? And so the lessons go on and on until we reach perfection.

It is not easy to understand what I am saying and perhaps a rape victim would be very annoyed by this statement. Nevertheless this is true. Do you understand?"

"I see what you mean; I think I would also be very angry to hear that if I had been raped."

"There are times when a positive outcome occurs from a terrible negative act, such as the victim becoming a rape crisis counsellor and helping numerous people. This could well have been the reason the soul agreeing to the rape in the first place. Helping others can bring about a good healing for the victim.

If this was not a pre-birth plan for your friend, this could cause the victim to be traumatised for years and often take this emotion back to the spirit world, which will cause more karma; she must try and forgive. In such a case the rapist will pay the price for this act of violence. However, the motive is always taken into consideration, for example.

There are times when extremely dark roles are agreed upon with a soul mate before incarnations, including murder. In such a case as I have said it is an act of charity and the perpetrator will not suffer for this act.

When you have done a wrong, the first point is to repent, or stop doing wrong and ask forgiveness, and as you forgive yourself so you are forgiven. Providing you have repented, you have paid the karmic debt through your suffering. You may now invoke the Law of Forgiveness!

In truth, however, there is no punishment, simply a desire to balance karma. Similarly, because you have chosen the roles you play, you are not victims. My dears, have I made this clear to you?"

"You are saying if someone harms me whilst I am on earth, I am not the victim, then who is?"

"That is correct. How can you be a victim if you have chosen that life knowing you will be harmed? No one is to blame; in fact, there is no blame."

Jane queried. "I don't understand. If someone

hurts another person surely this would be an evil act?"

"Obviously I have not made myself clear enough to you. Before incarnation, before you leave the spirit world you voluntarily choose your next life including all trials, suffering and hardships in order to pay back, to balance your karma, or the need to experience that particular act. Sometimes the perpetrator agrees with you to fulfil this act so that it will help you. Therefore, if a soul hurts another to balance karmic debt, there is no blame. Now do you understand?"

Jane went on to say. "Are you saying, if a person is hurt by the hand of another, the spirit already knew of this before incarnating?"

"Yes that is the case most of the time but do not forget what I said, if this was not a contract and just an evil act, the perpetrator will suffer. You can only evolve to a better place, a more beautiful plane of existence if you learn from your trials."

"Thank you, I think I understand now, although I am not sure I like it." Jane admitted frowning.

Disabled, deformity and insane.

Beth another member of the circle spoke up.

"Daniel thank you for all the information you bring us, if I may ask? If you select your body, then you must select whether you will be deformed, disabled or not. Is that correct? And what could be the reason for anyone to want to have a disabled life?"

"Yes that is what I said to the first part of your question. Those who are born deaf, blind, disabled, or deformed, or even become so later in life is what that spirit individual chose to endure as lessons on earth. However, they will not remember this when they are in a physical body.

Your health is part of your karma and your thoughts and emotions do affect your vitality and health. For example; the reason why someone would prefer to be deaf or blind, perhaps in a previous life could possibly be that they have heard or seen something dreadful that left them traumatised, something horrendous that perhaps happened to someone they loved.

When the soul returns to the spirit world this experience remains in the subconscious and when it is time to incarnate again it makes the spirit decide out of fear to be blind or deaf in this life, not wanting to hear or see anything horrendous again.

Being disabled could give that person the opportunity to be more in touch with their inner feeling, their intuition and thoughts, helping them to know themselves. For some individuals, being disabled is an opportunity to explore avenues of growth that they couldn't explore before.

Any form of disability does increase sensitivity, and that soul perhaps later helps others who are experiencing the same, enabling them to feel compassion towards people with other various sorts of disabilities. Do you see what I am trying to say? "

"Yes I do, thank you."

A visitor to my development circle asked Daniel. "Do souls actually agree to be the parents of handicapped children? If they do make such plans and contracts, is it because they need the experience, or could it be an agreement with another soul's birth-plan? If the former, what does the experience offer that will make such suffering worthwhile from the viewpoint of the soul?"

"My dear that is a very good question. Having handicapped children is one of the most heart-breaking challenges one can face. When a child is born with, or later develops a handicap, there is often anger at God the Great Spirit. Asking why would this be allowed to happen to an innocent child? Parents who give birth to a handicap child may also blame their partner or themselves for 'faulty' genes. It may cause bad feelings and affect their marriage putting more stress on the situation when they need to be united, helping each other and their new born child to come to terms with it.

If a soul planned before incarnation to be handicapped from birth, and if the parents wanted the challenge to have a handicapped child they would have arranged their life plan with their guides and elders beforehand. In both cases the experience gave each soul the opportunity they needed to learn from this. Does that answer your question?"

"Yes, I understand what you are saying because I believe in karma; still quite a lot to take in."
She continued. "Can you explain to me why are children born with defects, such as being crippled or blind through no fault of their own? Is that the same as the previous question?"

"I have already explained this to you. You must not confuse the progression and development of the soul with the growth of the physical body. Usually what you call a defect is caused by the natural law of their parents' genes, inheritance from the father or the mother, or both parents. Remember what I have just said, this has been planned before birth. Therefore you will find those who start their material lives with a physical defect will show in their character more kindness, tolerance and gentleness to others; this is the lesson they wanted and chose to do before incarnating. There is nothing that escapes the law of cause and effect."

"If a soul is insane and is not responsible for his or her actions, what happens to those souls when they pass to the other side, since we are all judged by whom we are and the way we have lived our lives and dealt with our challenges?"

"My dear, again you are confusing the physical things with the things of spirit. When the human brain cells are not working properly this causes confusion during the soul's life on earth, nevertheless, the soul is not damaged and knows its own responsibility even if it is unable to express itself in your world because the bodily functions are impaired.

The progression of every soul is governed by the laws of the Great Spirit, the soul is not judged by the standards of the earth, but with the standards of eternal wisdom. If a soul is not responsible, then it is not accountable in the spirit life. Neither are moments of madness, as you call it, when a person takes another human life or even their own. They cannot be blamed because they cannot function properly. In the spirit world, it is the soul's motive that matters. Do you understand?"

"Yes I think so. Thank you. If the soul has been unable to learn its lessons in its life on earth, because of the defects, what happens then?"

"The earthly experience is null and void, invalid because of the defects; it will not register its experience on the soul as it would have done. However, the soul could have come to earth in service for another soul to learn from this. Incarnating again is not always for self to learn lessons.

When you understand karma, unaccountable events, trials, emotions can all be easier to accept if they relate to events in former lives; debts left unpaid.

You have heard people say, they have been dealt a bad hand of cards, others a good one, it is a true saying; each card is directly related to events in your character, which you have previously created within yourselves. You see my dear; it is up to you to play each card correctly. Your future and your development of your spiritual growth is down to you. Do you understand what I have said thus far?"

Jean responded with. "Yes I think so, but it's not easy to absorb everything, there is so much to think about.

Selfishness.

190

Beth asked. "Daniel what happens to those people when they die who have been selfish, thinking only of themselves, who are ruled by pride, greed and controlling everything and everyone close to them. They lack the simple feelings such as compassion, caring and understanding?

My sister is married to a man who is very controlling and selfish. He would never let her learn to drive, I presume it was so that he could be in control of where she went; he takes her everywhere. It is the same with the bank account and mortgage they are all in his name; she has to ask for every penny she spends. There are more selfish acts and I don't know how she puts up with it; I couldn't live like that."

"Those souls who have been shallow whilst on the earth plane are held by their own actions after death on the lower astral plane of existence with those of like mind; this is near the earth plane, until such time as these tendencies have been conquered.

Everyone goes to the place that they deserve, what they have earned by their actions during their many lifetimes. The lower a person is spiritually the more earthly is the place where they will go because the vibrations are more gross; the higher in the realms of spirit, the finer the vibrations and more beautiful the place where they will reside.

Your sister will be creating karma by allowing herself to be ruled by another, unless, of course she is paying back karma from things she has done previously. You must always remember, as you give, so you will receive. Bad deeds and thoughts return to you. So does the opposite, kindness, love etc., all karma is recorded with debits and credits. Loving thoughts, words, deeds are positive and bring you credits, whereas, negative ones are debits. If you have a problem with someone, it is better if you wish them well and this with help to heal the karma. You only carry karma until you have learnt the lesson."

Beth replied with. "Thank you Daniel I will tell my sister what you said. It sounds so hard, cold and indifferent to me."

"My dear child, can you not see that she has allowed this to happen to her, therefore she must have drawn it to her like a magnet. The Great Spirit does not punish you by making 'bad' things happen. Karma is a neutral, impersonal law by which the universe operates.

Instead of seeing bad karma as punishment for actions in your past lives, try and understand karma. Karma helps you to move forward, particularly with those who have experienced major traumas or setbacks such as drug and alcohol addiction.

Do you see you can better understand it as lessons toward living in harmony with all people and all things? Positive beliefs and actions create good karma in your life, therefore it is down to you how you think and act.

As I explained earlier, and I will continue to say, before you are born into this world, while still in the realms of spirit and along with spirit elders, teachers and your guides, you decide the lessons you need to learn on your next visit to the earth plane. They help and encourage you to pursue these lessons by creating the correct conditions necessary for you to proceed on your chosen path.

My dears, it is not easy for us to see you suffering and there are times when we weep for you but we know and understand all your trials are for your own good, your evolution.

You choose your family before you are born as a chance to resolve problems with lessons your soul needs to learn and grow. You also select your body and your genetic tendencies this has an important part to play. Some may choose some form of illness or deformity, so that they can fulfil their trials on earth. Do you see how important that is?

There are some souls who often refuse to accept the opportunities offered for their spiritual growth and changes of their karma, instead, they prefer to carry on with the old ways or feelings because they feel it is too difficult for them to make changes; they will remain static and not move forward until they see what is best for them."

"Thank you. Each time I listen to you it helps me to understand a little more." Carol replied.

"That is very good. I will go over anything you are not sure about. It is better for you to ask me to repeat something than for you to go away from here not knowing what I have been teaching you."

"Thank you so much, I do try to understand and I don't wish to be a nuisance."

"My dear you are never a nuisance I am only too pleased to help. Let me continue and explain, even though you chose your partners in a pre-birth plan, you have been given 'Reason' to reason with. Without this power you would be like a robot obeying every whim of whoever suggests any given thing just like your sister.

Now then, suppose someone suggests a 'thing' or asks you to do a certain thing. Well, what shall you do? Shall you blindly obey every whim of another or shall you sit quietly and reason the 'thing' out for yourself? If you have been given reasoning power, then use it to reason with. Then do the thing if it seems right or best for you.

As long as human beings are governed by

what others think and suggest, they are the slave. You have been given Reason to use, then you must use it. This is the Law of Reason.

I think it is a good time now to explain to you all another law, the Law of Transgression. Every transgression, wrongdoing against your fellowman must be wiped out, it must be erased and put right, it has to be paid in full; this is the law. Owe no one anything, whether it is a service, a kindness, money or a gift.

If someone does you a service or kindness, repay that person by returning the service or kindness or to another person, by doing this the first individual is repaid.

Do you see that if each person follows this way of life, then everyone looks after each other, because this is the way that brotherhood can be recognised, established on the earth planet? Each must do their utmost to this end. It is law.

Now, transgression: If you have wronged another person in any way and you are unable to make amends with that person. In your heart, ask for forgiveness. Then do something good to someone in need of the thing you haven't been able to put right with the one wronged, then there is no injustice. Therefore, forgive all transgressions against you and right all transgressions against your fellowman. This is the law of transgression."

"Thank you very much, it all makes sense."

"After all that has been said I think it is time to follow on with the law of forgiveness.

No one can be forgiven, unless they are also willing to forgive themselves. I'm afraid none of you are perfect, but you are all striving for perfection that is why you have incarnated to the earth plane, which is good. Nevertheless, in the striving you make mistakes, but that is the only way to learn.

When you have felt that you have learnt your lessons, not by just thinking it, you must feel it deep inside of you, within your being, then do not sin any more. If you repeatedly make the same mistakes over, and over again you have not learned the lessons, therefore you must experience the effects of such a mistake again and again until you learn. There is no escaping the law of cause and effect.

When you sin, or make mistakes it will cause dis-ease in the body because there are the Great Spirits laws governing the universe, governing all and everything, and when you obey our Creators laws you will live in harmony, and harmony is health, because you are balanced. Do you understand?

If you do not forgive, there can be no harmony within, which causes unhealthy bodies and you will be sending out negative feelings of hate, intolerance, criticism. If you truly forgive your fellowman, you are forgiven because you have first forgiven.

It is simple, learn this Law; obey it always and it will bring you true happiness on earth. Forgive all wrong doings against you, real or imaginary. This is the essence of the law of Forgiveness. I know sometimes it is not easy, but remember what Jesus said, he said 'sin no more' what he was also saying is you are healed!"

"Thank you for that Daniel. When you tell us these things it sounds so right and easy to do. We will try.

I am sorry Daniel it is the time to end our lovely spiritual talks with you this evening, thank you good night."

"Yes, sleep well and we will speak again soon."

We talked as usual for quite some time about everything Daniel had told us so far. I must say some of the information took some swallowing with some members. We talked and talked and talked it over again and again until we couldn't talk anymore. In the end we all felt much better about what Daniel said, discussing these subjects amongst ourselves helped us no end.

It reminded me of what Daniel said to me about the group soul discussing a souls past life and dissecting everything to find various ways of dealing with the trials. (This is talked about later).

We said goodnight and they went home to their family.

Chapter Seven.

What are Guides and Controls?

The weeks go by so quickly, I don't seem to have enough time to do any serious thinking about our lessons with Daniel, or anything else.

I am pleased that everything is transcribed by Elsie, we now have written work to use as reference. We met again at the usual time and greeted Daniel with affection.

Beth asked. "Daniel can you please tell us what guides and controls are and what is their role?"

"Yes I will explain to the best of my ability what you need to know, so that you and others might understand the simplicity of the Great Spirit and the love for us all.

Without the constant influence of spirit guides the earth would in a very brief time be reduced to a state of complete and absolute barbarity and chaos. Man believes he can get on perfectly well with his own powers and volition. He is conceited enough to think that he requires no help from any source whatever. Your world looks very dark to us, and we try very hard to bring a little light to it. We try to make our presence felt.

Spirit guides and controls are knowledgeable,

developed spirit beings who are devoted in helping those who dwell on the earth plane. They bring knowledge, to those who seek and have a thirst for spiritual truths.

Not everyone knows about spirit guides, therefore there are a number of spirit guides who carry on their work unknown to their students. It would be much easier for all concerned if the students were aware of spiritual things as it makes their tasks so much easier. Therefore, we must spread spiritual knowledge to all who seeks.

The word guide speaks for itself because they are there to guide and assist you throughout your many lives. They try very hard to communicate and guide you through your intuitive senses, your gut feelings, they also let you know by thought what is right and what is wrong for you, your conscience tells you. You hear people say 'I will go with my gut feelings, they are usually right.'

Most guides and spirit teachers do not need to incarnate anymore because they are extremely evolved beings. There are some other guides who are knowledgeable and have reached a high level of growth but sometimes they still need to incarnate again because there are things they still need to experience. Your highly evolved guides have remained with you from the beginning of your lifetimes, this could be hundreds or even thousands of years for some, they chose to help and guide you whilst you learn and grow spiritually. I must say it saddens them to see the mistakes and errors of judgement that students make, and because of their karma and free will the guides have to stand to one side and watch.

Guides find with those who have no knowledge of spiritual life near impossible at times to penetrate the wall that human beings have built around themselves.

My dears, it is not an easy task to communicate as some in your world may think. Your guides have to alter their consciousness down to a level in which you can understand and it is very frustrating at times but they try very hard to keep you on your preferred path that they discussed with you before you incarnated.

Once you become aware of spirit and connection is made, there is also the difficulty when something needs to be described; often there are no words in your vocabulary to describe what they want to say.

There are times when your guides have to make things happen, such as making you slow down when in the car because further on the road there is a problem that may cause you to have an accident, injure yourself or even die and return you to the world of spirit before your allotted time. Having said that, they cannot let you change your path without trying to help you and cannot change the reasons you have come to the earth, you have free will to do as you will, rightly or wrongly. As you know, what you do today changes tomorrow; this is what creates your karma, good or bad.

Guides and controls often get together and discuss what they are doing to help their students, they sometimes speak of their near-despair at their inability to explain more than a very small part of what they intended because their charge cannot understand.

They have awareness and a vision into their character, and with their advanced knowledge the guides occasionally discuss their future. The insight of a guide to his student does at times seem to lead a little into his or her future.

Your guide has a different role to your control, much wider, he or she brings spiritual wisdom and knowledge, and they are wonderful teachers of importance and their mediumistic performance, their demonstration excels and is in no way limited. They work behind the scenes of every human being, linking with each individual.

It must be amazing to you my dears, when you think that they possess a spiritual map or pattern for you, assisting you to fulfil your own spiritual opportunities within this plan enabling you to carry out on the earth the tasks that you need to do. And being aware of this, gradually prepares you the medium for heavy duties and trials ahead, that you would otherwise at times find yourself most unwilling to face. They help you with a challenge or entanglement, which normally would put stress upon you.

Working with your guides is a long-term process; they gently guide you and gradually broaden and deepen your consciousness. A responsible guide will always respect the free will of his medium, never ever imposing his beliefs upon them or making them dependent upon him.

As I have just said we do communicate with you when you have developed your six sense, as we are doing now. Every soul has this ability, you are born with this faculty however it all depends on how near the surface it is; a development class as you have, can improve this natural gift for those who seek help. 'The guide' endeavours to influence the whole life and destiny of the individual student, so that what they experience will enrich and deepen the understanding of spiritual truths.

Their guide and the spirit control generally remain with a medium throughout their lives, and there are many other spirits who join in the work of ministering to the medium, some of them are only around for a short period of time, some of them remain so long that they are mistaken for guides or controls.

There are other spirit people that want to help human beings and try to assist them and there are spirit beings that are like probationer guides who are not quite ready, not yet experienced enough to take on the responsibility of a guide's role.

There are always wonderful spirits beings who are engaged in missionary work and out of compassion they descend into the lower dark regions of the spirit world that are very close to earth, and lead lost souls out of their misery. Do you understand thus far?"

"Yes, thank you so much Daniel. If further questions arise regarding a guide's role I will ask you if I may."

"My dear I am always here to try and answer any questions you may have. However I have not yet finished. I will continue. Dear ladies, now you have started your mediumistic training; you will soon be aware of spirit operators around you, try hard to link with them.

You see it is difficult for a spirit control to reach the mediums mind and to be able to work with the breathing and bodily movements so that they respond to his (or her) will. In other words take control of the medium, with their consent of course. They are then able to pass on information and impressions first obtained from the sitter's dead relatives and friends and then passed on to the recipient through their mediumship. They do this because they are familiar with the process of working with their medium. This enables them to do a better job than the relatives can do for themselves.

They have a specialised role of giving evidence on behalf of those unable to communicate satisfactory by themselves. Their duty is to make sure order prevails during the process of the communication.

Most children when they are born are aware of their spirit body and the spirit realms. It is natural for them to communicate with the spirit world and they are able to see and hear spirit people, these are their 'invisible friends." It is a great pity that as children gets older the spirit world and their spirit friends fade and they are forgotten as the physical world and materialism takes over. Do you see how this can happen?"

"Yes thank you very much; we now know what your role is.

Reincarnation and karma.

"Can you please explain to us reincarnation and karma?" Beth asked.

"Reincarnation gives you meaning to each of your earth lives, however it is difficult for you to understand what exactly is involved, and it makes a great difference if you can accept that karma does exist in your many past lives. It will make things much easier once you understand that your difficulties and complications within your character come from a former life.

So many human beings find themselves facing unwelcome and unavoidable issues, which intrude into their life. This is usually due to karmic debts that need to be put right, or from things that had been left undone or not done correctly before in a previous life. However, each new life could quite well be an opportunity to create good karma, so live it well. It is always good to remember, what you send out in thoughts or deeds always returns to you as difficulties that you need to resolve, or, as opportunities.

Reincarnation is important and can lead you out of your treadmill existence, enabling you to move forwards towards your necessary growth of being, instead of walking the same path over and over again. Understanding reincarnation gives you some of the more unexplained, baffling episodes and problems in your life, such as the unwelcoming events of terrible illnesses like cancer, the sufferings of children and animals and the natural disasters, such as floods and earth quakes. Do you see?

I have heard many, many times human beings say when in a difficult situation 'why me, what have I done to deserve this.' Well now you know.

When you care for someone with an illness and give a great deal of love to that person it creates a step up on the rung of the ladder to growth and progression. When a person finds they have a serious illness it can make them think about what is important in their life, so they make changes with themselves and their beliefs, values and judgments.

Mostly it is a form of karmic balancing. Even so, all these terrible things make it impossible for human beings to believe in a loving God, or life after death in the spirit realms where everyone will eventually reside.

When you look at a person, their true character of the soul is not what you see. If for example a family member or a friend is harsh or perhaps emotionally distant towards you whilst you are in the earth life, you are only seeing the physical body, the external part, the school uniform, of the real individual.

My dears ask your selves what did I learn from this episode and those people I encountered that has given me knowledge and wisdom I would not possess if I had not been there or if he or she had never been in my life?

Once you believe in reincarnation you will stop blaming the Great Spirit for all your troubles. Do you understand?"

"Yes thank you."

"As I said earlier in our discussions, when you are incarnating to earth you play a role and

207

every role that a soul is given in their earth life has a purpose, and the struggles on earth does not only belong to you alone but forms part of your destiny as a member of a group soul. Jesus said 'I am in you, you are in me, and we are all in the Great Spirit'.

Every life you have lived you have acquired a number of identities of your own. You understand each body, the outer shell of each of your personalities; your school uniform. When you have finished your role, your school uniform is cast away at your physical death, and what you learned whilst wearing that school uniform is retained within your higher self.

Souls grow stronger with every incarnation, especially when it experiences hard lives on earth, longing to progress and express more of its spiritual self. Therefore a spirit incarnates again to earth with a double task. First it is to unfold a new part of them-selves as far as they can on the earth. In addition, they bring back things they haven't done, remnants from their former lives, their former selves, in other words unwanted 'baggage', their karma.

Souls both on earth and the spirit realms have found that the suffering they endured has brought them knowledge and wisdom and spiritual growth, they no longer see the Great Spirit as being an unjust God. The struggle on earth is all part of the destiny of the whole, the group soul; we will speak about group souls at a later time.

When you can accept and understand the workings of reincarnation, you are able to see a clearer picture and meaning of your own lives as they are lived out.

In the spiritualist movement there are some people who reject this idea even though spirit teachers with wisdom and insight communicate through mediums to teach reincarnation. However, there are more and more individuals who look towards the spiritualist movement for truth into life after death, including the possibility of reincarnation.

To answer your question, the aim of incarnation is a necessity and compulsory to all of us; it is the only way of attaining perfection. For some, as I have said before is an opportunity to make right their previous wrongdoings and for some it is a mission. All of you, even though you may not be aware of this, continually strive towards perfection by the means of progression by undergoing the trials of earth, your physical life.

You are compelled by the Great Spirit to achieve in your lives what you have not been able to do in a previous life. Therefore, in order to attain perfection you must undergo unforeseen changes on the earth plane of existence.

Once you understand life continues after death you are more able to face your trials with strength of mind. In addition, by incarnating again with new trials you are able to be more willingly to put things right that had been left undone in a previous life. It gives you the opportunity and the means of rectifying your mistakes, your wrongs doings and the experience required to atone, to pay back that which you have created in other life times, good or bad.

You are never alone; we draw near to your world because we love you. We will do everything in our power to assist you, but we cannot give you what you are not ready to digest, to take in. It is only through growth and understanding that knowledge comes.

Each plane of existence, as you climb upwards reveals the more beautiful level above, and all these spheres of existences stretch towards infinity. I cannot solve all your problems for you because there are issues, influences that cannot be revealed to you.

The knowledge which you already have received must be the ground on which you should build your faith, the faith which is created on what you have been shown, what has been proven to you.

My dears, with every new existence, you take a step forward on the path of unfoldment towards progression. In time after many lives when you no longer have imperfections, you will have no need to incarnate again, and then you enter the state of a perfect, purified spirit. This is the only way to explain the future and provide you with a sound basis for your hopes."

"Thank you." I continued to ask. "There are thousands, perhaps millions of people suffering in the world today. Are they all souls paying for past misdeeds?"

"My dear it is not possible to give you a simple answer to cover a complicated natural law at work. All souls are part of the one great evolutionary ladder; therefore, it is impossible to judge physical happenings without knowing the spiritual requirements. In other words what you sow, you reap.

Nothing is ever forgotten and nothing is overlooked or neglected. The law includes all. Every being, every aspect no matter how small or large, simple or complicated are all part of the unchangeable law, I repeat, unchangeable law. My dears your world is only one little aspect of being, it is not the whole of eternity."

"Does everyone have the same number of lives?"

"Not at all, the number of incarnations varies for everyone, some are quicker to advance than others, and those who grow more quickly spare themselves many trials. Nevertheless all successive incarnations are always very numerous because progression is infinite."

"Thank you Daniel you have given us such a lot to think about in a short time; we have to go home and digest all that you have said. Before we go can you tell us why you had to go through so much in your lives on earth?"

"My dears, how can I teach others unless I have gone through fire myself to become strong? And as I said earlier, we all have to incarnate many times, including myself.

I have only briefly touched on karma today, however all that I have given to you thus far is the result of karma. We have only spoken of serious issues, therefore I must explain less noticeable issues to you, because these are just as important.

The emotion of love and hate are not far apart, therefore they can quite easily turn into the other. For example, and I am afraid this example is typical. When a daughter or son is doomed never to marry, to forego loving relationships because they have no choice but to look after an elderly or sick parent, this love can turn to hate. It is a sacrifice that most human beings may feel and resented bitterly. However, it is what those spirit beings chose for themselves before incarnating to earth as trials for their spiritual growth.

Let me give you another example. When souls

find that they are always in a situation where sick people are around them, it is likely that they are being told that a lesson in compassion may be needed for that person to progress.

Remember what I have said, before incarnation is where they chose their lessons and why they are here, why they came to earth. When they plan a life they are shown the most likely path. All paths have crossroads and detours; these are all part of the road ahead. Every lesson, every challenge is what the spirits choose to experience.

Illness is dis-ease and when mind, body and spirit are not balanced you will find you are creating indications and displays of emotional or mental difficulties. This is all part of the natural law and if you do not learn to express yourselves on a higher level of vibration by thinking and acting in a positive way you will then find illness in your life. If you do raise your vibrations illness will disappear; it is that simple. It is always better to accept the lessons you chose and get on living your life without complaining knowing they are lessons you chose and you will receive your spiritual rewards. You will understand pre-birth planning later as we talk, it will be made clear to you all.

Let me explain another example of a young woman with breast cancer. First I must tell you that our bodily cells hear our thoughts and they respond to them. If you cut a lemon in half you will find your mouth waters, do you see this is your body reacting to what it has seen? Therefore in a way this young woman may have given herself cancer by not accepting how she looked, possibly her breasts were too big or too small or, she desperately wanted to breast feed her children and couldn't. This applies to all those who are unhappy with their appearance, more so with those who have been ridiculed in their life.

If I can remind you, you are what you think. Perhaps once she accepted herself the way she was, the cancer would be healed. One thing is clear her body had reacted to her feelings about herself. Another reason that is not karma; the experience, the trial of breast cancer may have brought people into that life that would not have been there had she remained healthy, it may well have awoken strengths she did not know she had. Or she wanted to experience this trauma to add to her other life experiences; this contract would have been made in the spirit world.

If for example a parent protects their children to excess by keeping them in the house never letting them play out or express themselves, in other words preventing them from doing what they came to earth to do; their free will. They may end up imprisoning themselves in their next life as payment for the karma they created for themselves in that situation.

There can be many reasons why people suffer

on earth. Usually it is lessons that the person needs to heal, a karmic debt. It is simply another layer of learning.

Do you understand a little more of the trials a soul has to encounter and how 'what you sow you reap' works?"

"Yes thank you very much." Jean said.

"Wow!" Elsie exclaimed. "One can't imagine the illnesses we unwillingly cause to ourselves through our negative thinking and some we agreed before we came here.

What about the women who desperately want to breast fed their children, do they get cancer? Or, what about women who can't have children are they at a higher risk of cancer of the womb? And what of those who were unloved, do they get a heart disease?"

I answered the question. "I think those who cause their own illness must have an obsession about something wrong with their body, or something they desperately want. There are millions of women who hate their breasts! It really doesn't bare thinking of." I said and continued with." I would like to tell you all about a couple of past life stories to do with karma and reincarnation if I may?"

Marie's past lives/Karma.

"But of course my dear."

"A young woman who I had never met before came for healing. She came as a patient to see me for spiritual healing and she told me she had been diagnosed with Lupus.

I understand it is an incurable immune system illness, probably genetic in origin; I understand only women are usually prone to this illness. It can affect any part of the body and that it is a very nasty persistent disease. Lupus can produce many symptoms and a number of major organs can be damaged in an irreversible way, principally the kidneys the skin, heart, lungs and brain.

Thank goodness, Marie did not have any major organ problems, although she had a severe skin condition, which was becoming more and more upsetting for her. This affected her head and face; it is horrendous for anyone especially a woman. Her hair was beginning to fall out and her scalp was sore and scabby. By the time, she came to see me it had started to spread onto her face.

Poor Marie couldn't stand the heat or light from the sun or any form of heat on her face. When she went out in the car, she had to cover herself in suntan cream and completely cover her face, leaving only a slot for her eyes, and then she wore glasses, otherwise she would burn.

Much later after the healing sessions, and after joining my development classes for mediumship and healing, I was told by my spirit doctors the condition was due to past life karma. I immediately checked her aura to find that karma was indeed causing this illness and went back several lifetimes. I know if it is past life karma or new karma by examining the aura for block in any of the seven levels.

Following a healing session I explained to Marie how to regress herself through meditation. I hoped that this would show her the relevant past life that would connect her to her Lupus condition. Regression meditation can take a long time, as with most things, the more a person practices the easier it becomes. Eventually, her patience was rewarding and she saw herself back in time. This is a good way to forgive past life karma and worth trying if you can.

She told me, 'I lived in the time when there was no electricity; we used candles when it got dark. I lived with my mother and father in, what looked like, a farmhouse in the country. There did not seem to be any other houses nearby.

One night I went to bed as usual with my candle to light the way. That night I was not particularly tired and played with my dolls. I wasn't allowed to play when I went to bed but I didn't think mum and dad would find out.

Eventually I must have fallen asleep without extinguishing the candle. Sometime later, the flame of the candle must have set fire to my dolls clothes and then spread to the rest of the house. I awoke coughing from the smoke; my bedroom was on fire. The next thing I remember, I am outside and crying, I can see the whole of the house is a light and my face hurts from burns I sustained. Someone told me my parents were killed in the fire. I was devastated; I knew it was my fault!'

From what Marie had told me, I concluded that she blamed herself for her parent's deaths and she had carried this guilt with her into the spirit world and then to this lifetime. I believe from what she told me, that it was because of this tragedy she had Lupus and was feeling the pain of heat on her face. I explained this was karma and that she must meditate again and try to go back into that lifetime and forgive herself for the death of her parents. She would then recover from her illness.

It was not easy for her but she did manage to do what I suggested. Soon after that, Marie started to get a little better with the help of healing. That wasn't the end; future regression meditations showed other lifetimes where she had similar experiences. I am pleased to say she is completely better now.

I believe it does not matter how much healing a person receives if they have karma to pay back they will not get better until they have learnt the lesson and paid the debt.

Second past life story.

Marie also told me of her second past life experience. This past life of Marie's was connected to the nerve pain in her face and mouth; it was activated when she went on holiday to France.

During her holiday, she developed a large lump in the roof of her mouth, which became infected. She was in a great deal pain and made many visits to the dentist and the dental hospital. Eventually the dentist had to remove the tooth and the nerve hoping this would solve the problem, unfortunately, it didn't improve and later was diagnosed with mercury poisoning. Therefore, the dentist advised her to have all her fillings removed and replaced with white non-mercury fillings.

Marie decided to regress herself again and this time was shown a previous life set in France; she saw herself as a nun. Her father, in that life was the head of the monastery and her present day husband in that lifetime was a monk.

Marie had an affair with the monk, which caused nasty rumours. She was taken and tortured, but never confessed. The head monk then put her into a dark cold cellar, where further torture took place. The monk with whom she had the affair was also tortured and kept a prisoner; he eventually confessed.

After some time as a prisoner, she watched whilst a mixture of herbs and mercury were being ground in a pestle and mortar, she was forced to take. She died in agony with a burning mouth and face.

After Marie had seen her past life, she made every effort to forgive her father for her death, and she forgave her husband for confessing. I am pleased to say that Marie is now a practicing healer and Reiki Master, and the karmic debt for that life is now paid and she feels much better."

"My dear thank you for that, now you are able to see for yourselves the workings of karma and how it affects what you take back with you into the spirit realms. You always have to pay back or forgive yourselves or others, something that has made a big impact on your psyche enabling you to rid yourself of the unresolved karma."

Astral travelling.

I turned my attention to the girls again and said. "Human beings have a spirit body besides our physical body. When we go astral travelling we take the same shape as our physical body.

Each night when we go to sleep, the physical body rests, and when we go into a deep sleep our spirit body leaves our physical body with the cord still attached and visit friends and relatives in the spirit world.

If you remember, Daniel explained to us earlier that the astral body is attached to the physical body with a permanent cord. Can any of you remember sometimes when you suddenly jump awake and your heart is thumping in your chest as if you have had a shock? Well this can happen when your astral body has forced itself back into your physical body and you often feel disorientated and find you cannot think straight for a while. I have found the best way to overcome this feeling is to go back to sleep and relax; you're alright there is no danger at all. Neither is there any danger connected with astral travelling, even if you try to do it consciously or not."

"How do you know about this?" Jane asked.

"She's probably done it." Beth interrupted.

"Well, have you Barbara and will you tell us about it?" Elsie chipped in.

Smiling at them, I said. "Yes I have, I have released my astral body from my physical body without severing the cord; this is done by will, consciously."

"How do you do it consciously?" Jane asked.

"Give me a chance and I will tell you all I know. You must have heard in the media, some people can recall seeing themselves lying on the bed, looking down on themselves from above, or stood at the bottom of the bed, looking at themselves. This is a perfectly natural thing and it happens to most people every night as they sleep, it is only the fortunate ones who can remember the following day when they wake up.

If you wish to project yourself away from your body consciously you need to be relaxed so it's better to try when you are ready to go to sleep. Don't worry there is nothing to worry about, the astral body can re-enter the physical body because it is still attached by the cord.

You must be aware that if you exit your body by willing it to leave, you may visit the astral plane and meet people who are physically dead. And you can also visit people who are still in the physical body, and communicate with them quite easily. I have done this when giving distant healing, I would go off with my healing guides to visit patients and one particular patient wrote to me saying she had seen me. She said 'I saw you when you gave me healing, you were with a doctor and you told me to turn over, which I did of course' she then went on to describe what she saw. Fantastic isn't it?"

They all said yes, and Elsie said. "I wish I could

do that."

"I will show you." I said. "You can do this by will power, although you may not remember the conversations you have afterwards or the feelings you experience.

If your astral body stays on the earth plane, you will find that your astral body can walk through walls. You can travel most places by sheer force of your will. I read somewhere that the astral body can go backwards and forwards in time. I haven't done that although you never know maybe I just didn't remember, that is the problem remembering when you return.

You can will your astral body to rise above the bed and with practice it will become easier, and as you look down at yourself you will be able to see that you are still attached to your physical body by a silver cord; there is no limit to distance. There is no danger whatsoever when you go astral travelling, the cord will not be broken or become harmed in any way. There is no reason to fear that you will die whilst you are experiencing this travelling."

"It sounds fantastic, but how do you know this?" Elsie asked.

"Because I was told by one of my other spirit guides when I was about 28ish, after that I went on my travels. Astral travelling often feels as though you have been dreaming, however the more you practice the better it becomes, most experienced people can make it happen whilst they are awake, then return to the physical body remembering everything they have seen or done.

I have many times mentally rocked my body, my astral body, out of my physical body and gone into the spirit realms and visited people there.

As you know there has been much on television about near death experiences, `out of body experiences. The most common story is when a patient is being operated on, or having been in a coma, the patient has been able to see what has taken place. Many people have been able to describe to doctors and nurses what they have seen, during an out of body experience. The doctors have then confirmed what the patient has told them. This however is of course only a temporary release from the physical body.

I have on many occasions visited friends and relatives at will, and not just in this country. Distance is not a problem when you are out of your physical body; a thought can take you anywhere. The mind is amazing, a thought and you are there. It sounds very difficult but it's not. Practice and more practice is all it takes."

"Oh! Will you teach us Barbara?" They all said.

"I'm first on the list." Elsie said.

"All in good time, sometime soon, I am very busy but I promise. Let me continue and explain all that I know about it first.

There are people in the spirit world that will protect you from dangers. Although, I do not recommend you travel until you are a more of spiritual things, and I must say you're all on the right road. You need to have some knowledge and insight to spiritual phenomena first because it is possible for a person to travel on the astral plane, and get mocked and ridiculed by low spirit entities, this only happens through ignorance. So you must be very careful what you do if you are not sure wait for me or leave well alone.

Something you can do mentally is to practice taking yourselves to a spiritual garden of reunion that you can create by thought, a lovely place to visit either in meditation or travelling, although we do not all go to the same place. For example I meet my spirit family in a beautiful place that I created.

It's a circular garden with wrought iron benches spaced around one side. I sit down to wait for someone to come to visit me, as I look around I am always aware of the beautiful flowers behind and in front of me. The colours are exquisite, much brighter than on this earth plane. Birds of different colours and sizes are always singing beautifully in the lovely warm sunshine and perch next to me on the bench. They never show any sign of fear when I reach out to stroke their lovely smooth feathered breasts. I cannot see, but I just know that other animals are playing nearby.

My spirit relatives always came from around the bend in front of me and when they see me they wave, then they come and sit next to me on the bench. We talk about all sorts of things, just like we used to do here on earth. When it is time for them to go, I know that I must not go with them, I am not allowed to attempt to follow them around the bend in the garden.

I have travelled to some beautiful spiritual places never experiencing anything that would upset or offend me. Every journey I take is always beautiful, loving and peaceful. It's a wonderful way of life that brings love, truth, peace, knowledge and a more sensitive and caring outlook to life in general. It removes all fear of death and brings a new insight to what this life is all about. Why we are here and what we have to learn, so that we can grow and improve ourselves as we are supposed to do. Our schooling on earth is very important to us, and now is the time to start and to understand. We will do this one circle evening whilst I am with you so that I can keep an eye on you."

"Great, fantastic, when?"

"I don't know yet, I am tired now, sorry, I think it is time for you all to go home." I said yawning. "Next time you come I will tell you some more of my astral travelling."

"I am sorry Daniel for talking for so long. Am I correct in what I have said?"

"Yes my dear. It was good to listen to you. Keep up the good work."

"Thank you Daniel, good night."

The following afternoon the telephone rang, it was Carol, she said 'they had all talked and decided if it was ok by me they could come around tomorrow Friday evening to continued our discussions on astral travelling.'

The problem with those you teach about spiritual 'things', they want everything yesterday On this occasion I agreed for them to come to see me an hour earlier at 6.30pm.

At the next meeting with Daniel they all arrived on time eager to talk with him. Emma jumped in first and asked. "Daniel where do we go in our sleep?"

"Good evening my dear children. The answer is, every night you travel cosmically in your sleep to the spirit realms, but you can also travel cosmically when you are awake, at will, wherever you wish when you know the way; this is astral travelling mentioned earlier.

In the divine mind, your soul mind, there is no time, no distance at all because 'all is'. You are spirit, who has taking on a fleshly body to function on the earth plane whilst you are learning. You are not alone, ever. You have constant connection the silver cord to keep you in constant oneness with the Great Spirit.

When you travel cosmically, you travel outwards with your cosmic cord still attached to you. It will always bring you back. If it were not for the silver cord, you would not find your way back. You can do this, however you must first have a desire or a need to travel to a particular place; nothing is ever done without a reason or purpose. You must believe you are able to do this and there must be complete faith in your spirit-self to be able to accomplish this, in other words there can be no doubt or fear. All that you need to do is just sit quietly, surround yourself in a great sea of golden light, the power of our Creator. Then ask to be taken wherever you desire. Ask also to consciously remember the journey.

Many travel cosmically but do not remember or know that they do, and yet, they have been seen by those they visited. So do ask to remember when you get back to the physical.

My instrument Barbara will direct you safely.
This is the law of Cosmic Travel."

"Thank you Daniel. We will look forward to
Barbara's guidance on this and other subjects.
It's not that we don't believe her it's just better
coming from you who knows best." Elsie said.

My story of 'Astral Travelling'.

It was a short meeting because I decided to take
the circle into meditation and development.
Something we hadn't done for quite a while. I
explained to Daniel and said goodnight.

"Goodnight ladies."

We had our development time and then we
spent about two hours talking about what
Daniel had been teaching us, agreeing and
disagreeing and not getting anywhere at all. By
the time we closed, we had gone round and
round in circles, in the end we said we would
write down anything we couldn't accept and
discus it later. Eventually we felt much better
about what Daniel had said. I agreed to see them
on the following Friday only two days away.
    They all arrived as we agreed on time just
seconds between them. All the problems the last
night we met had suddenly disappeared.
    When they were sitting down and comfortable

I said jokingly as they do on the television to children. "If you are all comfortable then I will begin." They all laughed, lifting their vibrations; laughter is good for the soul.

I started. "There has been so much speculation and research concerning life after death, and now as you must know there is more interest in the public mind than at any other time. So far, every attempt to prove survival after death has been carried on through spiritual mediums, myself included and eventually you will be able to do it. We must pass on to others this knowledge so that they will understand the reality of life after death, which we all have to face when we die and leave our present world the earth.

I was about thirty-two my husband was away on business, when I experienced astral travelling. I had often meditated to leave my body but nothing happened, until one day when I quite easily slipped out of my physical body and saw the real me. Wow! I felt exhilarated, a little apprehensive to be conscious of the fact that I was out of my physical body and I was in the next world, the astral world.

I was so excited; I was above my bed looking down on my physical body and for a moment or two I inspected my face, I noticed how pale I looked without any makeup, in fact I looked dead, although I had never seen a dead person before. My eyes were tightly closed and my mouth slightly open, I seemed to be lifeless, like a corpse. I gazed at my physical body for a few more moments and then looked down at my spirit body. It was strange to see both of my bodies at the same time, I must say I preferred my spirit body, it felt lighter and I could float around the room, my body was illuminated in appearance; what a transformation. For a brief moment it crossed my mind, why would I want that awful heavy body back. I wasn't frightened in any way, I was at ease now and very calm as I closely inspected my face and body once again.

Although the room was dark there was no need for the electric light to be turned on, the illumination from my body lighted up the room enough for me to see clearly. I looked around the room everything appeared to be normal, apart from lovely spirit coloured balls of light darting about. Astral travelling was new to me and I wondered what to do next, I wanted to take advantage of this wonderful experience and journey into the spirit realms. I didn't want to go back to my body and I didn't know how to get back anyway.

I was hoping a spirit guide or family member would come and show me around, but it didn't happen, so, I thought I would try to walk around the house first. I floated slowly across the room towards the door, I could see it was closed and passed through it anyway onto the landing. Wow! I walked through a door; I was thrilled. I floated and peeked in each bedroom and watch my children sleeping. I then floated down the stairs and into the large hall, as I approached the kitchen I saw myself in the full-length hall mirror. I froze for a moment because the reflection was of a young woman who looked so peaceful, it was my reflection and I was now infinitely more beautiful. I did look a bit like a ghost though, I could not see my legs, I was just a wisp of an illuminating body with my earthly features; it was a little eerie though looking into my younger bright knowing eyes. I was translucent and could see the hall table through my body; I wasn't afraid and I felt great. I looked closer and noticed my hair was long again.

I moved away from the mirror and walked out through the large solid oak door into the garden. I reveled at the feeling of the lightness of my spirit body. It was strange to be able to walk through doors and float around without any conscious effort, I know the realms of spirit are a mental world and everything is done by the power of thought.

I must have been sending out thoughts of my family and guides, wondering why they were not here with me, when I saw several shining beings coming towards me. I heard very loud, 'go back, go back to your body'. I was upset; I didn't want to go back it was the beginning of my journey.

A strong feeling of urgency came across my

whole being and I knew I had to return. The return was easy, as soon as I thought of my physical body in bed I was back to hear my daughter crying, she had been having a bad dream. I felt relieved that I had returned in time before she came into my bedroom and woke me up. I am not sure what would have happened to me if I had been travelling around the next world. I then understood the feeling of urgency my spirit friends had relayed to me. That was the end of my first out of body experience.

Has that whet your appetite?"

"It sure has." Jane said. "But it sounds a little scary, when your little girl almost interrupted you."

"That is why you really need to be alone, or it would work if someone was watching out for you."

We meditated as a normal circle day, approximately one hour including discussions. We then talked and talk about out of body experience and astral travelling but as usual the evening came to an end. I wondered if it was detrimental to chat before going to bed as it gets every ones' mind working overtime and then you end up not being able to sleep, so I asked the circle members if they would rather talk during the day. They left it up to me to decide. We said good bye and they all left.

Chapter Eight.

Downloading the Records.

Time between meetings goes so quickly, and our teaching from Daniel seems very fresh in my mind so that any questions we need to ask Daniel I think is much easier draw to the fore. We all sat for meditation before 'tuning in' to the spirit world and Daniel. I then sat at my computer waiting patiently for Daniel to overshadow me; it didn't take long.

"Hello ladies I have been waiting for you, I will start immediately.

When a spirit has chosen to incarnate as a new human being it needs some help and guidelines to live on earth. As I said it arrives on your planet with no memory concerning what it had agreed, what contracts it made. If it were to remember it would not be able to experience the lessons it came to earth to overcome.

Some of the paths a soul can follow are limited in the contracts it has made with other spirits. For example, it may need to experience addiction, therefore it would choose an alcoholic family or a family who were addicted to drugs, or it could be a lesson of sexual uncertainly, male or female gender that may have been selected. As the soul enters the foetus the necessary information is downloaded into the foetus for it to have the chosen inclinations. Also contained in the records downloaded into the new body is the remainder of lessons not completed in prior lifetimes, such as fears, desires and natural instincts that were strong in a past life. This is what you would refer to as Karma. My dears do you understand what I am saying?"

Elsie spoke again. "Thank you Daniel the picture you are painting is becoming much clearer now and I am sure the more you teach us the better we will become."

"Let me talk to you now about the law of obedience. If you hear the voice within, do you take notice and obey? This is the voice in your consciousness your higher self. Yes, because if you do not, what a waste of time listening for guidance in the first place. Your higher self knows you better than you know yourself; it strives to lead you in your own spiritual pattern, or in your work that you chose before coming to earth.

There is no purpose in meditation unless you are willing to follow through, or do the 'thing'. Together you can do all things through the Great Spirit your Creator, who sent his Son to guide you all in the way he walked, or by His example set before you.

Obedience is one of the greatest tests. Many

things are given to you to do, only to see if you will do them; you're testing time. Shall you pass these many tests? If so, there is no failure in you. Barbara has discussed this with you, regarding tests. This is the Law of Obedience."

"Thank you Daniel. Yes Barbara has told us about being tested during circle, sometimes we get silly things given to us by spirit people to see if we are trust worthy of passing this information on to the recipient."

"All things are possible my dears if you believe, nothing is possible unless you believe it is possible. If you want to do a certain thing, be a certain thing, a writer, a musician or an artist. What prevents you? You are the master of your life, your destiny. You have all the power within you, it shall always be sufficient. Do you believe this? Really believe this? If so, just begin by doing what you want to do, it must be more than just a mere wish, you must will it.

Nothing on Earth or in Heaven can prevent you from doing what you want to do. Why? Because human beings have `free will,' this is the greatest gift. You may use it for good, or evil. It is your choice.

All the forces of the universe stand ready to serve the one who wills to do something and believes he can. It is, indeed law: This is the law of believing."

The death process.

Beth said... "Thank you so much, it's wonderful to speak to you again Daniel, I have looked forward to this all week. If you don't mind would you explain the death process to me please? I am sure most people would like to know what truly happens."

"My dear child you can ask me anything, I will always try to answer to the best of my ability.

It is sad, but there are those who fear death, it is a mixed emotion and most human beings prefer not to think or talk about it and the subject is put to one side. The thoughts at the possibility of total extinction or of the unknown are horrendous, unthinkable and are the greatest fear of most human beings. They not only fear death, it's how they will die, will there be pain preceding and accompanying the experience? I say truthfully that is not the case.

Whatever the cause of death it is the physical body that is tired, it is like anything that wears out there is nothing much you can do, therefore when a body falls ill, too ill to repair, the soul withdraws from it and it ceases to function.

It is not just the person who dies that worries, it is those who they leave behind, you see naturally some aspects of the person becomes connected to other people, to their family and friends. This happens when a human being takes responsibility for another, such as a mother with a child, a link by an invisible thread is created, which holds them together until it is cut by one person or the other.

The mother or father who is leaving your world feels the need to continue helping its child on earth, even though they may be adults. Sometimes this link is so strong that it may prevent that person from being able to let go of their child and pull away from the physical world and return home to the spirit realms. This also frequently happens with husbands and wives when one of them leaves your world, the other finds it hard to let go and live alone.

If a person senses that someone is holding on to life because the two have a connection they no longer need, one person can simply disconnect it, or give the other one permission to do so and to return to the spirit realms."

"Sorry for interrupting Daniel, what you have just said reminds me of when my mother past away. She just wouldn't let go and was talking to someone in the spirit world who must have continually asked her to let go of the earth life, but she wouldn't. She kept saying to the spirit person, 'go away please go away.' I realised what was happening and said to mum, 'you can go now love, go see your mum and your family, they will be waiting for you, it is ok.' Within a minute or two she let go of her physical body and went peacefully back home.

It puzzles me why she wouldn't leave because she believed in life after death; it could only be because she thought I need her to stay"

"Thank you my dear, it is good that you can associate a situation with what I have to say, I think it will help others to understand better also.

Death is the term humans use to describe the ending of a physical life when the soul, the real you leaves the human body that it has been using temporally, which of course is only the shell which surrounds the soul. Without a soul the body ceases to function and that is when the physical body dies. Therefore, at the end of your incarnation, when your spirit has detached itself from your lifeless body you return to the spirit world where you came from. Is that clear?"

"Yes perfectly clear, thank you."

"Good. It is natural that eventually all of you must leave your physical body when death comes, slowly the cord dissolves from the physical body and the astral body, but until this is broken, death cannot take place. Although not everyone meets the same experience in the actual death process and neither the events preceding death are the same.

My dears you must understand after the so called death, your spirit body is very much alive in the spirit realms doing all the wonderful things that you wanted to do on earth and couldn't. You will meet your friends and family members who have gone before you and others who are your family and friends from previous lives.

You will soon realise that the person who you once were on earth is not the real you because you and all spirit people retain all the faculties and qualities from their many previous lives. Do you understand thus far?"

Everyone said. "Yes thank you."

"Good. The majority of people who pass over to the real world will find much to rejoice. They will be able to be with those they truly love, and with friends who have a common mental kinship, attraction and affection, providing of course they must be similarly evolved spiritually; on the same level of growth.

If you could only see my dears, it is delightful here, death is only a stepping-stone into the wonderful world of spirit, and it is freedom from all the trials and hardships you have had to experience and sometimes traumatic times. Death, releases you, the soul from mental and physical pain, it is a time of stillness and of rest.

I must explain to those human beings who fear

death. The first thing a soul experiences is the painlessness of the actual process of dying, and that often death is not recognised until it is over, and sometimes not even then. Most deaths are followed when a person has been unconscious; they leave their painful body and find the pain free freedom and lightness of their spirit body.

Many people after death want a period to rest and recuperate from the stresses and strains of earth life, it enables them to adjust to their new life. For some it is a tremendous shock to find they are not 'dead' but alive and have survived the grave.

Death is not something to fear it is a time to celebrate, to rejoice. They have completed all that they came to earth to do and have now earned their promotion to go home to the spirit realms. To leave the physical body is to enjoy the freedom of spirit. The soul has been set free from the prison, the bonds of the physical body; there is relief and a sense of being freed from the intolerable heavy weight. Now the spirit has the ability to roam all over the physical world in a flash and to taste the beauties of their spirit life."

"Thank you. Are all deaths experiences the same?" Beth continued.

"No not at all, there are considerable differences; this all depends on the individual. If a person is conscious before their impeding death some will see their deceased family and friends around them, and because of it, find themselves looking forward to meeting them again.

Those poor souls who have been ill for a long time often drift in and out of consciousness; therefore their readjustment is gradual, and greatly helped by sleep. The tired soul has to overcome gradually the weariness of the last days on earth.

Some spirit people adapt quickly to their new environment, whilst there are others who may resist and shut themselves away mentally, and there are some who withdraw, wait and rest. Many individuals are chiefly concerned with finding their spirit family and friends with whom they spent their earth life and also those who are still on earth."

"I'm sorry for interrupting you again Daniel but I thought everyone would be interested with what I have to say, it's to do with what you have just said.

I was asked by the nurse in charge of the hospice where my dad was being looked after if I wanted to go see him because he was fading quickly. I went to see him, he was unconscious but as I talked to him to let him know I was there, he smiled, so he must have heard me. I stayed for a considerable time and then left.

I was woken up during the night by the latch rattling on my bedroom door, I knew then dad had passed, he had come to let me know he had arrived safely. A couple of minutes later the phone rang, it was the hospice telling me that dad had just passed away.

When my mum died, she made the phone tinkle to let me know she was OK. And when my previous husband died he turned the bedside light on and off till I woke up, again to let me know he was OK. He didn't believe in life after the death process so what a wonderful surprise for him."

"Thank you for that my dear, I'm sure others will understand what you have said.

There may be an easy transition for the soul who returns home to the spirit world at the time when this was arranged before incarnation. The soul usually knows when it has completed its earth lessons.

There are some souls who, when they have finished and have understood all the lessons they came to learn early, may choose to return home immediately or to use their remaining earth time to assist other human beings to understand the lessons from which they have gained knowledge and wisdom, lessons the others are in the midst of learning.

When the trials and the work of the soul is completed they usually return to the spirit world, however, if the soul has not understood the lessons it chose to do on earth, it may decide to 'stay on' and choose another test, another similar example whilst on earth to see if it can understand it better the second time around.

If a soul returns to the spirit realms before fully understanding all the aspects of the lessons it will have to return to earth to do it all over again and most spirits do not want to do that. As you know this is what is called 'karma.' Some think it is a punishment, it is not, but rather an uncompleted task the soul wants to finish. Do you understand?"

"Yes. Thank you for that Daniel. Can you explain what happens to someone who has been killed rather than died naturally?"

"Those who are unprepared for death, who die quickly or through a violent act frequently do not understand what has happened and find it less easy to adjust than those who pass naturally, although this is not always the case. However, some poor souls remain for some considerable time wondering where they are thinking they are still alive on the earth plane. Those who are unable to understand they are dead are for a while temporarily unhappy souls and in need of help, they are unable to see their loved ones around them. Souls who are confused are not left like that, gradually and gently it is explained to them what has happened by a spiritual teacher. Eventually they realise and they are united with their loved ones.

There are many examples of sudden death: If a soldier was killed suddenly he would probably arrive in the world of spirit thinking he will have to continue to fight. Most souls who experience a sudden death have the feelings and thoughts that they had just before they died, and often think they must have suddenly gone mad, because the scene has suddenly changed, they are in a place they do not recognise.

Others may awake in a spirit hospital, which is also puzzling to them. Gradually we explain to them what has happened and explain they are in the hospital. Most soldiers are so weary in spirit that they are glad and rejoice to be free of the world of wars.

Those who believe they do survive death, and already knew something about communication with the dead, usually find it easier to make the adjustment. This is another reason why we need to tell people of continued life after their death."

"Thank you Daniel, I thought my question would be easy, just a quick answer but I hadn't realised it is more complicated. Can you tell us, do some of these souls who experience sudden death become ghosts, earthbound souls?" Beth asked.

"I must emphasise, in the very minority of cases, it can take a considerable time for some spirits to realise they have passed away. These are earthbound spirits and are often responsible for haunting people and places. They are drawn to the earth plane like a magnet, because of their lack of spiritual knowledge and growth even though they are in the spirit world.

As I explained earlier some spirits who have been addicted to some form of drug, be it narcotics, cigarettes or alcohol are responsible for being close to, and possessing people who are drug addicts and alcoholics this enables them to obtain some sort of satisfaction.

I must say, it is not usual for those who die suddenly to be earthbound and it does not take long for the average person to adjust, therefore, do not let this frighten you, the overwhelming majority there is nothing to fear from death.

You must not think when you die you go far away or disappear, that is not true you are but a breath away. Spirit people vibrate on a higher faster level that is why human beings cannot see them, but they are still there, they will still be around to see your family and friends from the beyond.

You have already visited the spirit realms on thousands of occasions when you are sleeping. Your spirit leaves your physical body and travels in the beyond, which eventually is to be your permanent existence. This is your preparation to help you when you pass over, you will remember your visits, your dreams and how real and solid they were and all the experiences you have enjoyed; the spirit world is real to us and your world unreal.

There is nothing to fear during your visits as the separation from the physical body is only temporary, and the connecting cord is not severed. You cannot die until the cord that is attached to the spirit body has been severed, until then you cannot leave the earth. It is like when the umbilical cord has to be cut before you can start your new life, your incarnation, your entry into the heavy world of matter of earth.

When the time arrives for you to leave your world, death takes you to what is mainly a mental world, a world in which everything is created by thought and appears to be solid; I have already discussed this with you. Therefore, you should not grieve when death comes; you are in truth grieving for yourself because you will miss your loved one.

I repeat what you already know from our discussions. The body cannot exist if the silver cord is cut; when it is severed the body would be dead and just a lump of motionless flesh. However, spirit can live without the body. The body is only the clothing for the spirit. As long as you are on the earth plane, you are at school; therefore you could imagine your soul to be clothed in a school uniform."

"How do we look and feel when we arrive in the

spirit world?" Elsie asked.

"My dear, you will definitely not be vague or a ghostly shadowy beings, but real human men and women. You will be precisely the same individual as you were before you passed over into the spirit realms, except that you will have discarded your heavy physical body and the real you now functions through your spirit body. Some spirits adapt quicker than others, whereas some feel that they want to look for their loved ones who are already in the spirit world and there are those who resist their new environment."

"Thank you very much, you said that spirit are not far away, are they around us all the time and do we not have any privacy?"

"Those who dwell in the spirit world are not always intruding into your private lives; they reside in the same universe but on a finer vibration. The ones, who have died, as you call it, are close and in many cases closer than they have ever been before. But if there is no love, then there are no ties

Your family in the spirit world remain human beings and continue to be interested in you as they were before. They are closer than you realise even though you are unable to see or speak to them. They know your thoughts, your desires and your hopes and fears. They strive to influence and to guide you through your earthly trials so that your soul may grow and evolve.

Oh my dear children to die is not tragic; living on the earth plane is tragic. When a loved one leaves your world you mourn for the loss of the physical body, this is because you are unable to see them. You weep for your own loss but you should be celebrating for the one who has become free, free from all the suffering the ills of the human body.

There will be no more hardships and no more suffering; you must agree it is a time to rejoice. I have said so many times, where there is love there is no separation; death cannot part you from the one you truly love.

I do know how difficult it is for you, and I do understand your grief. However, the tragedy is for those poor unenlightened souls left behind and what they must be going through when someone they truly loved ceases to breathe forever. What a shame that so many of you are ignorant to the workings of spirit; you will eventually make progress."

Elsie went on to ask. "Do spirits who have just passed to the spirit world see and feel the distress of their loved ones grieving?"

"Yes they do, that is why there are some spirits who will not leave the earth's astral plane, until they are able to comfort their family and friends in distress. They send their love energy to their loved ones. Apart from your loved ones there are angel-like spirits who regularly go to earth between lives simply to help people they do not know who are in distress.

I will leave you now to think about what I have said unless there is something you do not understand. We will talk again soon."

"Thank you for that; what you have said has been very helpful. We will look forward to speaking with you again soon."

Part two spirit life.

Chapter Nine.

Choosing to Stay.

"Good evening. We are now going to talk of life in the spirit world."

"Thank you, but can I ask you first. Do some souls find it difficult to die and leave their loved ones behind?" Beth asked.

"Yes very much so, there are a number of reasons why a soul may wish to remain on earth when it is time to return. There are those who feel they have personal obligations to others and do not want to leave them in the lurch. They tell themselves that their families need them and cannot live without them. Therefore it is very important that those in that situation watching their loved ones die should explain to them that all will be well and that they may move on when they are ready. Remaining on earth helps neither them nor their relatives."

"That is exactly what I said to mum, and then she let go."

"That was the correct thing to do, helping her slip into the next world without any emotional stress about leaving her loved ones behind."

"Could this be a reason for a soul remaining in a sleep state for a period of time? My mum seemed to 'hang on' to life and wouldn't let go."

"Yes exactly. But I am afraid there are some who remain because they believe that they are needed by family and friends still in the body. They stay close to try and help out even though they are not a physical being anymore and most probably are not felt by those they seek to assist.

These souls will in time be guided and counselled to return back to the spirit realms where they belong. Once there, they can always watch over and assist those on earth with all the power of spiritual unconditional love.

There are many people who are ignorant of what happens to them when their body dies and fear that death is final and that they will exist no more. It is sad to see how they cling with their last ounce of breath to their physical body, their physical life, when their journey back home to a beautiful spiritual place of love.

There are some souls who are very negative and remain out of hatred or revenge, seeking to get even with whoever may have treated them badly or perhaps been involved in their death. These souls have one foot in both worlds, they are neither in the spirit world or the physical world, they remain stuck between two worlds until eventually they will be helped from other spirits to understand what is happening to them.

On a more positive note, there are souls who may decide to leave after a certain period of time but then find they have gained much knowledge and wisdom and are now in a position to help others if they remain around for a little while longer."

Survival.

"Thank you for that. Can you explain if a soul is shut up in the body like being in a cage?"

"No. The soul radiates outwards in all directions, and displays itself outside the body as coloured lights; this is known as the aura. Therefore you might say the soul may be exterior to the body, but it is not, it is within and surrounds the body."

"Thank you Daniel. Quite a number of people ask me if we survive death. I have given them proof of survival and that doesn't seem to be enough. I feel very frustrated because I'm not sure what else I can do, except write this book and then will it be enough?"

"My dear child, regarding the truth of survival,

it is better to have knowledge than to remain ignorant and I am pleased that you seek enlightenment and try to pass on your knowledge to others. However, it is not an easy task to prove we do not die, that we do live on after the death process.

Many people do not desire to gain knowledge regarding our continued existence, they think if they don't talk about it, it will go away. Yet there is an interest that drives the human soul to wonder, and as you say, they ask if they do indeed survive. They really want to know if they survive as a human being and not anything else. Some individuals are looking for belief, something to hold on to, although there are many who state they do not care whether there is survival or not.

There can be many reasons that often hinder a human being from investigation into the subject such as intellectual, emotional and religious obstacles towards death. Nevertheless, human beings generally want to understand, to know what lies beyond their life on earth and as they search, some begin to understand and look for knowledge for themselves, especially when they get old. They begin to wonder where they will be going and what it is like.

Those with enquiring minds can investigate, and there is properly recorded evidence in existence for all those who seek knowledge; it is always better to have knowledge than to remain ignorant.

My dear, there will always be some stubborn souls who claim spirit communication is nonsense and untrue. Nevertheless, the truth is that most of those who communicate through a medium do report their survival of bodily death and speak of knowledgeable things from the other side, which they did not acquire on earth. And like you, most mediums are proving survival from spirit relatives all the time, passing on messages and information that the medium could not possibly know. You can only explain the truth to the best of your ability, and then it is up to them what they want to do with the information.

I can tell you, spirit do not die they cannot die, that is why I am able to speak to you. You are a spirit in a physical body; therefore you live for all eternity, beyond the grave, beyond the fire of cremation. Spirit is indestructible, immortal and infinite. There is nothing on earth and nothing in the beyond that can destroy your continued existence.

You are immortal spirit beings in a physical body, without spirit you are nothing more than a lump of flesh because spirit gives life to all things, spirit animates the body.

Your spirit is clothed in a body; I like to think of it as a school uniform, because you are on earth to learn, to build your own personality, your nature, your character and to accomplish your own soul growth and evolution. Therefore, it is very, very important how you live your life whilst on the physical plane. If you are unkind, uncaring, unloving and choose a path of selfishness you will pay the price. If you show kindness and service to others you will receive the rewards that come with the growth of character. The more good that you do the greater is your spirit. This is the Law of the Great Spirit."

Immediately after death.

"Thank you for that Daniel. Please can you explain what happens just after a human being arrives in the spirit world, and can you tell me where do we go and how do we spend our time in our new life? Everyone, I am sure would like to know." Carol asked.

"Yes of course that is why I am here, to help you. It will take a long, long time for me to explain all there is to know, and some things I will not be able to explain to you for various reasons; knowledge is infinite."

"Thank you very much; I have a great thirst for knowledge."

"That is very good my dear, I wish there were more souls interested; there is much to learn. I will try to explain in a way in which you will be able to understand.

Firstly let me say that life in the spirit world is not obscure, unclear, unsubstantial, vague or ghostly as some individuals might think. The spirit realms are real and are just as solid as the earth is to you.

The spiritual world and the physical world are constantly intermingling; all levels of existence over laps each other. The spiritual realms are not vague or intangible but are real and natural, a vast area that consists of a superior energy and substance.

On the earth, the physical plane of existence the soul obtains knowledge through experience and contact with impartial things, the soul gains intelligence by demonstrating through physical organs. Whereas, in the spiritual world progression of the individual soul continues through natural service of an ever broadening idea of life's purpose.

In the spirit world there are levels of existence within realms or spheres. There is the lower astral plane, the Astral, the Etheric, the Higher Etheric, and other higher realms. Every soul will go to the place they have earned, that they have created for themselves by the way they have lived their lives on earth. On their particular level of existence of consciousness, they will have no choice but to see their real self in a far more objective way.

When you die, at the moment of death, your

soul is once again a spirit person, the spiritual cord has severed, and it disengages itself from the body and returns to the spirit realms. Those who think after death their spirit joins the universe is wrong, you are still the same individual as you were on earth, with the same characteristics.

The majority of people are afraid of death but there is nothing to fear. You will find it is a surprise the actual process of dying is painless. It is such a pity there are so many souls who are unprepared for death.

Those who experience a sudden death such as an accident are often confused and do not understand what has happened to them, this can leave them feeling confused, bewildered. However, some spirit individuals become accustomed very quickly to their new environment; others may need to rest, especially those who experienced pain, or a long illness; they are tired, and feel in the need to sleep.

People on earth are afraid that they will suffer when they die, however the physical body often suffers more in sickness before death than at the moment of death. My dears usually the feelings experienced at the exact moment of death are often very pleasant and enjoyable.

What a surprise for those who were disabled mentally or physically, those with missing limbs, deaf or blind people when they find they are completely whole once again; I am sure they will jump for joy. They understand they have put an end to their miserable life confined in a heavy physical body.

Generally people will find a freedom from physical pain when they leave their physical body and this is usually preceded by the feeling of distance, of unconsciousness and may take some time to recover. It is a similar state of a person waking from a deep sleep and gradually regaining clearness of thought and memory.

You have heard people say when they have had a near death experience that they have a feeling of being above their bodies and then passing through the bright light of a tunnel, well this is true with some transitions; others do not.

There are those unenlightened souls, unbelieving human beings who think when you're dead, you are dead. They find it inconceivable and do not accept that it has happened and for some considerable time persist in believing they are still on earth, hence they suffer a state of confusion and some are unwilling to move on. They feel something strange has happened to them but they will not accept they have died. In order to completely shut it out of their minds they deliberately continue with their familiar activities. They proceed to live their life as normal, going to the office; the housewife gets on with the usual household chores. Those who were at school continue to go to lessons and the tutor takes his class and wonders why they are not responding and so on. They seem unable to reason clearly about where they are until slowly they adjust to the enormous change to their life.

Eventually family and friends who died before them try to persuade them that they are dead to the earth world. In some cases they refuse to believe what their family is saying also. In reality there are many spirits inhabiting the earth believing they are still alive in a physical body.

There are people in the spirit world and on earth who are rescue workers who assist souls that prefer to stay close to the earth for various reasons, they help them to come to terms with their death and help them to see the light, and show them they are in the realms of spirit.

Those who pass over with the knowledge and understanding of life after death do not need help, unless they have been very ill before passing. Many are chiefly concerned with finding those whom they loved they shared their earth life."

"Thank you very much; I'm fascinated with all that you explain to us." Carol replied.

Emergency treatment and recovery of damaged souls.

"On death of the physical body some souls experience an extremely bright tunnel opening and closing synchronising its movement with that of the soul. They pass through the tunnel and feel much lighter. Most times they see someone coming towards them, perhaps a family member or a guide.

Spirit people who have had a hard time or been very ill on the earth arrive here in the spirit world exhausted and their spirit body is in a deteriorated state therefore their guides give them an emergency healing before they can move any further into the spirit world.

This is done by their spirit guides who completely envelopes the spirit individual with a large amount of their loving powerful energy; this is the most common method. Although healing acts do vary, there are some who have gaps in their spirit energy body therefore their guides heal those areas where there are gaps.

The guide begins at a specific point of the spirits body reshaping and smoothing out the rough edges and broken parts to make the returning spirit whole once again. This is followed by a deep penetration of energy.

In both cases there is an immediate blending of revitalizing, stimulating energy whilst they are moving forward into the realms of spirit on their journey to their destination. The more advanced spirits who arrive back home undamaged usually do not require the healing act or any assistance.

Most spirits who are arriving home to the spirit world and who are in need of rest and healing are met by advanced beings and taken to a beautiful, peaceful place to recover. Many spirits who are emotionally scarred from their previous life are usually deep rooted and they carry this damaged energy back home. In other words the karma they have made for themselves. Irrespective of the energy treatment received by their guides they will continue onto some sort of healing centre before finally joining their soul groups, their spiritual family.

I am sorry to have say, there are some spirits people who have become so contaminated by their physical bodies that they require special treatment and handling. Their behaviour would chiefly include those who have been associated with evil and have caused harm to other people deliberately because they desire to cause damage, having said that, there are souls who slowly become more tainted and spoiled from a series of previous lifetimes. Whatever the reason, these spirits are taken to a place of isolation where their energy body undergoes a more deep-seated treatment than with a normal returning soul.

Soul contamination does not only come from the physical body. It could also indicate that they are themselves impure beings.

The more advanced spirit people appear to get

over hardships more quickly than others after their lives on earth. As I explained earlier every soul has karmic choices their free will."

"Wow. That sounds like a spiritual 'wash and brush up'! Can you describe what a spirit body looks like?" Jean enquired.

"Let me first say, following the death process all forms of disabilities and deformities will no longer exist, they left these with the physical body; they are whole once again. And because the spirit world is a mental existence, what would be the point of keeping their old bodies, most old people prefer to be younger when in a spirit body. Howevera spirit person feels thinks and acts just the way it did when in a human body and they continue to retain all the memories of earthly life, good and bad. They remember their families and the happy times they spent together, the taste of food and drink, smells, sights and sounds.

They can reminisce about all things especially their family birthdays, the festive season, holidays, family outings, everything is much clearer and the mind is able to read other spirits thoughts and ideas. Spirit beings are able to see everything in the physical world as well as everything in the spirit realms, without any limitations. They may remember every detail of their past life on earth and be perfectly aware of who they are, and what happened up to the time when they passed to the spirit world.

The spirit body is lighter and composed of a much finer substance that vibrates at a different rate than their physical human body, that is why, or one of the reasons most human beings are unable to see spirits.

Although their spirit body is a duplicate and it is not permanent, if spirit wish to change their body, they can later and create a colourful, radiant shape of energy, or take on one of their many happier, comfortable and pleasing former lives. Whatever, a spirit decides to do; there is no age as you understand in the physical sense, the spirit body cannot grow old, but there is always growth towards spiritual wisdom and maturity. Do you understand?"

Meeting relatives after death.

"Yes thank you. Can you tell us if the spirits close to the earth are what we call lost souls?" Jean enquired.

"Yes in some cases. I will explain this to you later."

"Thank you Daniel. Is there someone to great us when we die?" Jane asked.

"But of course, when a spirit first arrives in the

spirit world they are usually greeted by a loved one, friend, and or, guide. Those who are united by their bonds will find one another again despite all the obstacles that may be in the way. People in your world do not understand the tremendous power of love. Love is the greatest power in the universe, where there is love there is no separation."

"Thank you for that. I was hoping to see my mum and the rest of my family when I die. Can you tell me if spirit relatives wait to see their loved ones before they incarnate again?" Jane continued.

"As you already know, we are energy and the energy of a spirit is able to divide into identical parts. Therefore, part of their light energy, their spirit self always remains behind in the spirit world. Thus, it is possible to see your mother and your family and friends when you return to the spirit realms even though they died several earth years earlier and incarnated again."

"Oh, that seems strange; nevertheless I am so pleased to hear that, thank you. What happens after they have met their loved ones?"

"My dears, as I have just explained to you there are many souls who arrive back home with damage to their energy; if they have had a very hard life it can cause physical and emotional scars from their life on earth. This needs to be healed first; therefore, their guide decides the healing procedure essential for the condition of the spirit's energy at the time, or they may just need to rest a while."

"Thank you. I am pleased to hear I do not have to retain an old wrinkled body. Do we retain our earth names, or can we change these also?"

Orientation with guides before soul group.

"I will explain that later. I will continue, when a soul returns to the next world their homecomings can take place in different ways. Some spirits might be met briefly by a friend at the gateway to the spirit world and then left for a guide to take them through some preliminary briefing, directions. It is a time for their guides to counsel their charge, with the opportunity to discuss any problems they may have regarding their previous life on earth. However, there are others who may need to rest as I said before any discussions with guides take place. The length of time will depend upon the circumstances of what they did or did not accomplish with their previous life. They will discuss any special karmic issues that need reviewing at this time. Often, they wait until the spirit feels more relaxed and returns to their group souls.

Whatever the case some kind of spiritual guidance and direction is needed, it may be intense or moderate in the initial debriefing of the life just completed. Later there will be a more in depth counselling with guides and with their council of elders.

Orientation periods with guides, vary between spirits and between different lives for the same spirit. This is a quiet time for counselling sometimes held in a beautiful garden; this is an opportunity to discuss any frustrations they have about the life just ended. These meetings are intended to be a primary debriefing session with gentle probing, perceptive, caring teacher guides. These gatherings may be long or short depending upon the circumstances of what they did or did not accomplish with regard to their life contracts."

Judgment day.

"When we get to the spirit world are we judged and if so, by whom?"

"Yes. Not long after spirits return to their soul groups and once they have adjusted to their new life, judgement can take place when the spirit meets with the council of elders for their debriefing; there is no courtroom with a judge, nevertheless they are wise beings, a step or two above their guides, these are what we call

Ascended Masters and they are the most advanced identifiable beings in the spirit world; they are responsible for spirits still incarnating on earth.

When the time comes for spirits to meet with the council they move towards the domed building where they are waiting; I must say with mixed reactions. Some are looking forward to seeing these knowledgeable beings so that they can find out how they performed and hopefully progressed, whilst others are very apprehensive but this soon passes once the proceedings begin.

Spirit people give the council various names, the two most common names to describe these highly evolved masters are Council Elders. The elders have a way of making the spirits who come before them feel welcome almost at once.

Everyone in the chamber is telepathic; therefore all who are there know the whole truth about every aspect, every detail of their conduct and the choices they made in their last life. My dears I am sure you will agree it is understandable why spirit feels nervous and apprehensive, although there is nothing to worry about; everyone has made mistakes and done things they are not proud of.

The domed shaped building where everyone meets looks like, and is symbolic of the churches on earth. In the centre of the assembly room is a large table raised up on a pedestal; this is where the large number of elders sits. Usually there are between seven and twelve members in the council, although this depends on the spirits development, they may at times require more specialists on their panel.

The spirit person stands in the middle of the room facing the elders with their guide standing next to them giving support. Council members send out energies of comfort and calm that brings a relaxed and loving meeting, however there is a higher presence above who concentrates the wonderful light energy on the entire proceedings, which is full of compassion; usually the elder in the middle of the platform asks the questions.

The council elder's colours are most beautiful. Purple is the colour of wisdom and deep understanding. Council members with purple and violet robes reflect their ability to govern the affairs of the spirits who come before them with benevolence and live born out of vast experience. Those who wear green are skilled in healing...mental and physical. Red is the colour of passion and intensity. However, this colour can have several meanings depending on the settings. The colours they display in different forms also relate to the topics under discussion.

Hoods, four-squared hats and skullcaps, all having antiquarian flavour, may be seen on the elders. Hoods are usually thrown back from the head, which is less ominous to the viewer. These trappings engender respect and reverence to wise beings, who, like oracles, interpret events in a spirit's existence.

These robed beings question the spirits activities during the time spent on the earth, and they evaluate all the contracts and lessons the souls agreed before incarnating. In addition, during the meeting the spirit people receive blueprints of past life-times brought forward into the spirits consciousness.

First of all the mind looks at the whole plan of life and tries to sort out the information before them. This is the first shock; a true overwhelming story of the spirits whole cycle of the life-term unfolds before them in a combination of pictures of their lives on earth, in minute detail. How it was, and how it should have been, good and bad so that they are able to analyse it. They discuss major choices that were made in the life just lived, the experience of all the acts of pain and pleasures given to others, followed by weaknesses of character, morals and so on. They are aware of their mistakes, especially if they have hurt others.

At this time spirit realize they have to face what they have brought with them, in terms of what they have created in their previous life. There can be no pretence, no cheating or deception and there are no secrets. Do you see my dears in my world, every individual is known for who they truly are, mentally and spiritually?

The council also looks at the help and service the spirit may have had time to give to others; serving others is very important.

Appearing in front of the spiritual council involves matters of accountability for the life just lived, a realization at what they see and who they truly are. They are aware they are responsible for the way they shaped their character, their spiritual nature they have formed over their many lifetimes. That is their spiritual identification, their classification in the spirit world; therefore, they have 'judged' themselves.

Some spirits have to be shown again to help make it clear, so they are able to absorb what has happened. Guides are their primary teachers, therefore they may want to interrupt and clarify, or explain some idea for them if they think they are confused at any point during the proceedings. It is shown with the assistance of their guides and they make notes to include that in its next incarnation.

Everyone has something that needs to be addressed or to be rid of, no matter what they think of themselves, therefore they are evaluated carefully, their accountability for their actions is very important. Spirits are not punished but they go through stages of self-illumination, self-enlightenment. There is always both compensation and retribution, because the natural laws of cause and effect are perfect in their operation.

With all this knowledge in hand the spirit tries to combine all the wisdom and experiences made available. It may take a while (in earth times) for everything to be understood. In addition, judgement does not end there; all spirits appear again before the council just before leaving, to be reborn, to be incarnated again, and also on each level of advancement. Spirits people are always grateful for this and need the wisdom and assistance to grow and move forward. However, the first council meeting has much more of an impact on the spirit than when they leave.

If a spirit person is not ready to face the first judgement, they can postpone it until they are ready, but they cannot put it off indefinitely. Seeing their past lifetime and the self-correction can be very painful indeed. However, there is always a gentle loving teacher nearby to help and guide.

One must always remember earthly belongings no longer exist in the spirit world. Souls can only bring with them possessions, such as their character, memories and the power of thinking, feelings, understanding and how they see things; these are the only things they can carry in their new life."

"Thank you for that. Can you explain more

about who the council members are? Are they spiritually higher than our guides?"

"These highly evolved masters are known as the 'Council Elders' and are higher, more knowledgeable and wiser than guides and are the most advanced distinguishable entities in the spirit realms. These beautiful robed beings question spirits about their past life performance and have great compassion and forgiveness for human limitations and their weaknesses; they demonstrate infinite patience with their faults and give them many chances in future lives. They do not select lives that are easy; otherwise, they would learn nothing by going to earth.

I have said this many, many times, your actions, words and thoughts create and that is why every soul is what they have made themselves to be. I find it sad that when the time comes for human beings to leave earth; they have a fear of their 'judgment day'. Religions are to blame for this, talking about heaven and hellfire and harsh judgment for human mistakes, for those who violate the laws of the Great Spirit. Although I must say, fear of divine justice has helped to make human beings behave better than they would otherwise have done.

There is no heaven or hell in the theological sense. Only the heaven and hell they have created themselves by the way they have lived their lives. "

"I see, but can you not change things?"

"It may seem harsh but the answer is no, the past is not changeable it is irreversible, although, its consequences are not final and can be overcome. This is done by learning and paying back old debts on earth, your karma. This is why spirit people keep returning to earth. This is the only way to achieve perfection and to climb the spiritual ladder of enlightenment, which is what all souls aspire to and to gradually rid themselves of all the trash, the rubbish from who they are, their character through many incarnations."

"Thank you, it sounds horrendous. I must say that I am not looking forward to that, even though I am my own judge. How do souls feel when they come away from their meeting with the elders? Is it all goodness and light for those who have been good and who have not been involved with cruel acts, or do some spirits come away unhappy from the meeting?"

"Some feel they could have done better to show themselves in a more willing and compliant way, whist some spirits come away with a sense of awe, penitence and the need for atonement. Nevertheless, however a spirit feels there is always room for improvement, there are many lessons to learn, many lifetimes before achieving anything near perfection.

When they have finished their discussions with the elders, they carry their feelings back to their soul group who assist them by helping each other to grow and evolve.

Elders are always available for meetings and discussions; it is their desire to boost the confidence of the spirit for their future tasks. They are like loving but firm parents and teachers. The spirit has great respect and admiration for their council."

"Does the outcome of the judgement reflect on the spirits next incarnation, and would that be karma?"

"Yes it is. I have said many times 'what we sow, we reap'; this is true that is karma."

A Guides role.

"When your work as a personal guide is completed, do you expect to be assigned to the council of elders?"

"Not all spirits want this. All spirits must become a master teacher working with younger teachers first, helping them to get in touch with their students on many levels."

"You told me you have lived thousands of years.

Do you still have to go before the council of elders following a life on earth?"

"I no longer have the need to incarnate."

"Where would you rate, classify yourself?"

"I have progressed beyond a master teacher."

"Is this the final level? Would the next elevation above the level of a guide be a position on the council?"

"The answer to your first question is no, this is not the final level there are more levels. The answer to your second question, there are many other choices for specializations. One might not be suited to be on a council."

"Oh! Well let's say if you were suited and were given a seat on the council and were effective there, where would you go after that as a spirit?"

"I would go to the place of oneness."
"Can you describe oneness?"

"It is a creation centre of new souls, where we can shape light energy for certain functions."

"Please describe this process further."

"I am unable to tell you too much, it is a place where the energy of new souls is stimulated, initiated from the Over soul. Where we can help the young ones grow, to find their unique identity."

"Thank you. I'm not sure if I understand what you are saying, but we will discuss this subject and others before we meet again. I am sorry to say we must close our meeting today, and look forward to our next discussion."

Earth names.

"Yes, spirit people can keep their earth name as long as they feel it is necessary; however names are unimportant, their name is not the individual. Once they have moved on into the spirit world their light, their aura, the radiation that a spirit emits indicates whom and what the individual truly are. Similar to a finger print, no two are the same."

Partners.

I thanked Daniel and asked. "You said earlier that part of our loved ones remain behind in the spirit world so that we can see them again. Do we automatically join our partners and loved ones? I am always asked, 'what happens when we have had more than one husband, partner, who will we finally spend our time with.' Can you please explain how this problem is overcome?"

"I understand people often want to know, when they have been married more than once, who will be their constant partner when they all have passed over. The answer is the problem will never arise; there are no jealousies in the spirit world. Only those of like spiritual qualities can dwell on the same plane of existence in this new life. A husband and wife where no love existed and who were mentally divorced from one another will not be together in the spirit world. The natural law of attraction operates, there can be no incompatibilities, no pretending, no insincerity, no keeping up pretences or appearances."

"Thank you. You have talked about the law of attraction; can you please explain this law again so that everyone can understand how it works?"

"It is very simple, you attract, or draw to you only the qualities you possess, for like attracts like. You are like a magnet force, you draw to you what you desire, and you repel all other things. This is the truth; nothing will ever come to you unless you draw it to you, even though you feel you are not drawing it towards you; it comes through, because there is a 'like' thing deep within you.

Since you are a magnet, you must consider what are you going to draw to you? I think you should start with love. If you desire to be loved, you must be love. If you desire peace, be at peace, if you need harmony, live harmoniously. All the laws of the Great Spirit are exact unfailing laws. You want to love all; therefore you should try to love everyone, even those whom you do not like. It will not be long before this law of attraction will prove itself to you because you in turn will draw love back to you. And so it does work in all things, in all of the Great Spirits Laws."

Spirit world and surroundings.

"Thank you, you make things sound so simple. Is it possible for you to explain to us about the spirit world and what it looks like and what we can expect to see when we leave this world? Even though we know from spirit messages the next world is better than this earth life, the unknown is quite frightening to some. I feel it is hard to believe fully what the spirit teachers are telling us, because we receive differing explanations from different spirit guides. And because we cannot recall what it is like, we are still stepping into the unknown!"

"I can understand what you are saying and the apprehension about going back home to the realms of spirit. I will do my best to convince you that what is said is the truth.

There is nothing to fear, the surroundings in the next plane of existence is very much the same as you see on earth, everything you see is real but it has been created by thought. The spirit realms are mental existences where thought is real; you can change and create things by thinking them to change. However you can only change small things; you cannot change the whole scene around you because it belongs to lots of other spirit people too, but you can change little things that will not affect anybody else. You soon begin to realise that all things around you are really thought forms; this makes your transition easy from the material world to spirit life. Do you understand?"

"Yes I think so."

"Once the soul is free of the heavy human physical body it finds it is no longer heavy but light and can float away into the spiritual realms to enjoy the unconditional love that is the home of the Great Spirit and all other spiritual beings."

"When we are in the next world what do we see?"

"It all depends on the individual person. Firstly, a soul may find difficulty adjusting to its new body after the heavy physical body it wore on earth and because the spirit is not clothed any more it may choose to clothe itself for a while in a body form. And it may also be more comfortable meeting all its family and friends similarly dressed in one of their previous bodies; they will oblige. A younger soul with very little experience may believe that the body it wore on earth is its true self, until it finally adapts to its new life.

Because you create everything by thought it is so easy for a soul to think itself in a place or situation such as self-made hell if they have been a bad person.

Do you understand when I say souls see things differently? You must have gathered by now thought is powerful and the eternal soul is brilliant creating endless versions of where it wants to be.

An older soul feels very comfortable in its cloudlike state because it remembers its spirit life and allows itself to be part of all that exists at that time."

"Thank you. I know this may sound silly, but we need to get a better idea of what the spirit world looks like, therefore can you tell us if the spirit realms have roads, motorways and such like? If you can live in houses, could there be trains, buses, public transport?"

"Chuckling Daniel replies. The Spirit World has a number of spheres and realms; they are divided into many different levels according to the state of mind, the spiritual growth of spiritual individuals. The number is twenty one, (not including the very low levels,) each one more beautiful than the preceding one. The higher spheres are where spirits who are purer and closer to the mind of our Creator and as we spirits grow and ascend to the higher realms we become spiritually free limitless beings.

My dears, we do not have roads as they are known on earth, but we have wide, far-reaching thoroughfares in our cities and elsewhere. However, they are not paved as you would have them on earth because we have no traffic; our roads are covered with the thickest and greenest grass, which is so soft you can sink your feet into it. We don't need to mow the grass because it never grows it remains nicely trimmed and yet it is alive; the gardeners do like to create wonderful trees and plants for our pleasure."

"Wow! How do people travel then if there is not any form of transport? Again I feel a little stupid asking this, for I know you will have a simple answer."

"I do not think any of your questions silly, I am

here to help. There are no buses, trains or any public transports unless you want to travel by bus or train. If you think it, there it is. Travelling is not a problem; immediately you think of where you want to be, you are there."

Clothing.

"Wow! I like the idea when an individual is fed up with their surroundings, they can change them. Could a spirit make fabulous outfits just by thinking them; is that possible too?"

Chuckling again Daniel said. "Yes of course, although in my world clothing is not necessary, when a stranger approaches a spirit person immediately thinks clothes and then quickly they are clothed in the usual way.

What you need to do is to imagine about a world of thought, can you do that? Because when you come to my world a mental world of existence you will find everything including clothing is created by thought alone.

At first most spirit people usually create clothes that were in the earthly style, which they wish to be recognised. After a while, spirit change their clothing away from earthly fashion, which then consists mainly of beautiful robes.

I will speak briefly regarding spirit clothing so that I do not confuse you with too many details. There are energy colours displayed by spirits that relate to a spirits state of advancement. For example, pure white denotes a younger spirit and as they develop and advance the spirits energy becomes more dense, moving into orange, yellow, green and finally the blue ranges. In addition to these centre core auras, there are subtle mixtures of halo colours within every group that relate to the character aspects of each spirit.

Usually you would see younger spirit people wear pure white or purple this is the most common, whereas when an individual spirit develops and gains knowledge their energy moves upwards into various shades of orange, green, yellow and finally to the higher stage of blues. Greatly advanced spirits are seen as having a deep indigo colour.

Elders wear wonderful robes which vary in colour from beautiful bright silver to stunning deep shades of violet. Not only do they have beautiful robes but they also emit pure deep shades of purple energy, which is the colour of knowledge, wisdom, perception, sensitivity and understanding; truly these are magnificent beings.

Further advanced spirit beings have no bodily shape of any kind, but they do wear robes, which symbolises and indicates dignity, honour, purity and clarity. They are identified by their wonderful radiance, their wondrous light, which they emit.

The council members who meet spirits during their judgment and again before incarnation are benevolent beings known as 'Elders'. They wear as I have already stated robes of silver, purple and violet; this mirrors their ability to preside, to supervise over the affairs of the spirit people who come before them; they have vast knowledge and experience.

If you have any further questions regarding this you must ask."

"We will think about all that you have said. Thank you."

"It is my pleasure. I will leave you now and give you time to absorb what has been said today."

Chapter Ten.

Look like.

The following meeting Daniel was asked. "Can I touch on what you said last time we met and ask if there are higher spirit people than you have already talked about and if so what do they look like?"

"In the higher spheres of purity there are beautiful shining figures of radiance, love and light, their personality, body shape and expression have gone."

"Thank you Daniel I will try to visualize a light being without shape, if that is possible, I feel sure it's not going to be easy.

You haven't told us what we actually look like, do our facial features change and what about our build and so on? If as you say we have lived many lifetimes which person are we?" I said.

"I thought I had explained this to you. When you first arrive here you are exactly as you were when living on the earth plane, without bodily imperfections. Because anything of the body has been left behind when your spirit leaves the material world. You are now spirit and no longer have the need for a physical body. After you have settled down to your life in the spirit world you will be able to decide which identity you wish to take on and how you wish to be known, usually it is one you were most comfortable with from all your many other lifetimes. Does that answer your question?"

"Yes thank you, that's interesting because I have always felt I had lived as a Native American Indian and feel that I loved that lifetime. Therefore, because I know I have Native American Indian guides I can't wait to meet them. When does this happen?"

"I have already answered that question, during cleansing or on entry to the spirit world, immediately after the death of the body."

Sex in the spirit world.

I asked Daniel. "Sex hasn't been mentioned yet. I am often asked mostly by men, if they can continue to have sex in the spirit world. Can you please explain this to us?"

"I said earlier you have to experience a situation before you can understand and learn from it, and this is no exception, but I will try. When human beings return to the spirit realms their feelings towards one another do not change, they are the same as they were on earth but without the human natural urge.

We in the spirit world feel love and this love varies in strength, it is difficult to measures passion but the greatest degree is accompanied by a kind of absorption, a merging, fusing temporarily with one another.

There is a difference between sexual relationships in the world of spirit and those on earth. Where there is magnetism, attraction, charisma, fascination between sexes, the urge is to draw close and share the warmth and beauty, the desire is a pure emotion of love, mutual love, which is so different from the sexual acts of human beings.

When a sexual union takes place it is the blending of the two energies, a blissful ecstatic, fulfilling and satisfying experience. There is nothing more beautiful than anything you could experience in a physical body. It is a very sacred and emotional private act of complete love. Are you able to grasp what I am trying to say?"

"Yes we can try and understand but as you say until we have experienced it, we can only surmise. It's going to be difficult for me to explain that to those who ask."

Food.

Elsie asked this time. "What about eating and

drinking, is that created by a thought also? Having said that, I suppose if you don't have a physical body then you don't need food, nor do you have some other spirit sustenance?"

"Food is not necessary; however, if you think it, whatever it is, it will be there. Some spirits in the lower levels of existence have food and drink because they feel it necessary to eat; this includes habits such as smoking and drinking. It satisfies them for a while until they progress to higher levels where they know this is unnecessary."

Language and telepathy.

I went on to say. "Thank you for that Daniel. Do spirits have a language and do they talk?"

"Thought and telepathy is the only means of communication. However, unlike your world, there are no language problems in the next life, for nationality does not persist."

Interrupting, I asked. "Is it similar to when we receive inspiration?"

"Yes but it is on a different scale and it depends on the circumstances. When you receive inspiration, it is because consciously or unconsciously, your vibrations are tuned into some intelligent being in the spirit world and, for that time, you are able to receive that person's message. Sometimes it is conscious sometimes it is unconscious, as I said it depends on the circumstances.

We are constantly receiving and transmitting thoughts. Those who are on the same spiritual wavelength, the same spiritual mentality, receive thoughts that are sent to them and they transmit thoughts back. It all depends on their spiritual attainment.

Do you understand what I am trying to say, it is hard when in a physical body to understand things of spirit."

"Yes I do, thank you. So we will be able to read minds? What about private thoughts?"

"Spirit people do not intrude. However, an individual can prevent a person from knowing their private thoughts by blocking them. Whilst nothing is hidden in a general way, it is up to the individual spirit to allow or not another to enter. With experience, the spirit has the ability to conceal any thought forms at any moment. Having said that, guides and elders usually examine and search the minds of those who are below a particular level of existence; this is for their benefit."

Books and newspapers.

"Thank you. When we come to the spirit world are we able to read newspapers and books and listen to the radio?"

"Yes, there are libraries with countless books, which hold duplicates of every book known to your world, and many others of which are not known on earth.

We do not have newspapers in a physical sense, because there is no reason to record happenings, as you do on earth. When it is necessary to be told something there are specially trained people whose occupation is to sends information to those who need it. News is constantly distributed to those they think ought to have the information.

My world as I have said many times is a mental world, therefore we do not have radios because we communicate by thought; this is the common method of reaching one another."

"Thank you Daniel. We watch television here and listen to all sorts of other things on various gadgets, so can you tell us what there is in the way of entertainment? And how spirit people pass their time, do they have time as we do with hours of light and darkness, or is it another sort of time?"

"Such measurement of time by earth is meaningless away from your physical world, since there is no standard by which to evaluate the passage of time in the spirit world. All occurrences exist at the same time. We in the spirit realms do not have time as you know it. Time on earth is based upon the rotation of the earth and its relationship to the sun. Therefore, in my world we are not dependent on your definition of time, minutes, hours, seconds, or days.

We do not experience night and day, the measurement of time depend upon the individual's spiritual growth; they feel time in the sense of enjoyment. The residents in the lower spheres find that because life is not enjoyable their time seems very long. Whereas, in the higher spheres, relatively speaking, there is much activity that is much more congenial; therefore, time seems to move much quicker in the sense that there is always something new of interest.

Those on earth seem to think we sit around doing nothing I can assure you that is not the case. It is ridiculous to think when you pass from your world to mine that we are idle, there are endless things to do. As to the way in which you work, spend your time that depends on the individual. We do not have to worry about money, unemployment, slums, or selfishness, there is nothing to buy, no mortgage to acquire, no bills to pay. It is wonderful, rich and poor individuals do not exist in the beyond; there is

293

only poverty and richness of spirit. Do you understand?"

All the circle members uttered. "Yes."

"Good. There are cultural and educational hobbies and pastimes of the mind and spirit. There are endless pursuits, plenty of activity connected with the mind and the spirit, which will occupy spirits for as long as they wish to be so occupied. There are spirits people who continue to be interested and are occupied in the arts. They are happy to encourage those who are open and receptive.

Because we are spirit, does not mean we no longer take an interest in all the things that gave us pleasure, such as singing, the opera, dancing and so much more. There are many opportunities to express the real self and your natural gifts and talents. The spirit world embraces all your gifts and abilities, such as inspiring the writers, doctors, scientists, inventors and many more that are constantly at work attempting to guide and motivate those of like minds on earth."

"What do you mean by guiding and motivating those on earth?"

"Spirit people influence the minds of people on earth who are interested in the same things. This is done by sending energy and thought forms into the minds of human beings."

"Oh! That sounds fantastic. Thank you. Do you have famous men and women in the spirit world, or do they become ordinary when they die?"

"But of course my dear, absolutely, why not? There are many famous people on earth through sheer birth and for no other reason, and there are those who have won it by their life, their endeavour, or their hard work. The gifts and talents that people had on earth do not end when they die.

There is greater freedom when they come back home to the spirit world, unlimited opportunities to express their talents. There are so many famous musicians, dancers and singers from earth whose desire is to continue so that the largest possible number should enjoy their talents, therefore, there are always concerts available, without having to purchase or queue for tickets. There are various theatres, for drama, cultural purposes, and others for educational purposes.

In my world, as in yours there are halls of learning, dedicated to all the arts, there is music, education, literature and culture; everything is possible. We have museums, which hold wonderful collections of varying kinds, objects relating to earthly life throughout time, also collections of interesting forms of spiritual life. For example, we have many other phases of natural life unknown to you and flowers that have never bloomed on earth all these wonders for you to see.

There is only one religion, and no sacred books, only the operation of Gods laws the divine laws to instruct you. The spirit world, the real world is where the artist and poets realize and understand their ambition, where all gifts and talents can be expressed, and used in the service of one another.

I am pleased to say, there is nothing in your world that you can compare to the life of spirit and the freedom from the prison of the physical body. We have liberty, the freedom to go where we wish, to see our thoughts take shape, to follow out our desires, to be free from hardships, struggles and poverty.

Those of you in the physical world do not yet comprehend beauty as it can be. You have not seen spirit light, colours, scenery, trees, birds, rivers, streams, mountains, flowers-and yet your world fears death."

"Thank you. I had not realised there would be so much to do, or that spirit influence those of like mind on earth. I understand now about what you said earlier about spirit leisure time, it is similar to when I am enjoying myself, time just flies by and when I am bored time seems to drag."

Houses and homes.

"Am I right in thinking that since it is possible to recreate any reality in the spirit world, is it likely that some spirits may wish to spend time in the houses where they lived on earth, or recreate their previous home?"

"Yes that does happen, although not everyone desires houses, they prefer to build them to their own styles of architecture, whereas, some prefer to include beautiful ideas of lighting, which are not known to you, the people on earth. This is a matter of personal taste and the creative ability of the spirit concerned. Often spirit may want to construct mentally an exact duplicate of their previous home and the familiar settings around where they used to live.

There is always a helping hand if needed to implement fully these projects, which are created out of pure thought energy. All they have to do is conjure up these places from memory and use energy beams for the images to appear. If a spirit prefers to have their home open to the sky, they can have it and they may change homes as often as they wish. There is no packing, no expense, no hard work involved, just a thought. These things are largely controlled for a long time by individual habit.

Those who have lived only in the town or the country are accustomed to certain styles of houses and so they continue to live in the style in which they were accustomed. Once the old habit has gone, they have other types of houses. Individual habits persist after death; this makes life smoother and more harmonious. I am sure you will be pleased to know spirits people may wish to have their old pets around too."

"Wow so much to take in! Are all buildings created from the thought process and are they all an illusion?"

"I have already said we live in a world of thought. People on earth are accustomed to thinking their world as being real and solid. In addition, the vast majority of human beings believe that spirits are ghostly, shadowy and vague, but to us who live in the beyond, spiritual and mental are real, and your world is the shadowy, the dream world. I know it is difficult for you to comprehend but our thoughts, hopes and desires are more tangible and solid, as your surroundings appear to be on earth.

It is only when you are in the spirit world and awake, you are stimulated with all your senses functioning, you are able to understand you are now living in a lighter world a different dimension and the world you have left is the dream world. Can you understand that?"

"It is hard to imagine. Is it similar to when we are dreaming; it is real and solid. Is that how you see our world, like in a dream? Apart from the spirit who recreate their earthly homes, can you tell me do spirits live in other types of houses, they must have somewhere to live?"

"I thought I had explained this to you, yes; they have houses of their own if they want them, if they desire them although these are not made of bricks and mortar. For example, there are those whose home is made up of trees for walls and the roof open to the stars. Everything in the spirit world is constructed out of thought, which is the most malleable, flexible, the most impressionable of substances in a world where thought is a reality. Does that answer your question?"

Appointments and time.

"So you think of a place and in a flash you are there? If spirit wishes to meet someone at a specific time, what do they do?"

"They simply send out a thought mentally to the particular person requesting a meeting, it is received, and if it is convenient then they meet. There are no diaries. It is a world of mind and of spirit."

Overcrowding.

"Daniel, I am often asked 'is the next world overcrowded and where do all those dead people go'. Can you enlighten us?"

"The spirit world has no separate geographical location from earth. It is part of the universe each blending with the other. The spirit realms is not in one place and is not divided into separate spheres or planes, each level or phase overlaps, blends into the next; the process is infinite. Therefore overcrowding is not possible; it does not exist.

When you die, you automatically travel; you rise to the spiritual place, sphere for which you have evolved by the nature, by the character of how you have lived your many, many lives. You cannot occupy a higher sphere than the one, which you have earned, your spiritual status determines. Neither will you desire to occupy a lower one, unless it is for a specific purpose, such as to be of help in some way.   The aim of the soul is to progress, to perfect yourselves and eventually gravitate to the higher realms."

"Thank you that is very clear."

Suicide.

Jean asked. "Daniel, can you explain again what happens to the spirit of someone who commits suicide?"

"It does not matter how people kill themselves and break Gods laws, all suicide cases are treated with kindness and understanding.

These poor souls take their own lives for a number of reasons, which I have discussed already. However, I can give you an example of souls that have lived on another world, another planet less harsh than earth. They may find it very difficult to get accustomed to the intense density and the heavy weight of the physical, human body, and the uncomfortable crude, primitive earthly emotions.

Both young and older souls who incarnate on another planet before coming to earth, may believe they are in an alien body, which of course they are. Therefore, they have great difficulty adjusting, merging with their current physical body; this is because they feel their existence is threatened because earth is so harsh, so cruel and they have never experienced anything like the earth planet. However, these souls before incarnating agreed to accept a life contract with a human body whose mind and thought process is drastically different from their spirit self. This leads them to feel they cannot remain in this particular lifetime.

You see my dear, and I have said this many times, earth is a very hard place to reside and is one of the lowest evolved planets in the solar system. Nevertheless you are there to learn and must remain until you have played your part on the earthly stage. Having said all that, I must say that most spirits immediately regret taking their lives.

Spirit guides, master teachers and the incarnating spirit give a great deal of thought into selecting certain bodies for their use, therefore in suicide cases, especially those who were physically healthy are sent back to earth to start a new life; they know this will happen sooner rather than later therefore this is done rather quickly, usually at their own request to make up for lost time.

They have to understand life is a precious gift; therefore, they are responsible for their body. Their teachers consider this as an act of gross immaturity and of cowardice especially with those who repeatedly commit suicide. They trusted the soul's courage to finish their life no matter how difficult it turned out to be. When all said and done they were at the council meeting when the choice of trials were discussed and accepted.

After much thought by guides and elders, the souls who continue to commit suicide when things get tough are eventually sent to places to repent to consider what they have done. They are not sent to lower spirit realms where sinners reside, neither are they sent to dark miserable places. Most individuals would rather go to a place of isolation where they can reflect and self-evaluate their lives. Wherever they decide to go, their spirit guides assist them with infinite patience and wisdom.

I am not sure if I have said this before, in addition there are souls who take their life because they are so ill that their physical condition has reduced the quality of their life to almost nothing and there are those who die from their life support system being turned off in your hospitals. Alternatively, a loving, caring, compassionate member of the family who ends their life where there is unbearable physical pain, are treated differently in the spirit world than those who have healthy bodies, whether they are young or old it does not matter.

Human beings and most souls fight to stay alive, that is their natural instincts."

"I am not sure I can go along with suicide no matter what. Jesus said, 'you will never be given more than you can bear." Jean replied.

"My dear, put it to one side until such a time when you are able to accept it."

Law & order.

Jane asked. "Thank you, can you tell us if there is some form of law and order in the realms of spirit?"

"There is no need to make laws to control the lives of the people who dwell here. The natural law takes care of people in the spirit world; they are now expressing themselves in spiritual body and the natural law is in operation. They no longer have physical bodies; therefore, earth life no longer concerns them."

"What is the natural law?"

"Natural law embraces all the circumstances of life, there are many of Gods Laws; some I have explain to you the others I will in due course."

"Have we been given Gods laws and the means of knowing His law?" Elsie asked.

"All may know it, but all do not understand it. Those who understand it the best are those souls who seek goodness. All, however, will one day understand it; the destiny of all spirits is progress and must be accomplished."

Elsie went on to ask. "Can you tell us before the union with a physical body do spirits understand and know the law of God more clearly than after incarnation?'

"The spirit knows the law according to the degree of development it has achieved."

Elsie has always been a deep thinker and asked. "Can you tell us Daniel what is the most perfect type of a spirit being that the Great Spirit has given to human beings as their guide and model?"

"My dear that is a very good question and easily answered, the type of moral perfection to which humans may attain upon the earth is that of Jesus of course. Jesus was animated by the divine spirit as you are, and He was the purest being that has ever appeared upon the earth.

The teachings of Jesus were ten and conveyed in parables; because He spoke according to the time and place, in which He lived.

The time has now come when the truth must be made clear for all to understand. It is necessary to explain and develop the divine laws, as we now are doing, because few among you understand them, and still fewer practice them.

It is sad to watch those who spread teachings that are not the truth, therefore, our mission is to attack, so to speak the eyes and ears of everyone, in order to unmask the pretence of those who accept the outward appearance of virtue and of religion as a cloak for their wickedness. We must prepare the reign of good announced by our Lord Jesus to provide the explanations that will render it impossible for men of your world to continue to interpret the law of God according to their own passions, or to pervert the meaning of what is wholly a law of love and of kindness. Everything will come in time."

"Thank you very much Daniel."

Other Planets.

Emma changed the subject completely by asking Daniel. "There are many people here on earth who is interested to know if there is life on other planets. Can you tell us Daniel if we are alone in the universe, or if there are other life forms elsewhere?"

"Yes, despite what your earth scientist and astronomers say there is indeed other life in the universe; how can they think otherwise? Such great minds and yet they are quite infantile, immature in their outlook. The Great Spirit our Creator did not only create human kind but many other species in your solar system, the universe and in all the galaxies.

Each planet varies in a number of ways from earth. Earth is a heavy, dense and a harder planet to live and survive on, with many hurdles to overcome; therefore it is a good planet for those who need to learn. It is the only planet where duality exists, which provides a good schooling with the balance of negativity and positivity. The concept of heaven and hell is of polar opposites and exists only on earth."

Interrupting Daniel a member of the circle asked. "Sorry for butting in, that's quite exciting; I am very interested in life on other planets. I always believed there is other life, could you tell us what these people look like and are they friendly?"

Laughing Daniel replied. "There are other planets which also have souls experiencing different types of lessons. None of these planets duplicates earth's energetic duality.

The individuals on these planets are very different to the humans on earth, even though they are from the same creator. Some of the non-human souls are contained in body-shells that appear similar to the human body, some are different and some souls maintain their energetic formlessness without having a body.

This information probably is perhaps not what you would normally take or understand. But I feel it will give you food for thought,"

"Thank you for that. Yes, it sounds very complicated."

The lower regions and where we go.

When we met Daniel again Elsie asked. "What can you tell us about the realms below earth?"

"My dear it is very sad to reside on the lower realms. Nevertheless we are all naturally drawn to where we are best suited to our spiritual growth, those spirit people who are bad and evil will go to one of the six spheres below earth. Hell will be a self –inflicted punishment for a selfish life that forces the individual to live with those of like minds and nature.

These realms below earth are realms of negativity, addiction, bad behaviour and evil for spirits who in the physical body were lovers of drunkenness and debauchery, they reside with others of like minds. And there are addicts who still hover around their former places of gratifications, around the bars and places of vice, lost in self-respect and shame.

The lower six spheres are occupied by all those imperfect spirit beings that are on the lower rungs of the ladder; I am afraid their instincts and desires are for evil acts, they are ignorant and selfish people and this will prevents them from progressing upwards to the spirit realms.

Every spirit, who has evil intentions, may be placed in this order.

Some individuals do neither good nor evil; but because they do, no good indicates they are unknowledgeable, that they are inferior. On the other hand, there are those who take pleasure in evil acts and are satisfied when they find an opportunity to do wrong. Therefore, any wrongdoing, intentional or unintentional, will create karma and will need to be put right in some form of a future life.

This will be an opportunity for spiritual growth, a time to pay back; it is not considered a punishment or even penance it is the law of the Great Spirit. It is really very simple, whatsoever a man soweth, that shall he also reap.

It all depends on the nature of their wrongdoings most of these souls would probably be quickly returned to earth to put right the wrongs they have done and to learn by their mistakes. The souls who have been associated with and been in contact with evil have also violated the laws of the Great Spirit.

When it is time to incarnate some may feel the need to choose to serve as the victims of others evil acts in their next life on earth. Whatever they choose there is no getting away with such terrible behaviour; everyone has to pay back for their actions. However, if they continued with their cruelty over a number of lives, this would indicate they are not learning, neither are they prepared to change. Therefore such spirits would be placed for a very long time in a solitary spiritual existence for many, many earth years.

Those who are driven by such selfish or evil tendencies look for a way to channel their foul behaviour, and because they no longer have a physical body they are attracted to those of similar behaviour on earth, and consciously or unconsciously attach themselves to them. They find they can influence these human beings by way of obsessing or possessing them, making them do everything they want. They can weaken their will power and often control their actions, producing great distress, mental confusion and suffering."

"That sounds terrible. If a person killed someone for example, they could be the one who is murdered in the next life? Alternatively, if they were very cruel, they could suffer cruelty in the next life. If they raped someone, they could be raped in the next life. Therefore, they would not be victims because they would have agreed to pay back their karma. Have I got it right, is that correct?" Elsie asked

"Yes my dear, that is correct, that is, if a spirit wanted to incarnate to repay debts in that way. However, it is not as simple as that, there are other ways a spirit can pay for their wrongdoings.

It is always better to do unto others, as you would have others do unto you."

"Yes, I do try to live like that. Thank you. Please can you explain what the lower realms look like?"

"As I have said before, whatever souls have attained spiritually, this is where they will go eventually; to their rightful place in the spirit world. Depending which level a spirit has evolved will depend on their surroundings, each one being better than the preceding realm.

Oh my dear, the lower regions are bleak and barren without beauty, they contain squalid dwellings inhabited by unhappy, tormented beings that pursue their warped existences.

There is no devil and no damnation only what they have created for themselves, the hells are of the mind, of their conscience. They are confining states of misery, which are dark and depressing and are real as the tortured consciousness of the dweller makes them to be.

The gates of hell are locked from the inside! Because they may feel more secure in the hell they have made for themselves.

Let me give you an example how unwillingly a soul can create their own hell: Hitler the German soldier who committed horrendous war crimes during the second world war, could have caused his victims of those atrocities through hatred to be tied to him; they would then share the same level of existence with him, lodged in the shadows until they were able to let go of their hatred and forgive.

In these lower realms there are missionary spirits who attempt to help these poor spirits to make the first step to progression. They try to convince them to introduce light into their lives and that no one is condemned to hell forever. However, some want to change but there are those who are not ready. Do you understand what I am saying?"

"Yes I do. Because of hate that person is not much better than the perpetrator. Is that correct? That sounds very frightening, especially the victim of a crime ending up in a terrible lowly place."

"Can you tell us what it is like in the world immediately after this one? I believe it is called the Astral World, is that correct?"

"Yes that is correct, but first I think it is better if I explain the realms and spheres to you. Within each sphere there are varying levels of knowledge and spiritual growth; these are what we call realms of consciousness ascending from lower harsh existences to higher lighter realms that are more radiant. As you evolve you move higher up the realms, the ladder of progression; each more beautiful than the preceding one.

Each realm blends and overlaps the preceding one just as the astral world overlaps the earth. This is completely invisible to the inhabitants of the realms and spheres below, because spirits belonging to lower realms cannot see more refined realms and in this respect, at least it provides its own boundary. Each level is a path of light which leads upwards and onwards into realms of unimaginable beauty and wonder.

The Lower Astral is the place where those poor ignorant spirits reside who has just been released from their human body. These spirits have no idea, no insight of spiritual things, when they were on the earth they were only concerned with material pleasures, and base desires. It is the place where earthbound spirits reside, whose minds are open only to the desires and influences of the earth plane. They linger there for some time, and have no wish for spiritual development, until such a time that they are rescued.

When a spirit believes that their death is the end and there is nothing beyond the grave, it is a big shock to find that they are indeed alive. Many others are lost or confused and there are those who have a conscience and suffer in anguish or remorse for their earthly conduct.

It takes time but eventually it dawns and they begin to understanding more, which then makes them feel very uncomfortable, they feel that they are in the wrong place. They are now dead to the lower astral world, and begin to move on and live in the world of spirit. I must say, this happens many times on every sphere and realms of spiritual growth, progression and evolution; spirit cannot move forward and upwards until they are ready. Once this has happened they can naturally and easily pass to the next stage of spirit life.

Spirits do not lose their astral bodies in quite the same way as you would lose the physical body. Spirit bodies become more indistinct; more purified and refined, as their lower-self fades away. This is death, for death really means transformation, resurrection, the rising of the higher out of the lower: Spirit is now free.

As I said, life in the spirit world is in many varying levels, from the lower reaches to the higher stages. Spirit people have to grow and evolve to enable them to move from one level to another, you 'die', and are born repeatedly. You go through the process of loosening, gradually letting go of what seemed to be yourself, adjusting to your own spiritual individuality, which may take quite some time.

Astral Sphere.

On a brighter note, the next realm after the earth is the Astral and is the place to meet loved ones and friends who died previously. This realm is a duplicate in every detail to your lives on earth. If it were not, many who are ignorant of the spirit world would be in shock when they arrive. The astral body also is a duplicate of your physical body, except that it is of a finer vague, unsubstantial substance. That is why so many arrive here believing themselves to be still on earth, they do not know they have passed beyond their physical life.

The spirit world has Spheres that individuals have to pass through on their way to perfection and within each sphere there are seven realms, 21 in total that we know, and there are six reams below earth, earth being the seventh.

The first astral realms have cities with streets and buildings, cars, buses, trains and the most beautiful countryside. That is why, as you can understand, some newly arrived spirits are still ignorant of their death and continue their activities as usual not knowing they are dead, because everything looks the same.

A large proportion of spirits who dwell on the first realms of existence are those who are struggling to make every effort to raise themselves to a higher realm.

The higher the spirits consciousness the less need there is there for adjustment: As a result, they are drawn like a magnet to the level they have earned for themselves. Most spiritually developed spirits pass almost directly to higher spheres, whilst others less developed with some spiritual knowledge go initially to the first astral sphere of consciousness. There is no pretense; every soul carries over with them their old selves, their former personalities of all their previous lives.

As I have said before, all spirit realms are mental existences spirit people can only reside on their level of consciousness, therefore, landscapes and pictures can create a barrier, as to how far the spirits can wander. For example, they may see beautiful mountains in the distance and no matter how far they travel towards the mountains; they will never reach them until they attain the required level of consciousness.

Can you understand spirit people may only go to a level of consciousness below theirs but never to a higher realm; they would not fit in, they would feel uncomfortable? Eventually they will grow in consciousness and gravitate to a higher level with those spirits of like mind and moral standards. It could take many life times before they are ready to learn and move on; it is their free will.

All spirit beings that reside in the astral and higher astral realms have incarnated many times on the earth plane so that their spirit may gradually evolve and earn the right to a true place in the higher spheres.

When it is time for a spirit to move up the levels of unfoldment and when it has graduated, so to speak, the student along with other students from different areas, gather in a temple, where guides and council members are waiting along with many great teachers: as you would on earth when receiving your degree at university.

As one moves up the ladder to the higher reams you will see they are more beautiful than the preceding level, with wonderful scenic landscapes, lush green meadows, fields undulating as far as the eye can see and tiny brooks flowing into great lakes towards the colourful purple mountain chains, the sky above, cloudless and blue. And because the spirit realms are of a mental nature people are able to build their dream homes and anything they require by thought. There already exist exquisite gardens with beautifully coloured flowers beyond your comprehension with delicious cent filling the air.

There are Botanical gardens and delicious fruits, thousands of colourful birds and animals that have never lived on earth, magnificent great animals that walked the planet thousands of years ago before man.

There is a spiritual sun which lights our world. Our sun shines always, but for a few hours of each 24 is not as bright, which is our night. We do not have extreme weather conditions, it never rains, but there are occasional gentle mists.

On all spheres and realms there are superior beings everywhere who are sympathetic and who are there to guide and assist. They are easily recognized, by their light, which indicates their high spiritual state. They are always ready to help by way of instruction, or of giving strength, or encouragement."

"Thank you so much for that Daniel. It makes me for one; feel less fearful or confused about passing on to the next phase of life."

"I am pleased about that, but I haven't finished yet. We have libraries containing all the books ever written and more. We have halls of music, theatres, art galleries and many museums of life forms, animals, technology, engineering, machinery and more. There are halls of learning to teach and inspire, of every imagine-able subject, dancing, singing, poetry, all the things you wanted to do on earth and never got round to, or wasn't able. Nothing can compare with the world of spirit."

Etheric Sphere.

"Thank you Daniel it sounds absolutely wonderful. Please continue and tell us what the next realm or sphere is like?"

"As I said there are seven realms within each sphere that blend and overlap the previous level. When spirit people have aspired to and arrive in the etheric realms, they will need to understand other parts of their life. Those who reside on this level, are shown a 'blue print' a 'map' of their lives on earth. They are then able to see clearer what they need to do in their next incarnation to satisfy their karmic debts and, or lessons they need to finish on their journey through the higher realms to perfection.

When souls pass through all the realms of their sphere and reach a new more beautiful world, they will become lighter and grow purer in spirit. Their old self has gone and a new more beautiful energy soul body exists.

Increasingly, step by step they remember all their earth lives and the outcome, including, their true identity, which has returned to them. They have now connected with their spirit; this is their true self, their individuality, they can see and understand the real meaning of their many previous existences."

"Thank you, but you haven't told us what it looks like."

"The etheric realms are similar but much more beautiful than the astral realms. The seas and lakes are a beautiful reflection of the blue sky above and the surface of the water is pure and calm, with various beautiful coloured fish and other life forms to be seen.

The cities consist of numbers of grand, majestic buildings each surrounded with perfectly cultivated magnificent gardens, flowers and trees.

Usually spirit people do not feel the need for houses or anything of a material nature. However, some are inclined to choose to live in a house that they created by thought, and these are usually dotted around the countryside.

The Higher Etheric.

The etheric and higher etheric spheres are strictly limited to spirits who have reached the degree of attunement to those around them. And at this level the spirit bodies are formless white light, and pure reason reigns supreme.

In the higher etheric world it is likely that most resident spirit beings will no longer have a need to reincarnate, but work extensively helping human brings move forward.

On this particular level of consciousness, they have changed in that their emotions and passions as they knew them no longer exist. Such serenity, such self-possession becomes the possession of the spirits in this last kingdom of experience, they are capable of living now without a body, shape or form.

There is on higher levels of the etheric world unending panorama spread out before them, magnificent buildings built of precious stones such as diamonds, emeralds, amethysts and pearls. A kind of paradise with lovely bird song, forests, meadows, seas and lakes, warm breezes and clear light emanating from the central sun. My dears you cannot imagine the richness of colours when the sun reflects on the jewelled buildings emitting beautiful colours radiating in all directions.

Light and music are always found together and it is possible to control light in the process of making music; the result, musical architecture. A composer can build and create wonderful buildings.

When spirit eventually rise up the ladder to this realm they may be called 'pure spirits' and have reached, accomplished, conquered, attained a supreme degree of perfection. Because of their achievement those spirit individuals are able to climb, ascend even further into the advanced realms more quickly. However, not all spirits progress at the same rate and express a variety of abilities and gifts along the way.

On this level spirits behaviour change, they now begin to develop and expand their outlook and are so immersed, so captivated in their training they are totally engrossed in their goal; they want to become even more talented. Some spirit beings are more focused on perfecting and adding certain skills that will contribute to the universal consciousness, such as becoming specialist rescuers and saviours of lost souls.

Some prefer to look after animals, becoming their caretakers and there are those who would rather look after new souls; what we call incubator mothers and there are spirits who are directors of music and much, much more. Scientists are plentiful and much of their time is spent trying to transmit telepathically to those of like mind on earth their discoveries they have made that will help your planet. In time, they will become masters who teach others. These realms are a place where gracious beings reside.

I hope by now you have a clearer vision of the world of spirit."

They all responded. "Yes, we think so."

Advanced souls.

"Advanced spirits are often asked by guides to come and visit groups to teach. These spirits are very knowledgeable and have what looks like a silver of flowing water as they pass by. The silver stream is a cloak of passage, the purity of a translucent inter-dimensional intelligence. They seem to be very elastic spirit beings with the ability to pass through most physical and mental spheres and realms. They come to help, to bring knowledge, but these beautiful beings never stay long. They help to widen the soul groups vision so that they are able to see more probabilities in making choices by becoming clever at reading people.

On the advanced realms emotions and passions as known to human beings, are absent and white light represents the perfect composure of pure thought. Such serenity and tranquillity become the possession of the spirit who enters this last kingdom of experience.

Those who reside here are without a body of any kind and merge with the Great Spirit and remain in the perfection, the flawlessness of eternity. Having said that, they still exist as individuals and are wholly aware of the consciousness of our Creator and aware of the whole history of the universe, everything created is contained within this consciousness. However, very few pass on to the seventh advanced realm.

Those who have reached the high level usually remain there because generally they are not strong enough to make the big leap into timelessness. They are capable of living now as the pure thought of their creator. They have joined the immortals."

Story.

"My dears, you will find this exciting; some spirit people, depending on their spiritual growth may visit other planets as travel is not a problem. They must have permission, and if it is constructive and positive to the spirits evolution it will be permitted, a spirit person may ask also to incarnate on another planet. Of course a permanent change of body, of form would be necessary to live in another environment and these vary greatly. You will have to wait and see. And yes they are friendly; it is the governments, the rulers of the earth who are the ones who would be hostile."

"Thank you. I was told when I was in my teens by a medium that one of my spirit guides was a Native American Indian and his name was Grey Buffalo. I was thrilled to bits to be told his name, as I had been aware of him for a long time, and I had only seen him when I woke up during the night to go to the loo. I tried very hard to get back to sleep to talk to him but disappointingly that didn't happen.

One day when I went very deeply into my meditation I became aware that I belonged to everything and everything belonged to me; it was a strange feeling, I was only aware of my mind and not my a body, I just existed in the great universe, in the deepest of indigo blues of space and time. Very soon I became aware of my wonderful spirit guide and friend who took me on a journey into the unknown.

I can only say in a flash we were amongst the stars, they seemed alive and they were vibrating outwards towards me. Suddenly, I found myself looking down into space and below me was the moon and I could also see the earth. As I looked around I could see other planets, I was sat at the edge of the universe dangling my legs, so to speak! I felt exhilarated and truly alive and very happy. We didn't speak, it wasn't necessary because I belonged there."

"Thank you for that." Daniel said.

Going to earth to visit.

Emma asked. "Do spirit people visit earth whilst still in a spirit body and if so, why?"

"Yes there are spirit people who go to earth as invisible, charitable beings between lives specifically to help make earth a better world.
    There are some spirit entities who like to go on a vacation trip to earth, nevertheless there are some who find this sort of sentimental trip to be very disappointing and they are frustrated not have a physical body. Neither do they want to spoil their old memories that they hold dear, so naturally this can put off spirits from going back to earth between lives. Nonetheless, there are spirit people who still want to go back to earth and other planets for visits, despite the

negatives.

Some spirit beings enjoy roaming around their old haunts on earth especially those who have addictions to drink, gambling or taking drugs; these are spirits of a lower level and has already been discussed.

There are those who are not motivated by a vacation, their desire is simply to help and comfort their loved ones."

Psychic toys.

"I'm sorry for darting from one subject to another but what do you think of people who use tarot cards and such like?"

"As you know my dear life as a medium is not easy and I have watched you struggle with some human beings trying to put across spiritual truths and no matter how much spirit evidence you give you cannot put across spiritual truths to people until they are ready until their eyes have been opened. Nevertheless, this is why clairvoyance and clairaudience demonstrations are important.

Once you have given the demonstration to the best of your ability and that is all we ask of you, remembering spiritual truths you should not want to play with toys such as tarot cards and other psychic tools, for that is what they are, psychic not spiritual. Psychic is to do with vibrations around you, earthly physical vibrations and is not linked to any spiritual vibrations.

If you want to progress and I am sure some do then you must tread the spiritual path."

I interrupted Saying. "Sorry Daniel for interrupting but I have said this many times to circle members, but I think they lose patience with themselves and go for the easy option. And I have said also to them 'if it's worth having, it's worth working for but it hasn't made any difference."

"Yes I have heard you say this. My dears, take notice of what I am saying, if you bring mediumship down to the psychic level, you are failing in your work for spirit, it must always be raised to its spiritual level. You must teach spiritual realities, spiritual knowledge, however if you are content with the psychic, which is the lowest level, then you are not evolving; you are standing still.

The power of the spirit is not for titillation, therefore it will not continue to manifest. Do you understand how important this is?"

Everyone mumbled. "Yes."

"Good. Your free will is your responsibility from which there is no escape. Once you become aware of the basic spiritual realities and knowledge, you form a wonderful magnetic link with the spirit realms and loving spiritual beings, which can never be broken. There is unlimited knowledge and inspiration for you to 'tap' into; therefore, you should seek to become a pure channel for the power of spirit to flow. Your desire to serve must be paramount in all that you do and all other thoughts must be put to one side, self no longer matter anymore; only your service to other human beings counts.

The reason for spirit communication is to come closer to loved ones for a while and to comfort those who are grieving, to uplift the spirit and to prove survival of death, certainly not to reveal what tomorrow will bring, but you do have free will it depends on how you use it. To grow always aim for a good standard of mediumship and then others will try to follow.

You are not alone the way will always be shown and those in our world will never fail you, we will do our best and all we ask of you is for you to do your best. When you are convinced that what you are going to do is right, then you must do it. If you teach and help more and more human beings to become channels for spirit power to flow through and to prove survival as best you can, that is all that matters. You must always strive for perfection and always do your best that is all that can be expected of you

You do not need a special place to work with

spirit, spirit can manifest in any room you keep as a sanctuary for the power of spirit to express itself; this is important.

You are not perfect, perfection is an infinite process, however when you fall down, pick yourself up, we will help you. My dears, does that answer your question?"

"Yes thank you very much." I replied.

Witches story.

I have two rescued dogs, poor little souls they had a dreadful life.

One day a friend came to visit me, someone I taught in circle. She told me about how she has, is struggling with the dark powers of evil witches. I was shocked and said she shouldn't see individuals who bring to her door step negative energies and perhaps an exorcism was needed. She went onto say that she was able to control, with difficulty these evil forces. We talked for a while and then she left.

The same evening I was woken by Lottie. She was trembling and pacing and wouldn't settle, she was terribly frightened. I wouldn't wish that on any animal. I stayed up all night with her and prayed and watched her pace the floor for eight hours.

My prayers were not answered and I felt totally abandoned by spirit. This went on for a couple of weeks and I felt inadequate, I was unable to protect this poor little soul. Poppy my other dog couldn't care less, obviously she couldn't see the monsters attacking Lottie and neither could I for some reason.

I spoke to my friend about bringing evil forces into my home; her response was that I had this already. I must say, I disagreed with her and explained I had been working for spirit around forty five years, and during that time nothing has been brought into my home of an evil nature.

I had no choice but to perform an exorcism reluctantly. I had in the past experience some terrifying situations where I was psychically punched in my solar plexus which left me with awful pain for several days. It took many attempts to rid my home and Lottie from these evil forces.

I asked Daniel. "Can you please tell me if the fear and agitation Lottie experienced regularly were of my doing, was it something connected with me?"

He replied. "On this wrongdoing you have not transgressed any of the laws of the Great Spirit, therefore there are no repercussions.

Let me explain. The instant souls come into being they are given free will, to accept or reject anything that is repugnant or unacceptable to their intelligence and reasoning.

As you know from experience, it takes time to trust information from a source that is unknown to you. If you are not totally convinced then reject the information or put to one side for a later time when proof has been placed before you. Be on your guard for those who take pleasure in wallow in the suffering of those misguided souls whom they have led onto the path of wrongdoing, causing havoc on the way.

Finally, it would be a crime to do wrong by disobeying a law of the Great Spirit, a command or moral code. Therefore it is not for a spirit guide to interfere with a soul's free will. The natural justice of the universe governs the actions of all living beings. I hope this satisfies your confusion."

"Thank you very much for that. It has been worrying me whether it was something I had done to bring about what happened."

Soul energy and spirit body.

"Daniel is it possible for you to explain a soul to us in a physical way?" Elsie asked.

"It is not that easy to explain in your limited vocabulary, however I will try. The energy of a soul/spirit is unique forms of identity just like a fingerprint, it has an appearance, a vibration of waves of intelligent light, it is an expression of beauty, creativity and imagination; the energy of a spirit can be identified by distinctive shades of colour, because each spirit person has their own radiation of colours, which comes from their spiritual growth and knowledge."

Elsie responded. "Thank you for that, but it doesn't really describe what the soul looks like."

Jean interrupted and asked Daniel. "What is spirit and is spirit independent of our physical body?"

"That is a good question. Spirit and the physical body are separate from one another but the union of the two are necessary to give intelligent life and activity to a body. In other words, when spirit enters a physical body you have life. Without this union, without spirit, which is your soul, you would be just a lump of flesh.

We are all brothers and sisters because the same spirit, which is part of the Great Spirit the creator is within all human beings."

"I don't think that describes what a spirit is made of or looks like. May I come back to you if I feel the need to ask more? Are you able to tell me if a body is able to exist without a soul?"

"Yes it is complicated for you now; however, you will gradually understand, as the pieces of the jigsaw fall into place.

My dear I have already answered this question. However before birth the union between the spirit and the body is not complete; but, when the incarnating spirit draws closer and is definitely recognised with the child and the union has taken place, only death of the physical body can sever the cord that unites it to the soul, and this allows the soul to withdraw from it. Therefore the body would be a mass of flesh without the soul, the intelligence; anything you choose to call it excepting a human being."

"Thank you. Please explain what a soul is?"

"The soul is an incarnate spirit, a spirit that has entered the body of a baby."

"Oh, what was the soul before its union with a body?"

"A spirit."

"So, souls and spirits are the very same thing?"

"Yes that is correct, souls are spirits. Before uniting with a body, the spirit is one of the intelligent beings who live in the beyond, and who temporarily incarnates by entering a baby, a physical body in order to achieve its goals and to balance karma.

If you do not understand you must ask, otherwise my time will have been wasted. It is inevitable that I will repeat myself, nevertheless this will enable you to understand fully."

"Thank you very much Daniel. Can you please expand on what is a spirit and body?"

"First let me say again, when the spirit is in the body it is a soul, when it returns to the spirit world it is a spirit. You are able to live because you have part of the Great Spirit our Creator within you. All life is produced by the action of the soul on the physical body; the soul gives life to all beings, including the animal kingdom. And the body can only exists because of the soul within, without the soul the physical body is as I said before, just a lump of meat.

Spirit is immortal, infinite, indestructible, and imperishable. You live beyond the death of the physical body because you are a spirit being. Nothing in the physical world, nothing in the realms of spirit, can destroy the everlasting divinity, which is yours, bestowed on you on your entry into the world. Because you are spirit, you live, because you are spirit you survive the grave and continue to live forever and ever.

All that counts is one thing, and that is how you have lived your life whilst on the physical world, the earth, good or bad. You are placed in the physical body whilst on earth to learn, to grow, to evolve so that you can build your own characters and to accomplish your own soul evolution, the operation of LAW. Is that clear to you?"

"Yes thank you very much. Is incarnation necessary for the spirits who, from the beginning, have followed the right road?"

"All spirits my dear are created simple and lack knowledge, they are ignorant; they grow only from the lessons, struggles and hardships of their physical lives. The Great Spirit is just and being just, could not make some people happy and trouble free without having worked for it. All spirit must incarnate many times to learn, there is no other way."

"What do they gain by having followed the right road and still they have to undergo the pains of a physical life?"

"They will fulfil, arrive at their goal more quickly. One must remember the sufferings of life are often due to mistakes, wrongdoings not learning, which are the penalties, the costs of the imperfect spirit; therefore, the fewer their imperfections, the less will be their suffering. Those who live a good life, who are neither envious, jealous, avaricious, nor ambitious will not have to suffer the torments, which are the results, the flaws of character and growth."

"Is there anything else other than a soul and a body?"

"Yes, I have told you this earlier, there is a link that unites the soul to the body. It is a semi-material substance, which is called the perispirit and unites the soul with the body. This substance is in-between the soul and the body, there has to be a connection with both in order for them to be able to communicate with each other. It is the way this union allows the spirit to act upon the physical body, which in turn acts upon the spirit. Can you understand a human being is formed of three essential parts? The physical body, the soul, or incarnated spirit and the link the intermediary semi-material substance"

"Thank you. Can you tell us if a body exist without a soul?"

"If you mean a human body, then no, however, organic life may vitalise a body without a soul."

"What would our body be if it had no soul?"

"As I said earlier it is a lump of flesh without intelligence; anything except a human being."

"Is the soul outside the body and surrounds it?"

"The soul is not shut up in the body, it radiates outwards in all directions, and displays itself outside the body as beautiful coloured lights; in this sense the soul may be said to be exterior to the body, which is known as the aura."

"Thank you Daniel."

Spirit colours.

"It is my pleasure. The coloured auric lights are energy colours displayed by spirits that relate to a spirits state of advancement. For example, pure white denotes a younger spirit and as they develop and advance the spirits energy becomes more dense, moving into orange, yellow, green and finally the blue ranges. In addition to these centre core auras, there are subtle mixtures of halo colours within every group that relate to the character aspects of each spirit. Greatly advanced spirits are seen as having a deep indigo colour."

Animal souls.

"I believe animals live after death; can you tell me where they live etc.? I would hope they would be with me and I would see them again."

Jean asked.

"Yes, they do continue life after the death process. However, they do not live in the same spaces as human beings; therefore a caretaker looks after them.

After the physical body of the animal dies, their soul returns to the spirit world and exists in different spheres from that of the human spirits, they happily adjust and except and their new surroundings, which is similar to the countryside on earth where they can run around happily with their own kind.

All animals have some sort of soul energy; it is exactly the same in substance as the soul of a human being, because both come from the Great Spirit the divine source. However, their souls are not as complicated as a human soul and are less complex, they are made up of smaller particles of energy and there is less volume.

All animals were carefully planned in every detail by the Great Spirit, the Divine Creator including all form of life. The divine spirit animates all aspects of life, human beings and animals that share your planet and they have responsibilities towards one another.

Every animal has its own individual personality, feelings and a sense of what their owners need. The domesticated animals are able to extend love and affection to human beings.

Most of you who are animal lovers know that

your pets develop distinct individualities because of their close contact with you. It seems as if the association between human and animals rouses, encourages and stimulates the latent individuality of your pets the dog and the cat, which helps them to develop as a result of this interaction and the love you give them. In some small way you believe you can communicate with your pets. Therefore, when you return to the spirit world and you can see them again you will jump for joy and you will be able to communicate with them much easier because you are both spirit beings.

Do not worry about being with your animals in the spirit world; domesticated animal spirits are willing to give up their freedom to remain with their human friends in exchange for love and affection. You have had close intimate contact with your pets, therefore that bond will continue in the next life. You belong together because you bonded on the earth plane of existence and your mutual love for each other continues. For you and many animal lovers, life in the spirit realms would not be perfect if their pets no longer remained with them. All spirit people and animals must move forward together, the animals cannot be left behind whilst humans make their way forward and upwards.

Whilst the connection between humans and animals become closer, their paths have to be separate. However, in time, with the natural process of evolution, the group souls of animals will become more individual. Having said all that, in the world of spirit, domesticated animals do not follow the same path of evolution as human beings. Do you understand?"

"Yes thank you Daniel. I am pleased to hear that animals do progress and evolve." I responded.

"I have always believed beyond doubt that pet animals do eventually become what I call a 'raw' human soul. I must say I know it will take a very long time."

"Good. I knew you wanted to hear that, and it gives me great pleasure to pass this information on to you all. There is a line of separation between individual survival of domesticated animals and other animals, because they do not persist as individuals after death. However, some animals attain their individual consciousness similar to humans through association with them.

You must never forget human beings are responsible for all animals well-being; they have power over them whilst they are on earth. Nevertheless, it does not give them the right to slaughter them so that their carcass may be used for the decoration and beautification of human bodies; that is not part of the Great Spirits plan.

All those who are cruel to animals, especially needless cruelty, will pay for their crime tenfold."

"If I were on a level where I needed to have a home in the spirit world, would my dogs be able to stay with me within my spiritual property?"

"Yes because it is natural for them to be there."

"That's great news thanks you, can you tell me more?"

"Animals do not evolve into a higher form of life and a human being will not become a lower form in a future life. You will not come back to earth as a dog, or a cat as some may think, you remain a human being."

"I am sorry I disagree. I feel animals do grow and evolve, have a group soul and eventually become very simple human baby souls and then continue to evolve.
Can you please tell me what happens to wild animals, do they live in the same space as pets?"

"Do not apologise, you must not accept anything that is contrary to your intelligence, do not reject it either; put it to one side for a later time.
Wild animals live together in a completely different space, for example; farm animals live

together, horses and zebras are together and so forth.

There are specialists in the spirit realm who look after the animals and they are called Animal Caretakers, their work is much appreciated by pet lovers."

"Thank you very much. It's good to know they are looked after."

The group soul.

"I have heard various explanations regarding group souls; can you please explain this to us?" Beth asked.

"Yes I will do that. All spirit individuals who reside above the lower realms are a member of a group soul; therefore what they learn on earth during many incarnations and in the spirit realms is shared, and is part of the long loving relationships with their group. Their spiritual home is with their group, who will never fail them, and usually group members have about the same number of incarnations and are similarly advanced and at an equivalent level of knowledge and wisdom.

The group soul is an extended family of spirits, sometimes ranging from just a few to a few hundred. They live with each other and share their experiences and if they need any help they generally ask for assistance from their own soul group first. They have an affinity with one another, a connection and they also have similar characteristics, although each spirit is unique with their own strengths and weaknesses that complement each other.

The group do many things together just like friends and family do on earth; they have meetings and meditation groups and take time out to travel to old and new places, returning often to familiar scenes.

When the time comes for one or more spirits in the group to incarnate they will make important binding contracts with each other to help with a situation they have to endure on earth, because they know them best and they feel most able to depend on them when their presence is needed. Better to live that experience with those they know rather than a stranger.

Sometimes in a particular lifetime a soul can hurt a member of their group, this happens when more than one spirit from the group agree to incarnate at the same time to assist their member in a particular act, that will help their karma. For example, a young joy rider takes a car and hits that particular soul member, which causes that soul to be injured so badly it is left disabled; allowing the agreed karmic debt to be paid. In these circumstances they forgive because that group member chose the accident to understand negative personality traits that are in need of attention.

Every soul who has a group brings to group their personal lifetime experiences; these attributes add a wealth of knowledge and bring a balance and support to the group. They do not think in terms of their personal path, instead, they think in terms of being part of a group. My dears do you understand thus far? In these circumstances there is no victim and no crime because both parties agreed, they made a contract.

Eventually, in the distant future when the long process of incarnations, paying back debts and learning has been fulfilled by the entire group, they can move on as a whole to some area of existence they do not know outside the planet earth

There are some spirit individuals who have had a difficult time on earth and arrive back exhausted to the love and safety of the spirit realms. In these cases, the spirit may wish to be alone and in need of rest rather than celebrating with their family, guides and members of their soul group. Those who need to rest do so before moving on. All group members welcome their friends with deep love and camaraderie. It is a joyous time, lots of celebrations, hugs and laughter."

"I'm not so sure about going to earth to injure someone, I didn't know that could happen." Beth said in disbelief.

"Oh yes, oh yes my dear. Individual spirits of the group incarnate into your world to have the kind of experiences that will help the larger self, the whole group to achieve tasks that are part of the plan for all of them.

When they meet up again back home, the members of the group soul discuss and review each individual's life times, in the way they handled their physical and emotional feelings directly related to those experiences; their earthly lives. Karmic plans do not always work out in the way the individual spirit intended, therefore, they discus every aspect of a life and dissect it, they act out reverse role-playing within the group as if on a stage: The truth is in effect, each soul's life on earth is playing out a role.

Each spirit individual aims are for spiritual growth within the group where all members struggle forward and onwards towards perfection; this has always been a long-term process. Their aim is always to bring greater understanding, greater awareness to assist one another, absorbing information from all of their life experiences.

Eventually everyone progresses upwards through the realms and spheres of existence, their insight, perception and understanding becomes instant and they are able to absorb everything. This of course is because the members of the group have experienced many, many struggles of soul life with the ups and downs of emotional and mental joys and sorrows. Eventually the tiny spark within is fanned into a beautiful flame, the divinity, the eternal life that is within everyone.

In the distant future when the long process of incarnations, paying back debts and learning has been fulfilled by the entire group, they can move on as a whole to some area of existence we do not know outside the planet earth.

The final choice for an individual becomes available when they have paid their debt to the earth, and to decide for themselves whether they will dare to take the final leap and become part of the divine whole which will lead them away forever, from earth incarnations and further onwards towards the divine essence.

These evolved spirit beings often resist the final stride forward and hold back for a long time reluctant to take that final move because they have no idea what is in store for them. They know they will be absorbed into spirit, and what it becomes then is a mystery. So it is understandable why they are reluctant."

"Thank you. You said spirits strive for perfection, therefore, whilst they are in the spirit world do they go to school to learn or do they go somewhere else?"

"Yes of course, everyone in your world and in mine should always seek knowledge. They have educational posts and assignments. Their education depends naturally on the level of the spirits development, their growth rather than how many lives they have lived on earth. However, the educational exercises do not necessarily bring high achievement.

There are spirit schools and universities for students to attend study sessions, of which some are of self- discovery. Some take longer to get through certain lessons, the same as classrooms on earth and just as students in your world are disappointed if they don't achieve what they set out to learn, whereas, there are some students who cannot be bothered to learn and choose not to give their best.

There are times when beautiful pure inter-dimensional intelligent beings are invited by their guides to help teach groups to widen spirits vision so that they may see more chances, more possibilities in making choices by becoming more perceptive, sharper at understanding people. They come with their wisdom to show spirits how to reach the light of knowledge and to push away the darkness of ignorance.

I find it difficult to describe these spirit beings in your words, a way in which you will understand; they are transparent, they are see-through, flexible, adaptable, changeable beings with the ability to pass through many physical and mental spheres."

"Thank you for that. I understand that our life between lives is in a telepathic world, therefore, how do spirits keep any private thoughts hidden from their group?"

"Do not forget the spirit belongs to the whole and because of this the spirit no longer has such feelings of embarrassment, shame, guilt or any other such emotions; there is no motivation for trickery. They open their minds to each other to such an extent it seems impossible to conceal any thoughts. Do you understand they live in a group where there is complete openness on all matters? They work on their own lessons and those of their group. Nevertheless living in a telepathic world is of paramount consideration between souls to respect personal privacy."

"Thank you Daniel. Do you prefer being in the spirit world than anywhere else and why?"

"My dear child, one cannot compare earth life with the spirit world, there is nothing in your world that can be measured to the life of spirit. Spirits are freed from the heavy weight and the restraints of the physical body. They no longer have any worries; they are free to travel where they will, to follow their desires and to see their thoughts take shape. How many human beings long to get rid of all their worries? I feel sure everyone who suffers from stresses of earthly problems would be first in the queue.

If you could only see the magnitude of the beauty in my world, the beyond, there are mountains, scenery, trees, flowers, birds, rivers, streams, of magnificent colours. It is a world where there is no unemployment, no slums, greed or selfishness, where the operation of divine laws works. All this is beyond your comprehension, and yet those of your world fears death. Does that answer your question?"

"Yes it certainly does, thank you."

Twin souls.

"A long, long time ago, each spirit split into two halves, male and female, eventually they blended, re-immersed with one another again.
Twin souls are identical, they are at the same stage of spiritual growth and development, and therefore they will move forward together: They are the two halves of the whole. Furthermore, when they are apart from each other, (they can separate) they still remain part of the whole spirit person. There are affinities, kinships, similarities, ties for every spirit, every soul in the

universe; the difference is they do not often meet in the same lifetime."

Beth interrupted asking. "Sorry for interrupting Daniel, what you are saying is that the two halves can incarnate into different bodies. Is that correct?"

"Yes that is what I am saying, but you can never lose one another only in the physical sense. When they return and join with each other this completes the whole, that entity and whenever that takes place nothing else seems to matter to them. They share the wisdom of the ages in an aura of unconditional love."

"Thank you Daniel."

Soul mates.

"People on earth often talk about their soul mate; can you explain what a soul mate is?"

"Let me first say that as spirit beings, your growth actually began in the mental realm of the spirit world with other spirits before any of you incarnated. However, to answer your question, it is because two spirits from the same group soul are incarnating to earth at the same time and if they meet on their journey, and because they are part of the whole there is complete harmony between them. They are incarnating into your world to add knowledge, development and experience that will help the whole soul group in their evolution.

Soul mates are those other members from the group with whom they repeatedly incarnate, and on whom they rely for their most vital learning contracts. Each spirit has between many soul mates who work with each other time after time. It is not unusual for a person to have feelings for a soul mate even the first time they meet in an earthly lifetime. It is almost as if they have known each other for their whole life; which they have in the spirit realms.

A vital part of spiritual life is devoted to sympathetic relationships with other spirits, therefore, my dear your development as spirits becomes a communal, a collective one. Do you see?"

"Yes I do. Thank you. Are there any other types of soul mates?"

Main soul mates.

"There is another type of soul mates, which we call primary, or principal soul mates, they are closely attached partners. They regularly incarnate into the same lifetime, their lives and partnership on the earth plane could well be with any of their family members or friends, such as their husband or wife, brother or sister and occasionally a parent. Therefore can you see why a primary soul mate is more important to them than any other spirit? Their lives with these soul partners enrich and deepen their existence beyond measure. Usually the average spirit individual chooses one gender over another most of the time. However, they may change their genders from life to life if they are spirits that are more advanced.

I have already discussed karma with you and as you know most spirit people in time want to incarnate to have the opportunity to balance their karma. Primary soul mates are no different; it is the greatest driving-factors they have to express themselves in a physical body.

These spirits can divide their energy to live parallel lives; because they are twin souls, which I have talked about earlier. Although this is a tiring way to hasten their learning, therefore most spirits do not engage in this practice. All souls have the ability to divide themselves, which allows them to leave part of their energy behind in the spirit world as an exact duplicate while they incarnate; this is different to living parallel lives, where both halves have incarnated at the same time."

Souls of solitude.

"Wow! That takes some digesting. If a spirit

person incarnates before say, a member of their family and they leave some of their energy behind they would still be in the spirit world, wouldn't they? So they would be able to welcome their family when they pass over?"

"Yes that would be correct."

"Thank you. Can you tell me if there are some people who die and are not ready to return to the spirit world, such as ghosts?"

"Yes, there are spirits who are unable to function properly and are confused after their physical death, so they go into seclusion to rest for a while. They are not ghosts but they don't accept death and they won't want to go home. Their major symptom is of avoidance. Eventually they are coaxed by empathetic guides to return to the heart of the spirit world.

There are entities that are not what you call ghosts, they just want to be in contact with a human being, they do not accept death and they want to avoid going back to the realms of spirit. It takes time for some spirits, but eventually they are persuaded by sympathetic understanding helpers and guides to return to where they belong in the spirit world."

"Don't these spirits know they must go through the normal process of returning to the spirit world?"

"You are right, but spirit guides do not force those who are in extreme distress to return home until they can feel or understand the benefits of doing so. They give them time to sweat it out. This is a challenge for teachers; they know these spirits are concerned about their evaluations and the reactions from their soul groups. They are full of negative energy and not thinking clearly. It may take many reassurances by those who wish to help them before these souls agree to give up their self-imposed places of confinement. Eventually they will be released one way or another through different forms of encouragement or persuasion.

There are other spirits who are unwilling to let go as a result of something they did which was left unfinished; this could be traumatic and devastating for them; they are unhappy spirits. However, I must say this rarely happens."

"Why don't their guides take charge and pull them up deeper into the spirit world despite their resistance?"

"It is not that simple. If spirit people were forced to do what is right for them they would shut themselves away from everyone and learn nothing."

"Where do the spirits go who will not go home?"

"I explained earlier, the world of spirit is a mental existence therefore, they are able to create and design their own reality from memories of their earth life; they can create for themselves any space they want. They can construct various settings; some individuals live in beautiful garden setting, others, who know they have been bad and have harmed people for instance, may confine themselves by designing terrible spaces such as a prison cell for themselves, or remain in solitary confinement. Wherever they do they separate themselves; this is a self-imposed punishment."

"I still wonder why the spirit who wants to remain on earth, with no stopovers in the spirit world, can't be given a new body immediately."

"My dear you cannot place a spirit who is not ready, who is troubled into a new body; it would not work and be very unfair to the unborn child; a baby just starting their earth life.

We all have free will, therefore, spirit individuals have a right to be in seclusion if they wish, eventually they will come to the realization they cannot move forward, they cannot progress alone therefore eventually they make the right decision and ask for assistance."

"How do guides deal with all types of spirits who have put themselves in a self-imposed exile?" Elsie asked.

"Guides know these spirits are concerned about their evaluations; they are full of negative energy and not thinking clearly. They are worried, afraid and embarrassed at what the reactions are going to be from their soul groups and need to have time to think about it and prepare themselves for the time when they will have to face their judgement and soul mates. Helpers will reassure these poor individuals many times before they agree to their evaluation; eventually they will be persuaded."

"Thank you for that Daniel, I really enjoy our discussions, it's all very interesting."

"I am pleased you enjoy are meetings, I also benefit from our discussions."

Interaction between soul groups.

"Almost all the younger soul groups remain in their own study areas. I must say that spiritual classrooms are not like earthly ones where they need excuse slips for absences. Spirits individuals are free to avoid study activities with their own classmates at any time.

If a spirit wants solitude, or to be involved in

some private work which they feel is beneficial to them away from their companions, they are free to do so as long as this activity does not interfere with the work of another group.

As I have said, spirit individual are not forced to study and some take long periods of rest than others. Even so, most spirits feel left out is they are not with their classmates in some ongoing project. The excitement of mastering certain skills drives them on. Therefore, most spirits don't wish to get involved in the middle of projects by other groups. No two groups in the vicinity are exactly the level in all departments of study. So regardless of their development level, it is not all that easy to visit another classroom and gain something from a lesson."

"Thank you Daniel."

Chapter Eleven.

The Presence.

At the next meeting Jean asked. "Could you please explain to us if spirit people see God?"

"The answer is no, but they do feel the Creators energy all about them."

"I don't understand is there some place in the spirit world where there is a being superior to the elders?"

"Yes there is a higher force; an awe-inspiring, overwhelming loving energy that we call the Presence. The Presence is an entity that functions as an equalizer, harmonizing the greater awareness of elders to the lesser awareness of the spirits who come before them. This effect causes the council chamber to breathe with synchronized energy.

It is very difficult to explain in your words the divine energy that we feel. However, when we are at council meetings with the elders, we can feel this entity, there is a wonderful powerful energy that helps to bring harmony and arranges energy within the council chambers.

The elders know the Presence is a sacred and holy entity, or entities, with capabilities immeasurably superior to those on the council. We all agree that the Presence is not the Great Spirit exactly. As far as I am aware, this is as close to God the Great Spirit as we know it. We also agree the Presence is there to assist the work of the council. All spirits will eventually merge, unite and join with the Source of all life."

I asked. "Where do you think the essence of the Presence comes from?"

"Everywhere."

"How do you know of these things?"

"I discus these things with those who are knowledgeable, we ask questions about the ultimate reality."

"Does the same Presence move from council to council, is there more than one entity, or is, 'It' simply God the Great Spirit which is everywhere?"

"These questions of course I cannot answer."

"Thank you. Are there spirits from other planets in the universe and do they have councils? And how many types of councils exist who are responsible for all the souls from earth?"

"Yes it is true that other worlds in our universe have souls that need to be cared for by spiritual masters, therefore, they need councils. Regarding the planet earth, this too is impossible for me to gauge, but the numbers must be immense"

"I see. If the 'Presence' is not God, who is? "

"It is divineness, not God. The truth is, we do not know"

"Is the divineness the ultimate Creator of all galaxies, universes and all dimensions connecting these, including the spirit world?"

"Again I say we do not know."

"Have you heard or, felt a force above the Presence."

"It is impossible to describe in your words, nevertheless I will try. It is an immense power of energy of warmth and purity that is gentle and soft, like a breath of tenderness and sacredness. I do not know it may be a part of the same influence and force as the Presence."

"Does some sort of energy, vibration create sound?"

"No, if you can understand, it is the sound that creates everything, where there is sound there is light and energy. Spirits together are able to tune in and unite, to merge their minds to the sound and then they are able to see pictures in their minds of what looks like designs and patterns."

Reuniting with souls who have hurt us.

"If for example, I and another member of my soul group had a life on earth at the same time and that soul agreed before incarnation to harm me in some way, how would it be when we both returned home?"

"Initially there is bound to be some awkwardness when you return to the spirit world following your lives together. However, both of you are soon relaxed and happy once again in your soul group when you realise you had made a contract with each other."

Journey of the soul.

"How did spirit begin?" Emma asked.

"At the start of a spirit's journey there is the so-called 'breaking off' of the individual soul energy and small groups of spirits by our Creator. When they are separated from the Creator, spirits gain individuality, further enhanced by the irreversible Universal Law that all spirits have freedom to choose their own path.

Each spirit is then partnered by its soul mates, who work with it in a give-and-take system of helpful contracts.

The spirit still remains eternally part of our Creator, resonating with its energy and returning to contribute all its knowledge to the Akashic knowledge bank, adding the wisdom it gained on earth to the wisdom of the Universal whole.

The divine is everything, everywhere, and yet in the Creator we have a thinking, energetic force that sends itself out through individual souls to discover what it does not know about the perfection of its own essence, unconditional love. Divinity truly is in every such place because all energy is made up of the energy of our Creator and energy is everything and everywhere."

New souls, birth, soul nurseries.

"Can you tell me if there are new spirits and where do they come from and are they created?"

"These are difficult questions to answer; can you remember when you were created? The answer is no, because neither you nor spirit people are able to remember where they came from. I will do my best; the problem is there are different stories. I can only explain to you what I believe to be the truth.

The energy of new spirits is produced from what we call the Over soul, the pulsations of the energy sends out what looks like hailstorms of soul substance. They are carried forward in a stream with other new spirits into a bright enclosed area where they are met by very loving evolved spirit beings that take care of them, in a spiritual nursery.

These beautiful and loving beings known as Incubator Mothers then open what looks like membrane golden sacs, this is where the new baby spirits are kept. They are similar to the uterus of human mothers.

There is beautiful intense music surrounding them, with nurturing lights of swirling energy. What happens next is that the new souls become aware and gradually they join other children who are in a different place where there are what is called Incubator Mothers, they act like midwifes who are warm, gentle and caring.

All new souls have their own incubators where they stay until their growth is sufficient to be moved away from the Incubator room.

The swelling mass of new spirits increase and push their way out, becoming a formless shape and then a new spirit is born. It's totally alive with an energy and distinctness of its own. Then we are able to help the young ones grow, to find their unique identity."

"Thank you for that, I can imagine these small spirits being born. Where do you think the Presence, Oneness, Over-soul, whatever you call the Energy comes from?"

"Everywhere."

"How do you know about this and what does the energy feel like from the above Presence?"

"We ask questions from those who know. To answer the second question, it could well be the same force of which the Presence is a part, I don't know, all I know is it feels enormous and powerful, yet there is a feeling of gentleness. There is also a sound very quietly like a whisper, the sound of purity."

"What creates the sound? Is it energy? "

"Sound creates everything, energy and light. When I am with my group of friends we can unite, combine our minds to the sound and then we see pictures in our minds of geometric designs and patterns. I feel the sound moves and undulates creating everything; it sounds like a mother singing sweet music to her child.
    I am told the very young souls have very limited memories of being created from tiny

particles of energy. They say that the energy comes from dancing, colourful illuminating lights. And these lights seem to pulsate and send out showers of individual soul energies that move forward in a line into a very light room. They are reassuring, beautiful lights which seem to penetrate, and they have a wonderful soft delicate music that surrounds them as they become more and more aware.

When this happens they are then moved to join other children in a different place where these new souls have spirit mothers who take care and nurture them; these are beautiful and loving beings.

We are not sure what happens because there are varying stories for instance, some young souls say there is a place where spirits are hatched from egg like shapes of very small white living energy of love that exhibits all the colours of the rainbow. From the mass of energy, a new spirit begins to appear and take shape.

When they are ready, new souls who are fresh from the security of the spirit world start out with simple tasks to find out what each of the major emotions feel like in a body. Then they will move onto major projects with more complicated scenarios.

Each incarnation nourishes personal growth, knowledge and understanding. Life-lessons become more complex, and an individual soul may finish its cycle of incarnations by searching or the true meaning of love and bringing the sensation of unconditional love into the physical body. I do hope this answers your question?"

"Yes thank you very much. I now have a picture in my mind of these small lines of new spirits; it's fascinating."

Occupations.

I asked Daniel. "You told us a while ago that spirits do not sit around doing nothing. Can you please expand on that, and tell us what do they do?"

"Typical afterlife occupations are many and various, such as nurses, doctors, botanists, scientists, librarians, musicians, artists, writers and more. However, we in the beyond do have some relaxation and play time with many activities.

There is so much to do, spirit people often help those in need on earth in practical ways, for example, wounded people on earth need to be given the courage and strength to go on living even though they may be crippled. There are those who have lost their homes in floods and hurricanes, they need strength to rebuild their lives again. And of course healing the sick and helping to prove survival are all important. They also work with groups analysing hunger problems and try to transfer their knowledge, their solutions telepathically to specialists on earth working on the same problems. There are also scientists trying hard to inspire all those who are trying to help human kind. Individuals do not change when they come to the spirit world; they still want to continue with their work. The thought transference to earth of helpful ideas is a common activity of spirits."

"Thank you, it sounds wonderful."

Specialists and nursery teachers.

"I will continue with spirit Specialists; we do have spirit specializing in various types of work. It is just like when a person graduates from university on earth they receive a diploma, the same thing applies in the spirit world. This is a record of the students many work lives, it gives details of their winning achievements and how difficulties were overcome.

Following the ceremonies, the students like those on earth, gather around to talk of new coursework with the new spirits who they have met in the same special area. These new graduates, who are in fact advanced spirit beings, teachers in training and some are called Nursery Teachers, they are working with very young spirits who have not yet begun their incarnations, away from the realms of spirit.

The special project mission is to care for the young spirits that come from the Divine energy of all creation and nurture them with love and tenderness. Eventually the new spirits are taken to the nursery and after nurturing; they are passed on to trained, wise, knowledgeable spiritual teachers.

Usually a new spirit is not necessarily incarnated into a physical world such as the earth because they need time adjusting to planetary life free of a physical body. Your planet is such a very hard and difficult school for training, nevertheless they have eventually to experience your heavy and difficult physical world, that is why they are taught how to collect the earth's magnetic vibrations and to combine them with their own energy vibrations so that they are able to feel what it would be like in a physical form whilst they are safe in the spirit realms.

Working with new child spirits is very challenging and a great deal of patience is needed because many of them do not seem to be able to move on with their incarnations and will require some corrective helpful studies. They have a short energy pattern and their colour have smaller white lights, whereas very innocent child spirits have dim coloured lights; they are full of life just like youngsters on earth.

Spirit beings who have reached this level of existence are allowed to work with these spirit people before finishing their tiresome reincarnations to earth. They are capable of giving advice to those spirits because they have been in their situation themselves. However they are not allowed to help the very troubled, less developed or difficult spirits.

There are many women in your world who longed for children and could not have them, for whatever reason, will indeed be pleased as their longings will be fulfilled in caring for children who arrived here before their parents."

Children.

"Thank you Daniel. Please will you explain to us what happens to our children when they die before us?"

"I have just said that children whose parents are still on the earth plane are cared for by the most beautiful and motherly spirits who in their earth life were especially fond of children.

The children are educated in every branch of knowledge and those who have special tastes for music, painting and other accomplishments are given every opportunity to cultivate these talents.

Some children who had not lived on earth seemed to be more spiritual but not as sympathetic or affectionate as those who had experienced a mother love on earth. No one, let alone a child would prefer to leave this world to go to the earth plane of suffering and pain."

"I'm afraid that doesn't make sense Daniel." I said. "You tell us that we have lived many, many times, in fact hundreds or thousands of times; which I believe. Yet when a child or baby dies you tell us that they are looked after by a spirit person inferring they are children. How can that be true? If we have lived all those times we must be an adult spirit person and not a child as we are always told. Can you please enlighten us? I must say, I have wanted to ask that question for a long time now Daniel."

"Yes, that is a very good question, and I can understand your confusions; both are true. Some children remain in the spirit world to continue for a while, they need to experience a child's growth from my world; later to incarnate again when they are better equipped to learn. Whilst others are found alternative parents and are usually incarnated again very quickly.

Let me say before you ask, the child spirits leave some of their energy behind to welcome their earth parents when they arrive in my world. I hope that answers your question?"

"No, that does not answer my question."

"It is entirely up to the spirit whether it wants to remain as a child for a while longer. And sometimes they have to go through their childhood again for whatever reason. And you are correct in thinking that they are adult spirit beings. Usually spirit individuals return to their loved ones on earth as they would remember them. But of course they have lived a great number of lives and can choose which body they were comfortable with and take on that particular form."

"Thank you Daniel."

Chapter Twelve.

Spirit Schools.

"Every spirit no matter how far they have evolved has their own individuality and it is expected that all spirits in their group will stand out and contribute. Naturally their characters vary some are forceful spirits and some quiet, no one is in charge and no one dominates, just as no one is obtrusive. Each spirit is unique, with strengths and weaknesses that compliment others in the group.

These differences in character are honoured because spirits share their lives bringing a wealth of personal wisdom to every lifetime experience. Because of this they are allocated to certain soul groups, this is for their differences as well as similarities.

Spirit people are just like human beings they love to tease and have a great sense of humour within their groups, nonetheless they always show respect for one another. They are very tolerant and forgiving even with those who have hurt them in a previous life.

Spirit people volunteer both to teach and learn certain lessons that are one of the reasons they also have visiting teachers who come and go in spiritual study sessions but never interfere with a spirits self-discovery.

Within spirits study groups, there is a wondrous clarity of rational thought. Self-delusion does not exist, however I must say that the motivation to work hard in every life is not always the case for some spirits. People do not change because they are in the realms of spirit. Nevertheless some take a break and slow down their rate of incarnations.

Although the spirit's teachers and council may not be happy with this decision, it is respected, they have free will. Even within the spirit world, some students do not try; they choose not to give their best."

"Thank you for that. Do spirit people have time off, breaks from their schooling?"

"Yes we do, it's not all work and no play. We go to areas and chat with other spirit people. There are various places we can go, for instance I like to go to a garden full of beautiful flowers, the colours are exquisite and there is a wonderful scent in the air, the fragrance is quite intoxicating. There is also a lovely pool which has a vibrating restorative liquid energy. I suppose it is a sort of pampering time for us all, like you do when you go to a spar for treatments."

"Do spirit people get bored with their schooling? I hated school and I am sure there are many others reading this that wouldn't particularly look forward to going back to school in the spirit realms."

"My dear I can assure you, you will enjoy learning, schools are not the same here as on the earth plane, spirit never get bored and their desire is to acquire wisdom and spiritual growth. They enjoy their educational training and they are encouraged to use their creative and original faculties."

Viewing past lives in the library.

"A lot has been talked of karma and debts that we have to pay back. Is there some place where spirit individuals can have a look at their past karmic records to understand what they need to learn and what they have learnt already?"

"Yes of course there is, there are libraries just like you have on the earth plane, but these are timeless places where spirit people can see and study their missed opportunities and responsibilities for past life actions. Whilst they are in the spirit world between lives, their spiritual minds have knowledge of these records. The Akashic Records is a library where records are kept of past, present and future events in a soul's progression on their journey through various and many lives.

The memory or record of all events are implanted in some way upon the 'Akasha', which is a refined substance surrounding the planet earth, a gigantic image a statement, an account or reflection of the lives of all its inhabitants. You also have the imprint on your spirit of all your past lives.

The past life rooms are in a huge open space, which are very busy learning centres for past life viewings. The desks are placed in rows as far as the eye can see and most of the desks are occupied with spirit people studying.

In the books there are life- lines representing important experiences in their life and the age when this is likely to occur. In their own personal books, they can see their past lives good and bad, the mistakes they have made and the good they have done. All this comes alive in three-dimensional colours. There are screens to review past actions involving choices they made right or wrong.

There are also private rooms off the main library for those spirits who are in need of counselling, whilst viewing their lives; these wise souls are non-judgmental, they are very understanding and loving beings always available to assist.

All spirit beings have their own personal books, these are called the 'Akashic Records', we talked about this earlier, and these books hold 'karmic' records for every spirit person in the universe. They hold details of all past lives good and bad, with lists of all the mistakes they have made and the good they have done.

These Akashic record books are not as you would have in the physical world, although they look just the same with pages, but in reality they are made, constructed from sheets of energy that vibrate and form true-life pictures of events.

Spirit people are often occupying these libraries because they are valuable assets to their spiritual growth. They are able to review and evaluate their records by watching live on screen in three-dimension their actions of past life involving choices they made right or wrong.

I must say that this experience has a great impact on a spirit, as you can imagine seeing for themselves all their good and bad performances in their role-play on earth. If you remember, I spoke of your life on earth as being a role that you act out in a play.

Description of the library and future life rooms.

These libraries, which are really learning centres, is not restricted to reviewing past lives there are many various activities and skills. For example; spirit people who visit what is called a life selection room do this before their next incarnation; it speaks for itself the purpose for this is to view their future life, which is vital for them to study to enable them to make the correct selection, the correct life next time around.

These side rooms also have books that are three-dimensional and they also have illuminated viewing screens. The screens here are much larger than those in the libraries and classrooms, so that spirits are able to enter these life-sized screens of destiny.

All viewing screens are multidimensional, and are referred to as lifelines. Spirit individuals are able to scan and manipulate these by thought; they can take a portion of their energy, leaving the rest at the console (computer screen) and enter the screens.

My dears, I am sure that what I am about to explain to you may sound even more incredible. Nevertheless in the spirit world individuals can both observe unseen through screens on earth without having any effects on events, or, they can take part and play roles, be part of the action within the scene, they can even change reality from the original event by re-creating it.

The screens vary in size but that doesn't matter, the spirit can become part of a demonstration of cause and effect sequences; there are no restrictions. However, most spirits are interested in using the smaller screens for observing past events in which they took part.

Spirits are able to move events forward or backward on the screen. It can be shown fast or in slow motion or even suspended for study. It is similar to your video recorders, except spirit can go forward or back in time: Once reviewed everything returns to what it was. All incidences involving the spirit are then available for them to study, as if they were using a movie projector. They are able to blend past and future possibilities into the next incarnation from the present spirit time.

It sounds very complicated, but it is not. The more you go over what I have said in your mind, the simpler it will become and the more you will be able to understand and accept it. However, I have said many time, if what has been said is unacceptable to your intelligence, put it to one side for later."

"Yes it does sound complicated and very much like a futuristic film, sci-fi."

"It is hard to understand things of spirit that is why we are having these conversations so that you may understand and learn more of the real life, spirit life. My dear child, I will do my best to explain to you all that I can and as simple as I can.

Future life rooms.

Future life rooms are small conference rooms, which have tables with a variety of TV-size books. These so-called books have three-dimensional illuminated viewing screens and give the illusion of books with pages, but they are sheets of energy, which vibrate and form life picture-patterns of events. The size of these screens depends upon usage with a given setting.

Life selection rooms are where spirit people visit before their next incarnation. These screens are much larger than seen in spiritual libraries and classrooms. Spirits are given the option of entering these life-sized screens. The huge, shimmering screens usually encircle the spirit and they have been called the ring of destiny.

Despite the impressive size of the screens in future-life selection rooms, spirits spend far more time looking at scenes in the library.

The function of the smaller library screens is for monitoring past time on earth on a continuing basis. All screens large or small are sheets of film, which look like waterfalls that can be, entered while part of the spirits energy stays in the room.

Regardless of the screen size, the length, width and depth in each frame allows the spirit to become part of a procession of cause and effect sequences. While there are no restrictions for time travel study, most spirits appear to use the smaller screens more for observing past events in which they participated. Spirits take a portion of their energy, leaving the rest at the console, and enter the screens in one or two ways. First they enter as observers moving as unseen ghosts through screens on earth with no influence on events. I see this as working with virtual reality. Secondly, as participants where they will assume roles in the action of the scene, even to the extent of altering reality from the original by re-creations.

Once reviewed everything returns to what it was since the constant reality of a past event on a physical world remains the same from the perspective of the soul who took part in the original event.

It is obvious that an unseen entity is re-creating a past life scene, but with alterations. The adjustments are intended to prompt sympathy, understanding and teach the spirit an example of entering worlds of altered time and causality through screens found in books, desk consoles and viewing theatres, although these space-time training exercises do not change the original historical event on earth.

Events on any screen can be moved forward or backward. They can be placed into fast or slow motion or suspended for study. All possibilities of occurrences involving the viewer are then available for study, as if they were using a movie projector. Past and future possibilities in the next life can be blended in the next life from an always-present spirit time.

Evaluation with soul group members.

My dears, there is so much more to learn. Life selection rooms are very important because spirit people need to understand the meaning and purpose of their many lives.

Most spirit individuals are determined to re-examine their last life in order to see why they did certain things, not wanting to make the same mistakes again so that when the time comes for them to incarnate again, their guides will be there to help and view the scenes of their past life with them. Their guides show them their life pictures and discuss with them their good and bad times, including all their mistakes or errors of judgement they made.

Their aim is always to improve with each life, with each performance, with each role play, so that when they have finished with their review they can return to their group souls in a more positive way.

The group studies all the individual scenes that were played when on earth and the outcome of their past life are studied and compared in detail, the group write new scripts, new roles and act out various scenes of their last life, showing alternative ways that a situation could have been changed or resolved, so that they can perform better in their next visit to earth; this will help them to balance their karmic book."

"Thank you. That sounds very helpful and exciting for them."

"Yes it is helpful because they are able to see and understand their mistakes, and by re-creating their past life and seeing alternatives is a good way for them to understand their future life. As you can see it is very important that members of the group join in by acting out different roles, to get the best results for the incarnating spirit, especially when each scene is minutely dissected.

It eventually shows various ways, different choices the soul could have made in each situation. And as you said my dear, this performance is important and exciting for the spirits concerned, as they all play scenes differently thereby giving an even better view of any situation. It is a good way for spirit individuals to increase their perspective.

Their guides keep an eye on them, watching and evaluating the performance, they are wise and encouraging and they are always a motivating force, never judging or intimidating.

It is a long hard road for spirit to continually incarnate, but finally, after many, many incarnations they know when they have reached that certain level of skill and development that they worked so hard for and achieved."

Living between incarnations.

"There is so much information to learn, but I must say I want more and more. Can you please tell us what spirit do with their time between incarnations, apart from what you have told us so far about halls of learning etc.?"

"There are many and various ways spirit people spend their time between lives and this can change depending on their desires and of course the level of existence a soul has aspired.

We have talked about spirit people choosing their appearance whilst in the realms of spirit, but for some this can be very traumatic for various reasons.

There are some spirits who wish to remain as a child for a while longer, and there are some who do not like to be rid of their disability, they feel that they still need to be restricted for a time longer until they are able to understand the lesson they had to learn from this. Always, there are experienced souls who help all those in need. And of course it is very different for younger spirits (who have not been to earth many times) when they return, mostly they are confused by all the information they have gained on earth and the information that is now available to them in the world of spirit, they are inclined to suffer from 'overload' this including everything that has been experienced by their companions when they were in a physical body. They find all this information is very confusing so they have to ask for assistance and for advice on what may be done with it.

There are groups of spirits who had similar experiences of another member while on earth, such as having committed suicide or something equally traumatic. They find that by getting together to share their experiences they may better understand the implications of their own feelings and the reactions of other people. Souls who are more able to deal with this take the position of counsellor to help those who are experiencing difficulties.

There are many experienced spirits who communicates with those on earth, which often help them to see things differently and it gives them ideas of what they might accomplish next time around. As the spirits observe what else is happening on the planet and elsewhere it helps them to decide what new journeys and events would increase their knowledge, their wisdom. These spirits begin talking with the council to plan the next incarnation; this can take up a considerable length of time, as you know it.

Usually once the soul has had the opportunity to finish going over its most recent life, it spends time catching up with friends and soul mates, finding out what they have been up to during their earth journeys. Or, the spirit may have become involved in some activity or other on earth and wants to observe its ongoing development carefully, or if developed enough the spirit may even try to assist those souls on earth still engaged in the said project.

There is much more help needed in many situations and there are always a number of experienced spirits always available to help."

"Thank you, I must say I find it fascinating and mind boggling. I'm sure I will find some questions to ask once I have given it some thought."

"Call on me at any time if there is anything you do not understand. Meanwhile I will leave you now and say good night."

"Good night Daniel and thank you."

We do enjoy our evenings with Daniel and never want them to come to an end. However, we all need to rest and to digest all that has been said. In between our wonderful lessons with Daniel we all get together and discuss any issues not understood or rejected. We can then talk to Daniel about them at our next meeting.

Chapter Thirteen.

Reincarnation.

"Good evening and thank you Daniel we are all so lucky to have you here helping us, we are so grateful. Reincarnation can be quite puzzling therefore, would you please explain to us why we hear different stories from the spirit world regarding reincarnation? Surely if we are all in the same spirit world we would know if we had reincarnated or not. Daniel, we need to know if reincarnation is true or not. Whilst I accept reincarnation there are others who do not, therefore would you please confirm if it is true?"

"Good evening my dears. I feel what I am about to tell you will be difficult for you to understand but I will do my best to keep it simple. Let me first say I am here because it is a privilege for me to be able to teach those on earth who have a thirst for knowledge, knowledge is very important for your spiritual growth.

I will try and clear up the confusion regarding reincarnation so that you can understand it, and yes I agree there are conflicting stories about reincarnation and you do need to have clarification. There have always been differences of opinion in our world and yours, amongst those who know, and those who do not know. There are many who say there is no such thing as reincarnation. This is because they are on a different mental plane of existence, a different level. There are many spirits who know they have incarnated before and there are others who do not. Their consciousness may know, but the mind may not. Nevertheless, there are many accounts from spirit people who are just as insistent in rejecting the idea of reincarnation as there are those equally forceful in believing in reincarnation because of their experience.

The confusion is caused because spirit people who reside in the lower realms of existence have no memory of ever living before; this is because of their lack of knowledge. In addition, because of where they live all those on that level have never met anyone who knows they have been reincarnated.

Those who belong to higher realms state that reincarnation is a truth; both kinds of accounts exist and are true to those who communicate, that is why there is confusion. If, for example, you ask a spirit on the 'Astral Plane' to describe the place in which they live, you will find the description will be completely different in every detail to the place where a higher evolved spirit being belongs. Another example, if you were to move to a different country on earth, say somewhere warm, sunny and beautiful and a friend moved to a different country that is undeveloped and basic your descriptions of where you live would be completely different, and yet you both live on the Physical world. Do you understand how both descriptions are correct?"

"Yes when you put it that way, I can. Thank you so much."

"We do try over and over again to explain to those in your world but sadly they will only accept things of spirit when they are ready.

All spirits have a theoretical knowledge of everything, but they will not fully know the subject until they have experienced it themselves. For example, if you haven't experienced love, how can you know love? This is the reason why souls continue to reincarnate, coming back to earth time and again to the dense heavy conditions to learn, some are blessed on their travels by the knowledge gained on their previous spiritual paths. You will continue gathering knowledge and memories on your many journeys until you no longer need to reincarnate. When that time come you will have advanced to the higher realms, and your permanent spirit body becomes a much lighter and beautiful body.

Before you achieve your promotion to live on the higher realms, you do live many, many times as differing people with different beliefs, different backgrounds, colour and creed and lived in various countries of the earth. To gain knowledge you must reincarnate because a large part of your spiritual growth is information gathered for your individual evolvement on the planet earth, or other planets you may reside. The intention is to take a new body, either physical or other, depending where you go and to attaining spiritual growth through each experience from the trials and tribulations set out before you.

You have come across many people during your travels, learning and experiencing all that your soul needs to know to enable it to grow and evolve. And during those many lives, you have created good and bad karma; this has a knock on effect on your life today; cause and effect. What you sow, you reap! Are you beginning to understand? Is everything fitting into place? "

"Yes Daniel, thank you."

"Good. Let me tell you, some people have terrible fears, cravings and phobias, unable to see how they came about in that particular lifetime. And there are others souls who have a terrible life emotionally and or mentally, they have hard times with pain and suffering. Whereas there are those who seem to have everything, which seems to be unfair to those who are suffering; It is not unfair, I say it is mostly karma, they are reaping what they have sown in a previous existence, time to pay back.

However, there are those who ask for a particular incarnation no matter how hard it will be for them, they do this because they feel a need for that experience or they are incarnating to assist another soul; this would be a charitable act.

So my dears remember when you feel badly done by, you are only getting back what you deserve and at times you will feel miserable, instead, be thankful for your lessons and pray you will learn from them.

Regardless of the extent in which you learn, you are all created equal and remain equal, some spirit people learn quicker than others but that doesn't matter as long as you progress in your own time. The things that you experience and the knowledge that you acquire throughout all of your lifetimes helps to define who you truly are this is stored in your memory bank and in the Akashic Records, which we discussed at an earlier time."

"If we are to believe in reincarnation, and I do, would you please tell me the reasons why we have to live again many times?" Emma asked.

"I thought I had explained this to you. Every spirit needs to incarnate, all of you, including myself and those on the higher rungs of the ladder have had to return to earth in order to learn from their trials and abilities missed out before, as long as there is anything that has not been resolved or completed at the end of each individual lifetime, they will need to incarnate again, and again, and again until everything has been resolved. The only way forward is for the spirit to return to the earth plane to resolve and to heal the problems they have created within themselves through many lifetimes, many incarnations. And my dears, this can take a long time.

It is never easy for those who are incarnating, they are afraid and uncertain how their new life will turn out, they do not know if they are going to make the same mistakes again and if so will they be able to endure the trials all over again. They strive to be successful but sometimes for some it is not that easy. They have some idea from their discussions with their guides and the elders as to what lessons, what trials good or bad is waiting for them; it is a solemn moment. The experience is similar to what most of you feel when faced with death of the physical body.

You ask me why you incarnate many times. The answer my dear is you continue to make mistakes; therefore, you are trapped on the invisible tread mill getting know where. As long as you have karma to pay you will incarnate repeatedly to perfect the lessons and repay what you owe. It is not all bad you have credits too.

Earth is your school and your physical body is your school uniform, your lessons are available in the form of experiences. As I have just stated before you incarnate whilst in the spirit realms and with the help of your guides and wise spiritual beings, you decide the lessons you wish to learn and those you need to redo to enable you to progress, to get off the tread mill. Although, it is not that easy, there is memory loss during the process of incarnation into the heavy world of matter; therefore, you must live your life to the best of your ability, listen to your conscience it will lead you forward on your spiritual growth."

"Thank you."

"When you learn from your trials on earth and balance your karmic debts, you are progressing; however, not everyone moves forward at the same speed, some take longer than others. It does not depend on how many times you have incarnated, it depends on the evolution of the soul and how you have grown. You can be in the physical world and be a highly evolved soul in service to humanity, or you can be the lowest of the low."

"It is hard to digest, but I think I understand. Thank you Daniel, is there an organisation or someone in the spirit world to control reincarnation, to prevent mistakes being made?

"There can be no mistakes; everything is ruled

by the operation of natural laws. If a spirit wishes to reincarnate they do so at a time when they have a greater awareness and realise what they can achieve by residing again on the earthly plane.

The incarnating spirit will need guidance and assistance from those who are knowledgeable and also visits to the selection rooms, to choose the family and the body that will best serve the spirit individual to learn what is needed to progress, therefore the answer is yes; natural laws."

"Thank you. Please can you tell us if we complete all our existences on the earth plane?"

"Not all your lives, no. There are many different worlds, the earth being one of the most material, the most gross, and the furthest from perfection. Spirit will remain incarnating to earth or other low material worlds as long as the spirit remains insufficiently advanced to pass on to a higher place.

There are spirits who can return from other worlds and incarnate for the first time on your planet, just as you can go to other worlds; what you do not accomplish in one can be accomplished in another. Some are sent to accomplish special work on other worlds in connection with that world, by divine ordering. In addition, a spirit person can live in a relatively inferior planet to perform a mission; in that way, they are made to contribute their share towards the general state of wellbeing, while achieving their advancement.

Those of you on earth are at varying degrees of advancement; it is the same in other worlds and there are quite a few worlds which are of a similar degree as the earth.

There are many reasons for wishing to reincarnate, as I have said, to put right past wrongs, to experience and strengthen you, to learn more about emotions and other lessons. With each incarnation, there are new experiences to learn to help you on your way to perfection.

It is a long road for you all and earth offers opportunities for growth not available elsewhere. Once you have mastered the lessons of the earth plane, and other inferior worlds your spirit can reach to the higher realms of the universe in service."

"What you are saying is quite intriguing, thank you. When a spirit moves from one planet to another, do they remember, do they retain what they have learnt in previous lives and on different planets?"

"Spirits people never move backwards in their knowledge, they retain all they have gained when passing from one world to another.

Intelligence is never lost, however, they may not have the same means of expressing it, and this depends on the degree of advancement and on the quality of the body they use and how they can influence that being."

"Thank you, I always thought I had lived on a different planet." Can you tell me what happens if a spirit prefers to stay in the spirit world and does not want to go back to suffer all over again?"

"All spirit beings have to ascend; it is their destiny, it is the law of the Great Spirit. There are no exclusions. That is why reincarnation is so necessary for spirit to gain knowledge, advance and move upwards to the higher spheres. For some it takes time but eventually they will feel the need to grow. If you were to remain in the spirit world, you would not progress and would remain stationary; this is not good for any spiritual being. Even so, there are some spirits who are happy to stay as they are, not ready to undergo the trials and tribulations of physical life. However, they are not allowed to prolong this indefinitely and will suffer from the delay by putting off the inevitable. In some cases, the uncertainty of their future is too fearful to them, whereas some never give it a second thought. It all depends on the degree of advancement of the spirit."

"Thank you. Why does the incarnated spirit have no remembrance of the past, and how can they be responsible for their actions and atone for faults if they cannot remember? Surely it would make their life on earth much easier if they knew what mistakes they had made in a previous life."

"To answer your question, many do remember some things but in a fragmentary way. Because you do not remember the past you are more able to be yourselves, if you remembered your past you would behave differently, you would have no freedom of will therefore your actions would be false. Because of this you are better able to distinguish between good and evil and with each new existence; you become more intelligent and spiritually aware. Do you understand what I am saying?"

"Yes, I think so. We would pretend to care and do the right thing even if we would rather do the opposite; it would be false and wouldn't come from the soul."

"Yes that is correct. As I explained earlier, no matter how you live your lives, when you return to the spirit world, your actions are revealed to you during the time when you judge yourself. Your guides and the elders show you where you went wrong, all your faults and how you could have avoided them. Then when it is time to reincarnate you are better equipped with help, to choose your next body so that you can repair the mistakes you have made. You are never alone, superior spirits will help you in your new life, they will try to guide you so that you no longer make the same mistakes and rid you of your wrongdoings."

"You have talked about all our life-times and how we need to learn through experience but can you tell me how can a spirit reach perfection?"

"As I have explained by undergoing new lives on earth and experiencing other spheres many times, the number of lives differ for different spirits, this depends on the purity, the knowledge and wisdom of the spirit; the spiritual growth is always the deciding factor."

"Can a spirit choose what world to live in?"

"Generally it is not possible, nevertheless, a spirit can request to incarnate onto another world, but again it will be determined by the spirits achievements before any decision can be made. In addition, other worlds have various levels in their spirit realms and are only accessible to spirits according to the degree of their spiritual growth."

397

"I understand. Are the physical and moral standards the same on other worlds as with earth?"

"No, not at all, the physical and moral qualities of human beings are one of the least advanced of all the worlds in our solar system.

Every spirit is subject to the law of progression wherever they dwell, whatever world they reside. We in the spirit realms look forward to a time when eventually the earth planet will also experience a transformation, similar to that which has been achieved in other worlds.

Sometime in the distant future all classes, creeds, races that now exist on earth will gradually disappear and will be succeeded by more advanced, perfect beings. It will take a considerable time, as you know it, but what a wonderful place the universe will be, when all spirits have evolved and are perfect. Don't you agree?"

"Yes I most certainly do. Can you tell me if highly evolved pure spirits are restricted to any one particular world?"

"No, these spirits are able to travel anywhere they wish instantaneously. As I have said to you, those who are on a higher sphere can go down, but those who are on a lower place cannot go higher, therefore those on the highest, purist level can go anywhere."

"That sounds wonderful. It makes me wonder how many lives I still have to endure on earth before I reach purity, it doesn't bare thinking about. Never mind, I will have to wait and see."

"My dear children, there is a long way to go and there is much to do in the world of spirit, you have no idea, it is beyond your comprehension."

"Can you give us some examples please?"

"Let me see. There are some highly evolved spirit beings that look after all the planets and the natural world. And there are evolved beings sending radiations from the sun to other worlds in our solar system and there are many beings who are devoted to taking care of the whole universe, and much, much more."

"Wow. Thank you for that. I always thought there were other inhabited worlds. I have had dreams where I was living on a different planet; unfortunately, I am not sure where it was. I understand that we are all born as inferior spirits, so can you explain to me, what is the state of the soul when it first incarnates? I have a picture in my mind of what I call raw undeveloped souls, who have no idea of what is right and wrong."

"That is a good question. Very young souls, baby souls, in their first incarnations will be given a very simple life, because their intelligence is only beginning to develop, they are just starting to live. They don't usually stay very long, just long enough to test the atmosphere of the earth perhaps a week or month or two. Whereas, teenage souls, if I may call them that, go out into the world and sometimes create havoc. The same applies on earth, when you have teenagers they can make your life very difficult, not wanting to do as you ask, they think they know better than you. Both in your world and mine they create karma for themselves by misusing their energy. Then we have those who are middle-aged souls, so to speak, who are becoming wiser and are repaying karmic debts they have created during their many lifetimes. Old souls, as you would expect are much wiser and peaceful."

"That makes sense to me, are you also saying that babies who die early are usually young baby souls?"

"In some cases, but not in all, it is not quite as simple as that. We have discussed other reasons why babies leave your world early."

"Thank you. You say it is only young teenage

souls who will cause havoc but what about evil, bad spirits are they also in a state of infancy?"

"Of relative infancy but they are spirits that have already accomplished a certain amount of development because they have feelings of emotions, passions and desires to choose to do ill. Do you understand?"

"Yes I think so. But can you tell me; are passions and emotions a sign of development?"

"But of course, of development yes, but certainly not of perfection. There are passions and emotions of evil as well as goodness. All spirits must go through the various existences to reach perfection, morally as well as intellectually, this can take many, many lifetimes to accomplish.

My dear children, the only way you are able to grow and develop spiritually is to incarnate to situations that are difficult so that you may be successful through all the trials and hardship you need to experience. Whereas, if you are given an easier, more agreeable life, you may not understand, you may not learn the true meaning behind your many lives. Never forget the trials you take on board are what you chose before incarnation to help you move upwards on the ladder to perfection; this is what we all desire and what we aim for.

There is good karma as well as bad karma it is

up to you. Whichever way you decide to live your life on earth, you are able to return home to the spirit realms with the rewards of all your achievements as well as the debts you have created. You come back to the spirit realms with your particular qualities you have acquired, through each succeeding life. You must then concentrate on perfecting these qualities, these characteristics.

As you grow and evolve and move upwards through spiritual planes of existence, to the higher realms of consciousness, you are able to see and recognise the imperfections within you, within your being. Because you long to progress, to grow, to reflect and express more of spiritual reality, you choose to return to the heavy earth plane again to improve yourselves. However, as long as you continue to live your lives in your old ways you continue to create karma and endure the treadmill of having to reincarnate over and over again.

In every incarnation to earth, you are more than likely to be faced with what you did in a previous life, your inner weaknesses and flaws. You already know, what you sow, you reap, therefore, the seeds you have sown come back to you, as difficulties and trials for you to put right, to amend, or as gifts and opportunities. I always say 'if it is worth having, it is worth working for.' Therefore, all the suffering you endure brings rewards of an inner growth a spiritual step forward."

"Thank you for that Daniel. I believe in reincarnation, and karma. It certainly helps me when things seem impossible."

"That is good, for when you accept reincarnation, you will begin to understand many aspects in your life, you will notice how actions and situations come together just like a jigs saw puzzle, to show you the reasons as they are lived out. You are then able to comprehend a little more of the meaning behind all life, your life. Therefore, reincarnation must help to lighten your load and outlook to the idea and understanding the workings of the continuation of life after death.

When eventually your time comes for you to return to the spirit world, as I explained earlier, you will have to go through the process of self-judgment with the helping hand of your loving guide and caring and loving elders. You will be able to see what you have done in your life on earth, good and bad."

"Thank you Daniel. I can imagine why people do not want to go back home to the spirit realms. There are a lot of things I have done that I am not proud of."

"We have all done things that we have regretted

at some time that is why we have to incarnate many times. Therefore you must understand not to attempt to judge any ones spiritual stature merely by their earthly circumstances. 'Judge not, lest you be judged yourself.'

Poor homeless souls may be much further forward in terms of spiritual wisdom, than the person who derides, who looks down on them. It is always better to know the laws of the Great Spirit than not to know. It is always better to search for truth, carefully and patiently rather than not doing so, and it is always better to strive for progression because if anything is worth having, it is worth working for. I am sure you will agree?"

"Yes I do. If everyone has to make themselves perfect, does this imply that eventually we would all be the same and look like one another?"

"No that is not so, each spirit remains unique, distinctive with all their individual strengths and weaknesses."

"If a spirit has lived many times, it must have retained a vast amount of knowledge and wisdom, so why doesn't that show when in a physical body?"

"That is a good question. When a spirit

incarnates into a physical body the soul is restricted to the amount of wisdom it can express compared with what it has acquired, what it has earned during the many lifetimes before incarnating. The amount of wisdom that can be conveyed in your heavy world is very limited because all spiritual expression is restricted by the faculties of the physical body."

"If the spirit knows the experiences and sufferings that lie ahead, does it know the results of its life?

"Yes, before incarnation, the spirit knows, in the vast majority of cases, which path it is to tread.

Whilst the soul is on the earth it can gain necessary experiences to meet the requirements needed for the work it has to do when it returns to the spirit world. It does not matter how many books you read, or how many people you may speak to, all knowledge must be strengthened by experience. It is experience and your response to it, which determines your spiritual growth. Which path you go down, the path you agreed or a different one it is entirely up to you, you have free will. This is the whole purpose of your earthly incarnation, to learn and to grow."

"Is our life span on earth predetermined, or is it a question of the state of the physical body, or some other factor?"

"It is all part of your plan before you incarnate. The physical make-up of the body is important for the soul to have the necessary experience for its growth on earth; the two go together. The conclusion, the time of death in most cases is known in advance, there is no such thing as an accident everything is planned before incarnation.

Time to incarnate.

When a spirit has chosen to incarnate as a new human being it needs some help and guidelines to live on earth. As I said it arrives on your planet with no memory concerning what it had agreed, what contracts it made. If it were to remember it would not be able to experience the lessons it came to earth to overcome.

Some of the paths a soul can follow are limited in the contracts it has made with other spirits. For example, it may need to experience addiction, therefore it would choose an alcoholic family or a family who were addicted to drugs, or it could be a lesson of sexual uncertainly that may have been selected. As the soul enters the foetus the necessary information is downloaded into the foetus for it to have the chosen inclinations.

Also contained in the records downloaded into the new body is the remainder of lessons not completed in prior lifetimes, such as fears, desires and natural instincts that were strong in a past life. This is what you would refer to as Karma."

Elsie spoke again. "Thank you Daniel, the picture you are painting is becoming much clearer now and I am sure the more you teach us the better we will become.
We were wondering how spirits know when it is time for them to incarnate. Would you please explain it to us?"

"It is very simple my dear. Every spirit can sense when their time is near, they know when they need to make that decision to return to the earth plane, they can feel inside the need to move on and face the challenges that are waiting for them in the physical world; they know this will help them in their spiritual growth. It is for some a sad time a fearful time, but for others they cannot wait to return. No matter how they feel about their incarnation there are always spirit helpers to assist them in the first stage of their journey.
  Once they have made the decision to return to the earth plane they have a preliminary meeting with the elders to plan their next incarnation; this is held in front of the council. Spirit people feel very vulnerable about their past life performance, even though their guides have debriefed them first. Their guides are notified

when it is time for the spirit person to go before the council; the incarnating spirit is then escorted to the arranged meeting place with these wonderful wise beings, the Ascended Masters the Elders.

As spirit individuals grow and move upwards through the realms of consciousness, they can feel and recognise within themselves all their imperfections, so they prepare to return to earth with the knowledge they have gained from many previous lives, in order to learn, understand and produce a better outcome next time around. It is only by returning to earth can they acquire the experience through lessons and trials.

The Great Spirit, God has willed that their action should equip them with the means to progress and advance towards perfection. Therefore, when the time of their council meeting arrives there is mixed reactions. However, the wise ones make spirits who come before them feel welcome immediately. They are loving and resolute teachers who encourage these students who are preparing for their new journey to a heavy physical world again."

Interrupting Daniel a member of the circle said. "Are some spirits more intelligent and experienced than others and therefore have fewer incarnations?"

"My dear children, we are all created simple and ignorant; we gain our education in the struggles and trials of earthly life. So to answer your question, all spirits can only advance by following the right road, which will help them to arrive more quickly at their objectives.

Those of you who have imperfections such as, lack of compassion, love, envy and greed will have to undergo the torments that are the outcome of those defects. The sufferings of life are the imperfection of the spirit; therefore, the fewer imperfections, the less will be your sufferings. I have also lived many times on the earth plane learning and going through many trial and hardships just as you, therefore I can understand how you feel. Again and again I say 'what you sow, you will reap'.

As I have just stated the spirits who are about to incarnate have a second visit to the council just before reincarnation takes place; this is much more relaxed and a less formal discussion regarding their impending life choices, the opportunities and prospects for their next life on earth. The reasons for the discussions with the elders are to help the spirits achieve their objectives and their ambitions in the next lifetime; the questions are both well-founded and yet kindly. Every spirit individual is aware of their life review, but even so, they are still nervous. Therefore, it is of utmost importance for incarnating spirits to attend their second council meeting to decide their next incarnation.

I have said so often, spirit people live in a mental world, therefore they are all telepathic. Hence, the elders know everything about the spirits who are attending before their meeting, they know the whole truth about every feature, every facet of their behaviour, the choices and the mistakes they made in their previous life, cheating or lying is impossible. I am sure my dears you can understand how very crucial the meeting is?

The elders are already bearing in mind the spirits next potential body and future environment therefore, they must question and explore all the information for answers on how they think their previous body served or hindered development. In addition, during the meeting it is important to reflect over how the mind of their student connected with their human brain in a previous life; this is important and has to be carefully analysed.

The elders are looking to see if the students' honesty, their truthfulness in terms of values, ideals and moral actions during their earth lives were upheld in their inner nature, their inner character, the personality of their spirit. They want to know if the soul successfully blended in unity with the human brain as one agreeable and harmonious personality.

They are questioned as to how they feel about major incidents in their previous life and how they dealt with them and what action they took. The elders look at the necessary and desirable actions, and those that were not fruitful, that were not productive, then they are discussed openly with them without bitterness. They are also asked if they were influenced in a positive way, or did they need to control others. Alternatively, were they easily led by others beliefs or desires demonstrating no personal ability or control.

It doesn't matter how many times they continue to make the same mistakes, the council of elders have enormous patience with them. The council is not concerned about how many times the spirit person fell down in their progress through life, but whether they had the courage to pick themselves up and start again. Do you see how much there is to consider?"

"Goodness me, yes there is a lot. Are we allowed to select the body we are to control, including the imperfections if it is to help assist us, and are we able to choose the tasks ourselves, or must they be given to us?"

"Yes my dear, both happen although, to a point. There are spirit individuals who are too backward to be able to choose wisely for themselves; in that case, higher knowledgeable beings will choose the physical body that will provide them with different trials that is best suited for them. In addition, there are those poor souls who are very un-evolved, with little spiritual understanding; usually they are incarnated very quickly. Because of their lack of understanding and their consciousness nearer to earth they need to return quickly to help them to learn and to grow. Therefore, they will return sooner rather than later. Having said that, spirit people do have a choice, in that, they are able to delay the moment of return until they feel more able to cope with a new life. However, they are not allowed to delay indefinitely.

All spirit individuals are given many differing bodies and all of them are imperfect which will help them to grow, to learn and to evolve. Choosing a new life always depends on the spirits stage of development when it comes to the choices they are given in their next life. Their past lives are revealed to them very quickly in a flash, but not in every detail. They are shown what they can do and what they should do.

Each spirit person is advised by their council as to the kind of life that is necessary for them to undertake for the next stage of their evolution. The more evolved a spirit is, the harder is the task they choose. Those who have mastered most situations, naturally do not want elementary tasks, therefore evolved souls choose to face many difficulties when they return to your world to face and deal with. When this happens they are able to tap into their undeveloped qualities of their spirit that can now find fuller expression and when they return again to the world of spirit they have a bigger contribution to make than before.

As to the time that elapses between one incarnation and the next, I am unable to say, it will depend upon the process of learning, which will be very different for everyone. You see, each spirit chooses what to do and what to learn during its time on planet earth. The selection made both in the spirit world and on earth, involves the soul's ability to exercise its freedom of choice.

The only solution for all of you is to continue with the process to improve yourselves to evolve and become better than you are. One must always try to develop the element of goodness. Reincarnation will come about when the time is ripe."

"Thank you that's very interesting. I was wondering, when you leave the spirit world, is it a form of dying?"

"Yes, what you call death is spiritual birth and what you call birth is spiritual death."

Contracts between souls.

"Daniel I think you mentioned that spirit make contracts with other spirits within their group. Is

413

that correct and if so can you explain, give us more information?"

"Yes, as I have said, all incarnating spirits going back to earth meet with their guides and the council of elders who helps them to decide what lessons are needed for them to move forward. Having discussed the lessons or experiences the spirits needs to enable them to move forward and upwards. They will need help to decide what type of parents will assist the journeys of the spirits, taking into account the needs of the parents in their new life. In this process they will decide the gender of the spirit so that they will be able to accomplish the spirits plans, this will include whether they will be heterosexual or homosexual.

The spirits will also try to include any skills they have developed in prior lives that help in some way in their new life. It is very important that they seek to make contracts with other spirits in the group who may have planned to incarnate at the same time and are willing to help to fulfil those experiences; they would rather receive help from their group member rather than a stranger, but this is not always possible.

There is a considerable amount of details to discuss and plan, they have to work out that the spirits who aid their journey back on earth are incarnated at the correct time so that this will succeed. Sometimes these contracts are made with other spirits away from their group but on the whole they prefer to work with their friends and spirit family. Discussions then begin to establish how they may be able to assist the incarnating spirit.

When the planning stages begin, the spirits involved may discover that some major disaster or event is going to take place on earth. It may be a war, famine, a tsunami an epidemic, or some other global event or tragedy that would fit into the soul's lessons; major life lessons are decided well in advance.

Agreements are then arranged between them all to ensure they all will have the desired experiences; these arrangements are contracts.

Whatever happens to that soul at any stage of its existence, whether physical or non-physical, is determined by the spirits choice of free will."

Birth, incarnation.

"When contracts have been made for a spirit to become the child of a couple, it will need to decide the time of conception. Once that has been decided the spirit will connect with a small amount of energy to the foetus, thereby claiming that particular body.

How spirit enter the foetus varies, some spirit individuals like to watch how their new family is getting ready for them, whereas, some younger spirits may enter the foetus fairly soon after conception because they wish to experience the entire growth process. However, it is usual for an incarnating spirit to join the unborn child around three to four months. Whenever the spirit chooses to fully inhabit the foetus it must be before the foetus leaves the womb, otherwise the child will not live. It is not possible for a child to exist without a spirit, without a soul because it cannot sustain life.

When the time has come to enter the body of the baby, friends from the soul group of the incarnating spirit assist the member to incarnate into a physical child embryo. They do this by sending positive energy into the mind of the incarnating spirit of the unborn child. When a spirit joins with a baby, it should be snug like placing a hand into a glove that is the exact size for the soul and the child.

The instant the spirit incarnates they experience confusion, similar to that, which follows when a spirit body leaves their dead physical body, although the confusion in birth is much greater and takes longer. This confusion lasts until the blending of the spirit body and the new body is fully established.

Spirit friends and loved ones remain with the incarnating spirit and they continue to support them up to the moment of their re-birth back to earth. The spirits that love them remain with them to the last moment, encouraging them, and often follow them through their journey in their new earthly life.

My dears you see, you have nothing to fear. Reincarnation is part of the basic structure of events in spirit life, and life is but a chapter in a long story. When you return to earth, you are merely acting out a part in a play, a character you chose for the lessons you need for your spiritual growth. You must play this part to the best of your ability by overcoming all the trials, anguish and suffering placed before you, such as life's unpaid debts, old problems of your personality not resolved, all that is associated linked to tasks and events in former lives good and bad, karmic debts left unpaid. Therefore, you must see and understand that there are no injustices, you get back only what you have sown. You may not have the ability to interpret the exact cause and effect involved but it makes a great difference if you can accept that such karma, your destiny does exist.

We have now completed what I wanted to teach you all. Dear children I have explained enough for you to understand the beginning of a spirits earth life and the full circle of your spirit life in my world and back once again through reincarnation. I am always here to help you. Bless you all."

"Thank you so much. I know we have all benefitted from all that you have taught us. We now begin our life with true spiritual knowledge."

Other Books by the Author.

Water Made Clear. 2002

My Little Book of Inspirational Poems. 2014

Printed in Great Britain
by Amazon